SHADED LIVES

SHADED LIVES

African-American Women and Television

BERETTA E. SMITH-SHOMADE

RUTGERS UNIVERSITY PRESS
New Brunswick, New Jersey, and London

LIBRARY OF CONGRESS CATALOGING-IN-PUBLICATION DATA

Smith-Shomade, Beretta E., 1965–
   Shaded lives : African-American women and television / Beretta E. Smith-Shomade.
     p.   cm.
   Includes bibliographical references and index.
   ISBN 0-8135-3104-7 (cloth: alk. paper)—ISBN 0-8135-3105-5 (pbk.: alk. paper)
   1. African American women on television.   I. Title.

PN1992.8.A34 S48 2002
791.45′652042′08996073—dc21

                                             2001048840

British Cataloging-in-Publication information is available from the British Library.
For permissions see Acknowledgments section.

Manufactured in the United States of America

To
   Evelyn Inell Cain-Smith
   my passion
     The memory of Leo Smith
     my heart
       and
          Salmon Adegboyega Shomade
          my soul mate

CONTENTS

ILLUSTRATIONS

Publisher's Note: Using frames from television programs has produced less than desired quality in some cases. However, we felt it was important to include them for the purpose of illustration.

ACKNOWLEDGMENTS

It probably goes without saying that a project like this is never done alone. First, I thank my dream team—my dissertation committee, who, by sheer force of will, guided me strategically and successfully through the first process: Nicholas K. Browne, Teshome H. Gabriel, John T. Caldwell, Chon Noriega, and Valerie Smith. Extra special thanks go to John Caldwell for always being there (well beyond the dissertation and any reasonable call of duty).

I thank several colleagues/friends for sustained intellectual challenge and encouragement: Lahn S. Kim, Bambi L. Haggins, Daniel Bernardi, Karla Rae Fuller, and Gilberto Blasini. Further, much appreciation goes to family, friends, colleagues, and students who read the manuscript, critiqued it, and questioned me about what I have said here (or at least about what I have tried to say). Thank you Gabrielle Branch, Mike Budd, Maurice Cain Jr., Jacqueline Duodu, Haseenah Ebrahim, Deborah Jaramillo, Nicole Jefferson, Leslie Mitchner, Pamela (Troutman) Palmer, Shaquana Walker, and the participants of the University of Georgia Womanist Consortium (summer 1998).

For those who helped with tape, still, and book resources, I appreciate you dearly: Maria T. Brewster, Christopher Craddock, Hope Chirino, Warner Bros. Publications, the Faculty Center for Instructional Innovation staff at the University of Arizona (especially Matt Van Hoesen), the Interlibrary Loan staff at the University of Arizona, Nikk Franklyn, Demetria Gallegos, Michael Heard, Theresa Liu, the personnel at Jerry Ohlinger's Movie Material Store, Pamela (Troutman) Palmer, Tani Sanchez, Jennifer Siracusa (EMI), Warren Singleton, James Stafford, Tani Sylvester, Adrian Tibbs, the Vanderbilt Television News Archives staff, and Robyn Wheeler. Extra special thanks to Tani Sanchez and James Stafford for all sorts of stuff related to the making of this book. I am also grateful to have received a Provost's Author Support Award from the University of Arizona. This award helped immeasurably in acquiring many of the stills and permission rights herein.

I cannot forget those who provided much-needed general and spiritual life support and listening ears. These thanks go to Diane Brewer, Noella Cain, Denise Davis-Maye, Ruth Forman, Tracii (Patterson) Hunter, Edmund Landers, Mary V. Morales, and Marc A. Thomas. A very special thank you goes to my personal editor/friend/husband/lawyer, Salmon Adegboyega Ajebola Shomade, and my mother/friend/soror/#1 supporter, Evelyn Inell Cain-Smith.

These two give me the freedom, encouragement, and love to follow all my dreams.

I would be remiss not to pay homage to scholars, writers, artists, and personal acquaintances who inspire me by their dynamic worldviews. These include Daniel P. Black, Todd Boyd, John T. Caldwell, Patricia Hill Collins, John Fiske, Ruth Forman, Teshome H. Gabriel, Herman Gray, Beverly Guy-Sheftall, Bambi L. Haggins, Cynthia L. Hale, Stuart Hall, bell hooks, Audre Lorde, Kobena Mercer, Marlon Riggs, Tricia Rose, Ella Shohat, Robert Stam, Kenneth Ulmer, Gloria Wade-Gayles, and Renita J. Weems.

Finally, to my students at U.C.L.A., Spelman College, and the University of Arizona, I thank all of you for continually pushing me further, for making me think harder about my assertions, and for always teaching me something new along the way. With all of this help and inspiration, one would think that this book would be perfect. But alas, I know my own humanity crept in throughout the pages. Any errors found here are, therefore, mine alone.

Permission has been granted for use of the following works:

"Green Boots n Lil Honeys," from *We Are the Young Magicians,* by Ruth Forman. Copyright 1993 by Ruth Forman. Reprinted by permission of Beacon Press, Boston.

"If That's Your Boyfriend." Words and music by Me'shell NdegéOcello. Copyright 1993 Warner-Tamerlane Publishing Corp., Nomad Noman and Revolutionary Jazzy Giant. All rights administered by Warner-Tamerlane Publishing. All rights reserved. Lyrics reprinted by permission of Warner Bros. Publications.

"No Matter What They Say." Words and music by Kimberly Jones and Bernard Edwards. Copyright 2000 Notorious K.I.M. Music; Undeas Music; Bernard's Other Music; Crited Music, Inc.; Nile Rogers; Robert Hill Music; EMI April Music, Inc.; Special Ed Music; Promuse, Inc.; Howie Tee Music; Bridgeport Music, Inc.; and FAF Publishing. All rights on behalf of Notorious K.I.M. Music administered by Warner-Tamerlane Publishing Corp. All rights on behalf of Crited Music, Inc., administered by Unichappell Music, Inc. All rights reserved. Lyrics reprinted by permission of Warner Bros. Publications.

"Ruffneck." Words and music by Markell Riley and Walter "Mucho" Scott. Copyright 1999 WB Music Corp.; Daddy's Little Boy Walter "Mucho" Scott; Abdur Rahman Music; BMG Songs, Inc.; and Brooklyn Based Music. All rights on behalf of Daddy's Little Boy Walter "Mucho" Scott administered by WB

SHADED LIVES

INTRODUCTION

Twenty-first-century popular culture recalls the latter days of nineteenth-century cinema. White audiences, startled and intrigued with how a filmed train pulled into the station, flocked to the glow of this new technology. A love affair with film emerged from this initial interaction. Fast-forward to the now. The same iteration of that train arrives in living color on television as flying chairs on *Jerry Springer,* sight gags on *Martin,* and bouncing breasts on BET. As technologies constantly change, the awe of once-new ones wanes. Yet what has replaced this spectator fascination with technology is colored bodies. In this contemporary iteration of the new, colored bodies usher in a different and equally entertaining type of spectacle.

In the last twenty years many scholars have devoted themselves to interrogations of, by, or about African-Americans, especially Black men. Research on Black men's supposed pathologies, victimization, and interactions with American systems has dominated mass media—most conclusions offering limited hope for their survival or common sense. However, Black male voices did attain some privilege within the realm of popular culture—specifically within cinema, music, and television. Yet this same period offered fewer (and then typically derisive) works focused on Black women, although they have endured similar types of disrespect within American institutions.

African-American women compose an underaddressed population in visual popular culture; simultaneously, they command a substantial amount of coverage regarding their literary achievements, political activism, and perceived public welfare participation. In *From Mammy to Miss America and Beyond* K. Sue Jewell suggests that the plethora of progressive representations of Black women, or their "cultural images," belies actual Black women's limited access to societal resources and institutions.[1] This contradiction of public visibility and actual disempowerment remains unresolved and virtually unexamined.

Given this conundrum, I offer *Shaded Lives: African-American Women and Television* as an intervention. In it I examine visual representations of African-American women on television since 1980. From situation comedies and music videos to television news and talk shows, Black women's images emerged in virtually all genres, advertisements, and new technological manifestations of network and cable. In addition, 1990s hip-hop cultural capital forwarded a notion of racial togetherness that ushered Black women to the forefront of popular vision. Concurrently, however, the nation's climate of heightened divisiveness in the wake of Ronald Reagan's 1980 inauguration relegated the representation of Black women to depravity and display. This incongruity makes conducting a scholarly cultural study of this demographic not only useful but critical.

Discourses about African-American women appear within a historical continuum that looks only cursorily at Black representations in the visual media. Scholarly research of Blacks emanates primarily from three realms (and combinations thereof): film and television criticism, mass communications theory, and/or within larger historical or sociological studies of African-Americans. Specifically, a trajectory of film scholarship on Black images has evolved through such texts as Daniel Leab's *From Sambo to Superspade* (1975), Thomas Cripps's *Slow Fade to Black* (1977) and *Making Movies Black* (1993), Donald Bogle's *Toms, Coons, Mulattoes, Mammies, and Bucks* (1991), Ed Guerrero's *Framing Blackness* (1993), James Snead's *White Screens/Black Images* (1994), and Jacqueline Bobo's *Black Women as Cultural Readers* (1995). Excluding Bobo's groundbreaking work, these texts' importance lies in their arguments for the viability of studying Black cinema, recuperation of Black actors and actresses, and exposing clichéd and stereotypical characters, themes, and tropes in Hollywood narratives. However, for the most part, they forward largely celebratory, historical, and male-centered assertions. Even S. Craig Watkins's recent *Representing: Hip Hop Culture and the Production of Black Cinema* (1998) dwells in the realm of the male. Black women hold limited space in these texts.

J. Fred MacDonald's *Blacks and White TV* (1992) remains the definitive historical work on Blacks and television. MacDonald draws the history of African-Americans in television from 1948. He contends that as an economic structure, television has not fulfilled its bias-free promise of entertainment and uplift. Yet he believes that by virtue of communication's global reach and the proliferation of vertically and horizontally integrated companies that produce, distribute, and exhibit products for consumers, audiences are no longer perceived as "just the predominately white United States with its racial prejudices."[2] However, his assessment fails to account for the disparities in access to and control of opportunities or for the continued proliferation of racist and sexist images. Further, MacDonald could not have foreseen the pervasive demolition of U.S. antitrust legislation as companies began wholesale ownership of multimedia forums.

In a recent book about Blacks and television, *Prime Time Blues: African Americans on Network Television* (2001), Donald Bogle historicizes the changing roles of Blacks from the 1940s through the 1990s. In an insightful text he traces the recurrence of Black stereotypes throughout television history. He also argues that certain actors within television have helped to transform the medium. Bogle's book is useful in making connections between problematic characterizations across time, but it fails to center Black women or to engage in many of the larger cultural questions and implications that these representations signal.

John Fiske's *Media Matters: Everyday Culture and Political Change* (1994) engages, quite convincingly, the tensions bound up in racialized and gendered representation, in particular, television news. He notes that increased technological capabilities directly reflect and influence national constructions of marginalized figures in ways that do not improve scales of equity or our ability to, as Rodney King suggests, "just get along." Beyond these aforementioned texts, most other television criticism frames Black women's representations either as regressive/denigrative or as potentially enabling real-life women to resist hegemonic positioning.

Herman Gray examines the television construction of blackness in *Watching Race: Television and the Struggle for "Blackness"* (1995). Specifically, he analyzes the television texts *A Different World, Frank's Place,* and *In Living Color* as sites of assimilation, contention, and parody. His book complements *Shaded Lives* by engaging the contemporary discourses of race and gender while addressing some critical intersections and problems with definitions of blackness. However, Gray's work centers blackness at the expense of an in-depth study on what that means to Black women. Other books focusing on African-Americans and television include George H. Hill's *Ebony Images: Black Americans and Television* (1986), his *Black Women in Television* (1990), Donald Bogle's *Blacks in American Films and Television: An Illustrated Encyclopedia* (1988), Camille O. Cosby's *Television's Imageable Influences: The Self-Perceptions of Young African-Americans* (1994), Robin Means Coleman's *African American Viewers and the Black Situation Comedy: Situating Racial Humor* (1998), and Kristal Brent Zook's *Color by Fox: The Fox Network and the Revolution in Black Television* (1999). Except for Cosby's and Coleman's, these texts are much more listings of who's Black in television (and the author's relation to them) than critical interrogations or interventions.

Shaded Lives offers historical analysis, coupled with political, economic, and cultural specificity of the time. By assessing cable inventions, political changes introduced with conservative Reagan-Bush ideologies, and the binary and contradictory cultural notions of Black women as economically potent consumers against their positioning as "welfare queens," I hope to inspire a more comprehensive understanding of the depictions of Black women in this historic moment. To this end I offer narrative and structural analyses of selected television product and programs that aired from 1980 to 2001, concentrating specifically on texts in which Black women either dominate, are the primary focus, or significantly serve the narrative structure. Further, I introduce responses to said programming by Black women. Overall, the analysis in *Shaded Lives* seeks to contrast African-American women's positioning as objects, their to-be-looked-at-ness, against their agency or assumption of subjectivity.

Although Black women who address Black women's representations receive only marginal consideration within television scholarship, this work is grounded in Black feminism. Black feminism (or womanism—as coined by Alice Walker) insists on the inextricability of gender and race. This argument, enunciated in Patricia Hill Collins's *Black Feminist Thought*, forces recognition of the legacy of struggle against racism and sexism as a common binding thread. Further, it argues for the interdependence of experience and consciousness, the struggle for consciousness and self-defined standpoint, and the interdependence of thought and action. In this book I highlight and advocate moments where agency and emancipation occur within and between generally conservative and oppressive television texts and divergent audiences. By doing so I claim a subjectivity for fictionalized and real-life Afro-American women.

Experiences not valued by broader audiences, like Black oral culture, inform and infuse this study. Their inclusion marks my attempt at what bell hooks calls "choosing the margins as a space of radical openness." She asserts that "[p]rivate speech in public discourse, intimate intervention, making another text a space . . . enables me to recover all that I am in language."[3] Thus, as a part of my own womanist agenda I inscribe myself within this writing. This positioning allows me to articulate the dual voices of television academic discourse and African-American vernacular in complementary and subject-validating ways. Some may charge that invoking orality lacks rigor (as founded on written discourse) or reeks too much of the academy (from those outside the university setting). Even attempting to recognize and undermine the processes of naming for women and people of African ancestry faces potential attack. Nevertheless, I insist on the importance of writing and speaking in multiple and what may sometimes seem oppositional voices.

Further, studying Negro women requires an elaboration of the naming tradition of African-Americans. Since the Emancipation Proclamation of 1863, those designated as property in U.S. society have struggled with the issue of naming. Carole Boyce Davies suggests that the problem resides with negotiating the "original misnaming and the simultaneous constant striving of the dispossessed for full representation."[4] I maintain that all of the namings and misnamings have shaped and continue to shape the roles, ruptures, rationales, and resiliencies of the only people whose preamble to this country came with chains. Consequently, my use of various terms throughout the text *(Negra, Colored, Afro-American, Black, African-American, Sistahs, Women of Color, Sistah-Friends)* not only locates women in a particular place and time but also shows the arbitrariness and consequences of naming itself. This naming serves also as a strategy to keep identity unfixed and uncomfortable. As Trinh T. Minh-ha asserts, potential for contestation resides with the hyphen, a "realm in-between, where predetermined rules cannot fully apply." [5]

Shaded Lives focuses on the television genres of situation comedy, music video, national news, and talk shows as useful platforms to discuss Black women's portrayals. After giving a historical overview of African-American women in visual culture in chapter 1, I turn in chapter 2 to the situation comedy and the depictions of Black women in them. Framed by the tenets of whiteness, comedic texts host the largest number of Black women's representations of all genres I have examined. Under the proviso and parlance of this whiteness, this genre has maintained a tradition of Blacks in broadcasting since the 1950s' *Beulah* and *Amos 'n' Andy*. It repeated its stereotypical legacy in the 1970s. The 1980s and 1990s introduced a seemingly new crop of Black and female images yet, in many ways, simply reconfigured its previous offerings.

In chapter 2 I also address the 1990s' Fox, WB, and UPN phenomena and their shaping of African-American women. My analysis centers on four post-*Cosby* series: *Fresh Prince of Bel Air* (NBC, 1990–1996), *Martin* (Fox, 1992–1997), *Living Single* (Fox, 1993–1998), and *Moesha* (UPN, 1995–2001). [6] During the 1990s, situation comedy, as exemplified by these four series, positioned Black women as perpetual objects of laughter while allowing for the most prolific offering of their appearances.

In chapter 3 music video merits examination for two reasons. First, music video largely defined the look of post-1980 television. Quick editing style, urban rhythmic beats, and various racial and ethnic threats changed spectators' relationship to television. Between Benetton's "we are the world" parade of different ethnic and racial peoples and television's fascination with the most intimate, superfluous, and banal aspects of the newly rich and famous, Black bodies were altered and laid bare for mainstream television consumption.

Second, Black music video crossed generations. Although the genre favored young African-American women, older divas such as Diana Ross, Gladys Knight, and Tina Turner held their own. In other words, these "divas" survived the economic, visual, and stylistic changes of contemporary music. Each negotiated her constructed space. Women served routinely as spectacle and objects of the gaze in this genre, yet they provided a compelling textual cross between fictional narratives and nonfictional musical bodies and business. I deconstruct the performance, lyrics, and visuality of several artists, including Queen Latifah, Janet Jackson, and Lil' Kim. Vanessa L. Williams, another prominent artist of the period, bridges the terrain between music video and the world of television news.

Television news demands consideration particularly because the late twentieth century prominently featured Negras as objects of scorn on the world-news stage. Stories that offered Colored women's images collided when American media culture elevated the figure of Black womanhood while simultaneously castigating it. Often these women were visually relegated (and regulated) to nonexistent status. In other words, Black women were lauded in some literary and political arenas and rebuked in others because of their perceived improprieties. Thus in chapter 4 I focus on three national news stories: Vanessa L. Williams's dethroning as the first Black Miss America, Anita Hill's confrontation with Clarence Thomas in his Senate confirmation hearings, and the television imaging of welfare across the bodies of Black women. Positioned as objects of scorn, these women's racialized figures became national news events.

Chapter 5 looks at Oprah Winfrey as cultural icon and object of credible voice. Her success as a talk show host defied the norm previously held for Blacks in general and Black women in particular. Although not the initiator of the form, she became the preeminent force in the field, largely defining topics, look, and creative venues of talk show production.

Winfrey, the premier African-American woman figure at the end of the twentieth century, became an intertextual performer and performance. Both her name and figure evoked a certain cultural cachet. Her talk show format (intertextual itself) represented only a part of her iconic stature in American and worldwide culture. Celebrated for its host's credibility, Winfrey's program ranked among the top-rated talk shows in its first year. Oprah Winfrey, the woman, became synonymous with the talk show format, with self-help, and with the American ethos of hard work, all rolled up into one big, lovable mammy figure.

This characterization, however, overlooked the fact that she presided over a multimillion-dollar franchise and maintained an overwhelming impact both on television's construction of the talk show genre and on works featuring African-American women. Because of her advances into film (both production and acting), media ownership (Harpo Studios, *O, The Oprah Magazine*, "Oprah" Web site, Oxygen cable network), and television-movie production, she defined the talk show quintessentially and the scope of this project. Upon her figure America's spiritual search and multicultural impulse collided and bonded. This chapter contextualizes her status in American culture and in her industry, her professionalism, and America's response to her presence.

The final chapter looks at the future of Black women's representations in visual culture. The Internet and the five-hundred-channel environment include the growing numbers of colored women in the United States. I consider Black women's future within these technological phenomena. Also, I lay some groundwork for continued exploration of Black women and television representation via media activism. I conclude *Shaded Lives* with an assessment of objectification and agency and their use-value in discussing television genres.

Where fissures and pacts divide and meet, important meanings emerge about African-American women's representations on American television. I offer *Shaded Lives* to African-American women, to share with them (and other interested parties) an assessment of the last twenty years. This book should serve as a siren—one that incites action. That action might take the form of self-interrogation, change of career, critical debate, or screaming in the streets. Whatever the response, critical contemplation and action are needed to stop the nihilism informing the treatment, evaluation of, and prolific visual representation of Black women's actual and fictionalized bodies.

1

THE MADDENING BUSINESS OF SHOW

[Beulah] . . . spends most of her time in the kitchen but never seems to know what's cookin'.

> —Louise Beavers, "Beulah Helps the Hendersons," *The Beulah Show*

I used to do a character, a little black girl who wanted blonde hair. Everyone on television was blonde.

> —Whoopi Goldberg, *Book*

Whether it's *Beulah, Julia, Get Christy Love, Thea,* or *Moesha,* one of the most pervasive problems with Black representation on American television has been the lack of scope and depth offered in its purview. African-Americans' furious responses to images of themselves have been directed less toward specific programs than toward perpetually limited roles, histories, and reflections of Black life portrayed on American and world television monitors. Historically, one show on television every few years has borne the burden of reflecting all of Black American culture. Thus, both quality and quantity of representation have been, and remain, an issue.

In fact, Black image dearth continued so egregiously at the end of the twentieth century that the National Association for the Advancement of Colored People (NAACP) felt compelled once again to take the television networks to task for their 1999 fall season's literal Black-out of African-American characters. The NAACP's attack on the quantity of colored representation—both in front of and behind the camera—is an ongoing struggle in the visual media.[1] Yet quality issues continue too. Representations that approximate the diversity and complexity of those called Black Americans and of America itself are scant.

According to Jannette Dates, Black programs have followed "the pattern set in minstrelsy, which . . . [seems] destined to continue ad infinitum."[2] The minstrelsy ethos resounded on American television before 1980 and, some argue, since. Yet, as much as visual history discounts their presence, African-Americans frame every picture of the United States—despite disfiguration and disguise. Thus, this chapter traces the representations of African-Americans as part of American entertainment, their place in its historical memory, and their function in a racist and sexist society.

HISTORICAL ANTECEDENTS

Early Black performers played roles that primarily satiated White audiences. Slave performance, minstrelsy, and later vaudeville introduced Negro performance as a commodity for White consumption. Cinema perpetuated that same type of blackfaced utility. For example, in an early silent Edison film, *What Happened in the Tunnel* (1903), a Negra (actually a White woman in blackface) literally buttresses a play on Black women's (a)sexuality. The short film features a White woman and her Negra maid on a train. A White male passenger makes advances toward the White woman. As the train enters the tunnel, he leans forward to kiss her. Once outside the tunnel, however, he discovers that the women switched seats. The maid received his affection. The man expresses revulsion as the women laugh.

Beyond its obvious racist implications, the "racist and sexist joke" is complicated, according to Miriam Hansen, by the women's laughter and the White man's objectification through ridicule. Hansen contends that "[w]hile the figure of the prankster falling prey to his own prank is quite common in the genre of mischief comedy, the maid's direct glance at the camera suggests not only that she was not merely a prop but that she, rather than her mistress, might have authorized the substitution."[3] Yet as we know, a Black maid "authorizing" anything in 1903 is ridiculous. The joke remains squarely on the maid. The pun, based on the man's confusion, can ultimately only contribute to the maid's disillusionment. With the maid's large and dark presence, the possibility of the kiss's voluntary sanction by either the man or the maid seems ludicrous, at least in public. The maid, in her Colored, nonsexualized construction, possesses neither the authority nor evident desire implicit in Hansen's suggestion, unless one subscribes to the idea that Black women harbor unrequited desires for their oppressors.[4] These types of images, nevertheless, emblematized the nation's early cinematic efforts.

Such images did not appear only in Caucasian cinema. Although films such as *The Birth of a Nation* (Griffith, 1915) and its antecedents further demonized the figure of the Black woman and man in feature-length films, early filmmakers like Oscar Micheaux, Spencer Williams, and the Lincoln Brothers made films that followed Hollywood's problematic constructions. Although their films attempted to answer Hollywood's racism, they perpetuated sexist, classist, and color-struck ideas.[5]

In these decades before television's arrival Negras appeared in film as servants, harlots, mammies, tragic mulattoes, and religious zealots. The nation's carefree attitude during the 1920s forwarded the Harlem Renaissance and launched the Colored woman as feature performer on screen. Nina Mae McKinney distinguished herself as the silver screen's first Colored harlot. She played in King Vidor's 1929 sound film *Hallelujah* as a jezebel, of course, bamboozling a good man. In *Toms, Coons, Mulattoes, Mammies, and Bucks: An Interpretive History of Blacks in American Films*, Donald Bogle describes McKinney's character, Chick, as a Black, exotic sex object, half woman, half child: "She was the black woman out of control of her emotions, split in two by her loyalties and her own vulnerabilities. Implied throughout the battle with self was the tragic mulatto theme. The white half of her represented the spiritual; the black half, the animalistic." [6] This and the other aforementioned screen stereotypes presented themselves in both mainstream and early Black cinema. They stood as Negras' predominant roles.

During the Depression years Negro actors appeared more regularly, perhaps as a comfort to the economically strapped majority. "[W]hether that face was seen for two minutes or three and a half hours, it was invariably there to tidy up the house, cook a meal, or watch over the livery stables." [7] Even within the highly publicized *Imitation of Life* (1934), in which Louise Beavers earns the title of Partner, her lot remains cast to service. Actresses such as Beavers and McKinney, Fredi Washington, Josephine Baker (mostly abroad), and Thelma "Butterfly" McQueen all helped shape certain descriptors of Black women during cinema's first fifty years. Limited opportunities for other film roles surfaced and none focused on Black women specifically.[8] After all, Peola's (Fredi Washington) passions (and thus the story in *Imitation of Life*) revolve around a White woman's life—a lie for a woman scientifically rendered Colored.

To bolster Black participation in the World War II effort, the U.S. Department of War (with the prodding of the NAACP) worked with Hollywood to create more favorable images of America's "problem people." Films like *The Negro Soldier* (1944), *Home of the Brave* (1949), and the *Why We Fight* series all attempted to lure Blacks into the war effort by ignoring America's atrocities and elevating Hitler's.[9] This linking of patriotism to representation obviously negated Colored women—a fact not missed by filmmaker Julie Dash several decades later.

A retrospective look at wartime Hollywood, Dash's film *Illusions* (1983) tells the story of a rising entertainment executive, Mignon Dupree (Lonette McKee), who "passes" in order to make critical decisions within a major film studio. But in one touted and poignant scene Dash illustrates the impotence of Blacks' and women's imagery and highlights the illusionary lives real folks led during the 1940s. In the scene Dash layers images of Mignon at a recording session with a White actress lip-synching in a Hollywood film. Between the two screens (one fabric, the other glass) stands a young Black singer, Ester Jeeter (Rosanne Katon), doing the actual singing. The scene depicts the confinement of most Black women's representation—between screens, without credited voice, and virtually invisible. Ella Shohat and Robert Stam characterize the scene as "Black talent and energy . . . sublimated into a haloed White image." [10] These processes occur while a White male technician orchestrates and controls the entire production. The scene aptly illustrates Black women's cinematic history and legacy of powerlessness.

Whereas 1940s films cursorily examined societal concerns, early television generally ignored serious social issues altogether, choosing to show happy people with happy problems. Although perhaps, as some surmise, programs featuring Black characters or themes were considered inappropriate,[11] the *Amos 'n' Andy* series offered White ideals of appropriate Blacks and their concerns. The program featured caricatured African-Americans who emerged from the minds and mouths of two White southern men. In the radio program (which preceded the television series) Black women existed as phantoms— invisible (because it was radio) but also voiceless. Melvin Ely explains: "For years the program presented [women characters] through the male characters, who discussed the women, 'conversed' with them on the telephone, and occasionally read aloud from their letters. Amazingly, Godsen & Correll managed to give each of these silent female figures a vivid personality of her own and, at times, a crucial part in the drama."[12] Personalities and actualities, it seems, characterized sufficiently and in exchange for tangible Colored actresses.

When the program appeared on television in 1951, producers cast Ernestine Wade as Sapphire Stevens and Amanda Randolph as Mama. According to Ely, Mama "epitomized both the race-transcending battle-ax and the hard-edged version of the familiar black 'mammy.' [Her] considerable heft, baleful stare, and enormous hats rendered that image even more vivid on television than it had been on radio."[13] Wade's Sapphire spawned a character type of its own. In essence, this Sapphire-type translated to an updated, shrewish mammy. J. Fred MacDonald calls the pair "less than picturesque images of black femininity."[14]

Arriving in 1950 just before the televised *Amos 'n' Andy, The Beulah Show* appeared, starring Ethel Waters (and later Louise Beavers). Beulah's centrality came through her guidance of the White family through crisis. This Black maid "restored balance and normalcy to the household."[15] To give shows like *Beulah* and *Amos 'n' Andy* credibility for White television audiences, "rural black dialect, malapropisms, mispronunciations, and misinterpretations" transferred from their earlier predecessors of radio, cinema, vaudeville, and minstrelsy to television.[16] The NAACP condemned both programs in its 1951 national convention, claiming, among other things, "Negro women are shown as cackling, screaming shrews, in big-mouth close-ups using street slang, just short of vulgarity."[17] Because of the NAACP and other external pressures, both shows were canceled by the fall of 1953. This, however, failed to alter substantially the portrayals of Blacks, especially Black women. Nor did it eliminate Blacks' appearance on television.

Black musical artists began emerging on television as singers, dancers, and comedians on variety shows such as Ed Sullivan's *Toast of the Town* (1948–1971), the *Colgate Comedy Hour* (1950–1955), and the *Jackie Gleason Show* (1952–1970). For one year (1956–1957) Nat King Cole hosted his own network variety program, the first Black performer to do so.[18] MacDonald suggests that the arrival of Black musical artists signaled a new era of racial fairness absent prior to the war.

In 1951 members of the National Association of Radio and Television Broadcasters pledged: "Racial or nationality types shall not be shown on television in such manner as to ridicule the race or nationality."[19] Bolstered by the 1954 *Brown v. Board of Education of Topeka* decision, by Black achievements in sports and sciences, and by Negro entertainers on television, Colored communities felt poised to assert their civil and social rights. With continued urban migration, undereducated Blacks occupied abundant manufacturing jobs, creating social divisions that would lead to increased economic disparity between Black haves and have-nots.[20] Institutionalized racism, however, proved a formidable force in maintaining cultural norms, particularly in television. People who produced television remained unconvinced of the profitability of Black television faces.

Yet by the 1960s worldwide attention centered on Blacks in America. With extensive civil unrest, protests, and frequent televised injustices, the living conditions of the nation's Black community burst across screens and into homes. During this tumultuous period Black representation erupted mostly within the genre of television news. Having done without previously, networks scrambled to recruit Black news reporters like Charlayne Hunter-Gault and Carole Simpson to cover those areas unknown to the television world.[21] Stories featuring beautiful, militant Black women with Afros vaulted into American homes. The images were often situated in a context of confrontation, characterizing perhaps some aspect of the Black Panther Party or children being attacked by dogs, city fire hoses, or bombs. Never before had America and the world been privy to such atrocities against U.S. citizenry. In 1964, pressured from within and without, President Lyndon B. Johnson signed legislation giving federal protection to Negroes in employment, voting, and civil rights. The legislation ended legalized segregation and illuminated a formerly hidden segment of society, all witnessed via television.

Capitalizing on both the uprisings of the period and Melvin Van Peebles's flawed protest film, *Sweet Sweetback's Baadasssss Song* (1971), Hollywood rediscovered Black America.[22] Studios found that Black power could translate into green power with negligible regard to context or content. Further, the 1960s brought the dismantling of the Production Code and implementation of the Ratings System. These developments virtually guaranteed cinema full freedom of expression.

Consequently, films aimed at Black audiences circulated from 1971 to the mid-1970s. This "blaxploitation" era characterized peoples of African descent as monolithic balls of anger, trapped in urban jungles, forever relegated to the margins. The films substantiated much of Daniel Patrick Moynihan's report on the Negro family.[23] Moreover, some argue that the Ratings System itself contributed to the rise of exploitative sex and violence in the new "R" and "NC-17" categories. Most Black exploitation films fell under this rubric and were directed and produced by White men. While demonizing blackness, the scripts often overlooked or subverted African-Americans', and particularly Black women's, legitimate anger.

For example, *Cleopatra Jones* (Julien, 1973) and her many adventures, *Coffy* (Hill, 1973), and its sequel, *Foxy Brown* (Hill, 1974), featured two angry Black women. These films' releases coincided not only with the Black nationalist and women's movements but also with the box office successes of their male counterparts such as *Shaft* (Parks, 1971), *Superfly* (Parks, 1972), and *The Mack* (Campus, 1973). Bogle suggests, "These macho goddesses answered a multitude of needs and were a hybrid of stereotypes. . . . They lived in fantasy worlds—of violence, blood, guns, and gore—which pleased, rather than threatened, male audiences."[24]

Antithetical to Hollywood film product depicting segregated and violent Black worlds, 1970s television delivered Blacks assimilated and functioning well in American society, as in the programs *Julia* (1968–1971), *The Flip Wilson Show* (1970–1974), and *The Jeffersons* (1975–1985). This alternative image was mandated in part by broadcast standards and practices departments, who policed all material for broadcast. *Julia*, in particular, operated fully within the American, safe, White, and middle-class mainstream.

Beginning in September of 1968, Diahann Carroll portrayed Julia Baker, the first Black nondomestic female character on television (fig. 1).[25] Julia lived in an integrated California environment as a widowed, professional nurse raising her son. This fictional integration aired across a real-life backdrop of White homeowners fleeing neighborhoods where Blacks moved. With government funds made available for the construction of federal freeways leading out of the city and government assistance for those who wanted to buy homes in the suburbs, Whites left the city in droves—taking their dollars with them. The Bradys, the Partridges, the Tates, the Douglases, the Mediterraneans of Brewster Place, and even Lucille Carmichael headed for the hills—where "farm livin'" or at least colorless existence prevailed.[26] *Julia* never alluded explicitly to this phenomenon nor to the civil and social unrest raging on American streets. This became one of the most potent criticisms leveled at the show from both the media and outside advocates. The show implied that the fires were mythical—harmony could be achieved if we could all just get along. Look, watch Julia do it. *Julia* ran for three years, with Julia never having a steady

FIGURE 1

Diahann Carroll as Nurse Julia Baker.
(Courtesy of Jerry Ohlinger's Movie Material Store)

companion, promotion, or confrontation.[27] This blind-eye approach paved the way for 1990s "no color lines" programming.[28]

The Flip Wilson Show began airing on September 17, 1970, and became the first successful Black variety series.[29] Wilson's brand of humor was perceived as particularly ethnic, which appealed to a wide (read White) audience. More important to this work, Wilson's character, Geraldine, became an American icon. S/he, with her "rotary drive hips," made the phrases "the devil made me do it" and "what you see is what you get" household expressions. This character served as a model and ideal for the characters Sheneneh and Mama in Martin Lawrence's *Martin,* which I will examine in chapter 2.

In a limited fashion television attempted to draw on film's blaxploitation notion of strong Black women. In the police drama *Get Christie Love!* (1974–1975) Teresa Graves plays an undercover cop for the Los Angeles Police Department. J. Fred MacDonald suggests that for its one season "the series was marred by an unbelievable character acting out poorly written scripts in a tired genre."[30] Although Graves's character was tough, smart, and sexy, she provided nothing new. Her character did, however, provide a modicum of empowerment to those who rarely saw physically strong and attractive Black women in visual culture. Young women, including myself, saw the possibility for a convergence of strength, respect, and femininity. The program also coincided with television's expanding view of Black life.

To their credit television executives attempted to explore different aspects of Afro-American life. They focused on working-class families. Yet that exploration confined itself primarily to female-dominated spaces and to humor. Programs like *Good Times* (1974–1979), *That's My Mama* (1974–1975), *The Jeffersons* (1975–1985), and *What's Happening!!* (1976–1979) limited Black women to the primary role of mammy or sapphire.[31] Qualities of strength, direction, and chutzpah, if you will, turned into Mother Jefferson's constant nagging; Dee and Florence's wisecracking, lazy remarks; and Florida's exasperated complaints.[32] The African-American women on these sitcoms emerged as domineering and consistently oppressive.

In its updated 1979 report on the status of minorities and women on television, the United States Commission on Civil Rights surmised that "[t]he black situation comedies and 'jiggly' shows, while certainly not the only ones in which minorities and women are portrayed, nevertheless represent recent and important trends in the portrayal of members of these groups on network television drama during prime time."[33] That trend was a marked lack of improvement. Yet with cable's rise in the 1980s, a shift in the labor market, and the browning of the country, networks began to alter their demographic focus and to recognize a new segmenting of the audience. This shift led to a transition from Reagan-Bush Willie Horton imagery to the hip-hop, colored Clinton reign.

EN ROUTE TO THE EIGHTIES

Historian W.E.B. Du Bois maintained that the "problem of the Twentieth Century [was and] is the problem of the color-line."[34] At the dawn of the millennium, no matter how this country skirts, circumvents, or denies it, race stands as the most critical malady of American society, particularly for those besieged by its ideological and social implications. According to Gerald David Jaynes and Robin M. Williams Jr. of the National Research Council, five major events transformed American race relations over the past forty years. Three decades of South-North and rural-urban migration by Negroes produced conditions leading to profound changes in their social status. The civil rights revolution moved Coloreds toward full citizenship rights, producing critical changes in the nation's political and educational institutions. During World War II and for twenty-five years afterward, the United States' economy grew at unprecedented high and sustained rates, facilitating efforts to improve Blacks' status throughout society. Yet during the early 1970s the rate of economic growth slowed, with thirty years of Black migration coming to a halt. Subsequently, the improved status of Blacks slowed significantly. Finally, rapid changes in the family living arrangements of children, beginning in the 1960s, split most of the Black population into two groups: those living in families with one adult head—overwhelmingly poor—and those living in families with two adult heads—largely middle income.[35] These five distinct but related events dramatically altered American life.

In 1980 the African-American population represented approximately 11.7 percent of the United States total population, or twenty-six million people. In 1998 that figure reached 13 percent, or thirty-four million.[36] Politically and culturally the 1980s marked the rise of buppiedom (Black urban professionals), the benefits of affirmative action, and a renaissance in Black intellectualism. Jesse Jackson bid persuasively for the presidency in 1984 and 1988, and multiculturalism (mostly commodified) reigned. Yet this period also ushered in the presidency and policies of Ronald Reagan.

Reagan's inauguration emerged from and fostered a new wave of conservatism with his encouragement of racial division and his celebration of the dominance of United States capitalism in the world. By the end of his term, in 1989, critics had lambasted him for the savings and loan scandal, environmental abuses, civil rights reversals, and consumer victimization. Ironically, however, according to a *New York Times* poll he left office with 68 percent of the American people (40 percent of Blacks, 72 percent of Whites) approving of the way he handled his job since 1981.[37] The Reagan worldview reproduced itself largely by way of television.

Coco Fusco suggests that during the Reagan-Bush era a form of social engineering transpired. She calls it the "commodification of ethnicity"—a commodification fostered through media production that claims a stake in maintaining multicultural diversity: "In this depoliticised version of the '60s, ethnic identity becomes the focus of ongoing spectacle and aestheticisation, and subaltern popular memory is its terrain. This simulation of ethnic diversity keeps each group in a fixed place, since we each have the spotlight only for as long as we express our difference."[38] Or, it remains profitable. The spotlight on African-American ethnicity advanced largely by way of two groups: one that Americans termed the "Black middle class" and the other contemptuously called the "Black urban underclass."

E. Franklin Frazier wrote derisively about a Negro elite in his 1969 revised text *Black Bourgeoisie,* suggesting that their behavior and mentality reflected White American values. Calling this group "exaggerated Americans," he proposed, "What may appear as distortions of American patterns of behavior and thought are due to the fact that the Negro lives on the margin of American society. . . . [The bourgeoisie] lacks a basis in the American economic system . . . [and has] shown no interest in the 'liberation' of Negroes except as it affected their own status or acceptance by the white community. . . . [T]hey have attempted to conform to the behavior and values of the white community in the most minute details."[39] Franklin's disdain notwithstanding, contemporary versions of his Black bourgeoisie, Buppies, include Black business owners, educated white-collar workers, professional athletes, entertainers (including media workers and politicians), and academics. Inclusion is based largely on income, attitude, and visual presentation. Members of the other group, the urban underclass (particularly men), garner a surfeit of scholarly articles, studies, and even political agendas. Rappers rap about them, news characterizes them, and politicians capitalize on their presence during depressed economic times. Despite this deluge of information on the urban underclass, coverage of the causes for, the tangible impact of media on, and solutions for this segment of American society is limited.

Black American income levels resembled a pyramid—a small portion at the top widening out to a large poverty base. Conversely, White American incomes replicated a diamond—a small top and base with a wide middle. In 1985, for example, 31 percent of Black families (10 million) and 11 percent of White families (29 million) lived below the federal poverty line.[40] Although the numbers were quite small, membership (or perceived membership) in the Black middle class encouraged a mind-set of much greater numbers and influence. This Negro nouveau riche produced a unique form of individualism, different even from that described in Franklin's analysis.[41]

Beginning in the early 1980s, many members of the Black middle class began to assume behaviors that were culturally anomalous to previous ones held by Black Americans and their ancestors. Their behavior exacerbated the chasm between Blacks with privilege and Blacks in poverty. In West African philosophy, the foreknowledge of African-Americans, a part of the notion of self was tied to the notion of community. As described by psychologist Wade Nobles, "the traditional African's view of himself; his self-concept is that he believes: 'I am because we are; and because we are, therefore, I am.'"[42] Thus in the U.S. past, because of smaller numbers of people actually in the middle and upper classes and because of restrictions on where people could work, survival for African-Americans meant cooperation. But with desegregation the requirement of contact with other Negroes no longer existed. A degree of disdain has grown between the two groups that actually furthers regressive conditions for both. Cornel West offers an explanation for a certain nihilistic behavior consistent with this widening gap of the two groups. In *Race Matters* his comments refer to the Black lower class, but I submit, they apply also to the bourgeoisie: "our black foremothers and forefathers . . . [created] buffers to ward off the nihilistic threat, to equip black folk with cultural armor to beat back the demons of hopelessness, meaninglessness, and lovelessness. These buffers consisted of cultural structures of meaning and feeling that created and sustained communities; this armor constituted ways of life and struggle that embodied values of service and sacrifice, love and care, discipline and excellence."[43] These buffers seem to be wearing away rapidly and readily with the assimilation of buppies and the misrepresentation of the poor.

Affirmative action gains helped create and sustain the bourgeois mentality by many who began to occupy upper- and middle-management positions in the late 1970s, particularly in the government sector.[44] Ironically, although affirmative action policies actually advanced mostly White women, the program became the whipping post for unemployed and reactionary White men, the Christian right, and new-niche-needing scholars.[45] Much of the monetary benefit of these advances fell to the young people sarcastically labeled Generation X, many of whom have seen only what the new status brings materially. In cities like Los Angeles, New York, Atlanta, and Washington, D.C., prominent Black families struggled to keep up with the Joneses—two paychecks from poverty. They pursued the American dream relentlessly—a dream constructed during the time of their ancestral enslavement. Some of these same people formed the Black intelligentsia.

Affirmative action opened university doors to Blacks that previously had been closed. Yet some of those who got in identified themselves as racially Black but were philosophically anti-Black. Those who earned Ph.D.s received university positions, book contracts, and network consultations. Despite this trend, the late 1980s saw a third wave in progressive Black intellectualism blossom alongside the conservatism.[46] Promoted by university presses and sometimes, necessarily, the scholars themselves, African-American academi- cians came to public consciousness as Sam Fulwood describes: "the acclaimed and celebrated to the obscure and ridiculed; the ultra-left to neo-conservative to the reactionary right; the Afro-centrists to the Classicists; the B-boy and go-girl posse to the buppie and Jack-N-Jill clique; the radical feminists and lesbians to the engendered men and gay paraders."[47] This new era of Black thought produced the likes of Houston Baker, Kimberlé Crenshaw, Patricia Hill Collins, Henry Louis Gates, bell hooks, Todd Boyd, Tricia Rose, Robin D. G. Kelley, Valerie Smith, and Cornel West. Unlike others of their economic and professional status, many of these new scholars at least reintroduced problems and concerns of African-Americans along the multiple axes of race, gender, class, ethnicity, sexual orientation, and generation.

In this cultural landscape Black women (such as Maya Angelou) became celebrities within academia. Within much popular discourse, however, they also became the corrupters of the Black family, the straw on the backs of Black men, and the primary pilferers of America's welfare coffers. All of the critiques laid a foundation for a real-life phenomenon in which by the end of the cen- tury 63 percent of all Blacks attending college were female, fourteen Black women served in the 107th United States Congress,[48] and Sheryl Swoopes be- came the first woman to have shoes (Nike) named in her honor. The 1980s provided a noticeable increase in Black women's television representations with the introduction of Black Entertainment Television (BET) in 1980, *The Cosby Show* in 1984, *The Oprah Winfrey Show* in 1986, and *The Arsenio Hall Show* in 1989. Black images doubled in number during the 1990s via all genres, pro- filing African-Americans in large numbers. Programs created venues formerly (and formally) closed to African-Americans and began a new trajectory for Black representation in the television spectrum.

CONTEMPORARY TELEVISION

In the 1980s the incestuous relationships among networks, advertisers, and production companies became further entangled with deregulation and the in- filtration of cable, forcing television networks to reexamine their ability to be profitable. In the 1990s corporate mergers reduced media offerings to essen- tially five companies.[49] Television executives began to see "narrowcasting" as one way to retain some of their dispersing audiences.

As defined by cable and accelerated in the 1980s, *narrowcasting* suggests en- tire programming devoted to a defined audience by elements such as gender, race, and ability to consume. The idea actually emerged in earlier years, with network programs like *Mary Tyler Moore* (1970–1977) and its spin-offs *Rhoda* (1974–1978), *Phyllis* (1975–1977), and *The Betty White Show* (1977–1978), the first example of gender counterprogramming. For example, by 1986, to counter ABC's *Monday Night Football*, CBS scheduled a distinctive women's night with the programs *Kate and Allie* (1984–1989), *My Sister Sam* (1986–1988), *Designing Women* (1986–1993), *Cagney and Lacey* (1982–1988), and, later, *Murphy Brown* (1988–1998).[50] This successful gendered counterprogramming strategy translated racially also, particularly on NBC. As early as 1981 Thursday night found *Diff'rent Strokes* (1978–1986), *Gimme a Break* (1981–1987), and *Hill Street Blues* (1981–1987) in the prime-time lineup.[51] In the two subsequent years, NBC continued to lead with Black majority casts or focus for one evening. With the introduction of *The Cosby Show* in 1984 and its spin-off, *A Different World* three years later and directly preceding it in the lineup, NBC's Thursdays became television's Black night. When Fox introduced *In Living Color* (1990–1994), *Roc* (1991–1994), *Martin* (1992–1997), and *Living Single* (1993–1998), it followed that same pattern.[52]

Postmodernist rhetoric played a significant part in the text and context of the programming subsequently offered. Talk of waning historical relevance, parody's lapse into pastiche, and level playing fields danced with American capitalistic euphoria. Network television felt empowered by this new diversity dollar. Yet not all applied evenly. From the promotion to the opening credits of these new Black programs, an explicitness marked their positioning. In all four television comedies that I focus on—*Fresh Prince of Bel-Air*, *Martin*, *Living Single*, and *Moesha*—urban (read Black) rhythms, dancing, or rap announce their arrival. Commercials for corporations sponsoring these programs, such as McDonald's, Nike, and Revlon, limit Black faces to eating, running, or simply needing makeup—at least before ten o'clock EST. After that time those faces disappear.

Television promotions for this night of Black programs introduced the hilarity of the Black faces awaiting both the colorized and Anglo consumer. For example, print advertisements for *Martin* and *Living Single* showed cast members grinning and wide-eyed, yet with chic and hip clothing—for Whites (who were not a large part of the viewing audience) that meant performing darkies; for Blacks (the majority of the audience) it was a chance to see what younger generations do with their contemporary privilege. Even the printing font used for these shows' promotion marks a difference—intimating a lower (read ethnic) type of humor. John Berger suggests, "Publicity helps to mask and compensate for all that is undemocratic with society. . . . Publicity explains everything in its own terms."[53] For the Negroes in this new era the terms of televisual blackness emerged quite defined and limiting. In some ways they reintroduced the minstrel mantra from film.

Moreover, during the 1990s a spate of Black gangster films emerged following the success of *Boyz n the Hood* (Singleton) and *New Jack City* (Van Peebles) in 1991, which served to situate and confine Blacks to violent, urban ghettos. More successful films like *Juice* (Dickerson, 1992) and *Menace II Society* (Hughes, 1993) gave Hollywood fodder and incentive to reproduce 1970s cinema. These films were different because they employed Black directors and writers, but they were also much like the Black films of the past. These films largely position African-American women in the space of bitch, gangster, hoe, hoochie, or welfare-receiving single-parent mother (or, in many cases, a combination). These films, along with the rise of rap music, particularly define Black women's representations. Prime-time television followed this same pattern of profit at the expense of Black women's imagery.

BLACK WOMEN FOR BEGINNERS

As I suggested earlier, Black women's visual presence intensified during the 1980s and 1990s. In literature African-American women were accused of usurping the Black males' voice and position. Yet this literary takeover contrasted starkly with television programs that heralded predominantly Black male protagonists and executive producers, as well as many predominantly male film directors. Black urban America's musical sound, largely expressed by the male voice, provided a lyrical check on Black women's supposed power. All these male-dominated media factored heavily in the visual representations of African-Americans and women. Yet the media and Negro men pointed to literature, film, and television programs as evidence of women's ascension to power at the Black man's expense. *The Color Purple, The Oprah Winfrey Show, The Women of Brewster Place,* and *Waiting to Exhale* all bore crosses for alleged Black male-bashing.

Beyond the media realm significant political and economic power within Negro communities remained with Black men (for example, Congressional Black Caucus, Urban League, Southern Christian Leadership Council, NAACP, and the Black church). African-American men routinely led economic enterprises and held corporate seats. According to the popular press, 1992 ushered in the "Year of the Woman," in which Black women gained or retained ten congressional seats. This proliferation occurred while Black men retained or gained thirty House seats. This imbalance resounded even more poignantly in work and domestic spaces.

Economist Julianne Malveaux suggests that Black women work in a multi-tiered system. This system positions women in either nontraditional jobs, professional jobs (as teachers, nurses, and social workers), clerical jobs, marginally employed service and private household jobs, or in positions that cycle women between work and welfare.[54] Black women find themselves congregated within the lower three strata. This contrasts with the fact that during the past twenty years more Black women have completed high school with declining dropout rates. Yet Black women lag behind their White counterparts.[55]

Furthermore, research suggests that although Black families headed by women are more likely to be on welfare, less than 10 percent of the composite income of these families comes from public assistance.[56] The average number of children in Black female-headed families is 1.89, about the same as other families. Little evidence suggests that these women have children to get on welfare or that the size of welfare benefits increases the likelihood of their being on welfare.[57] However, news coverage of women and welfare paints a vastly different, Colorful picture.

Determining which group, Black men or Black women suffer oppression more in the United States is neither necessary nor a goal here. Both endure it. Yet the aforementioned forms of institutional exclusion persist alongside the myth of female takeover. Black women's survival in such dichotomous realms defies understanding, unless one knows the history of Black women in the United States of America.

Afro-American women emerged in 1980s television comedy as upper and middle class (as represented by the Huxtables and the young coeds of *A Different World*). They embodied the Black bourgeoisie. Women play material-driven individualists who possess the education, ability, and means to achieve goals, all through their own efforts. Even Claire (of *The Cosby Show*) was shown as someone who could have and do it all, effortlessly. She could care for the family and laugh about her children buying $90.00 shirts because she had already made it to the top. Hooray for the Black superwoman!

Yet, as I mentioned earlier, individualistic tendencies that exclude overt homages to trailblazers, community, and familial responsibilities have traditionally been absent in Colored communities—placing these images in opposition to African-centered ways of being. Black women's television behavior fueled renewed debates/doubts about the need for affirmative action and collaborated with the popular perception/deception of Black women single-handedly destroying the Black community. Significantly, most roles for African-American women (and men) on television remained outside of drama and within situation comedy—making people laugh and perpetuating the image of Black women as sidekicks to leading men.[58]

Knowing Black women's difficulties, one should acknowledge their resiliency and constant resistance to oppressive forces. For example, bell hooks suggests that Black women's communities function as sites of critique and resistance that stand against forces that tend to objectify their members. She maintains that in these places the idea of specialness (exoticizing) is kept in check. Accordingly, your sister-friends may tell you that your "shit is just common." Much of this analysis seeks not to hold women back or devalue their

contributions but to pay tribute to those preceding and to check manipulative moves to power and assumption of individualism. Although community
appraisals reduce objectification and exoticism's existence, hooks maintains
that in racially integrated spaces, where White, male gazes are favored, it becomes easy for "individual black females deemed 'special' to become exoticized,
[o]bjectified in ways that support types of behavior that on the home turf
would just be considered out of control."[59] Those behaviors lend ammunition
to those same White men who label assertive Black women crazy (needing
containment) or supermammas who care for all those around them (and bear
the burden of the work).

In *Shaded Lives* I argue that objectification of Black women exists yet can be
undercut by showing moments of subjectivity achieved within television texts
and within the audience's own subjectivity and identification with the character. In other words, I advocate moments of agency conferred upon and taken
up by Black women within their circumscribed roles and within the audiences' readings of the text—defining *agency* as the mode of visual and content
awareness of women's authority, voice, and vision. Subjectivity enables Black
women to "define their own reality, establish their own identities, [and] name
their history."[60] It implies action and effectiveness either orally, visually, nar-
ratively, or consciously. Investigating representations of Black women situated
in the political, economic, and cultural contexts of post-1980 helps to both
rewrite television history and forward a womanist agenda.

Despite the obvious economic, political, critical, and theoretical disparities
that exist between Colored men and women, perhaps a word more is needed
about why Black men have been decentered in this study. Racialized discourses
have received validation in postmodern academia—discourses that now circulate within both popular and scholarly media outlets. African-Americans
and other marginalized people have been allowed dialogic space in almost all
arenas: sports (oh, but not management), domestic affairs (well, not policy and
only limitedly in foreign affairs),[61] crime (but not punishment), and white-
collar positions (but not merit-based compensation). These openings include
visual representations.

These gaps have placed a poignant focus on African-Americans, but, significantly, this focus has centered primarily on Black men. Scholarly film texts,
the popular press, New Jack cinema, and television all validate, condemn, or
otherwise spotlight Black men. It is a rare entity that does otherwise. With this
deluge of materials on the representations of African-American men and the
lacuna of similar material concerning Black women, I believe a focused study
on African-American women is desperately called for, solo.

2

LAUGHING
OUT LOUD

Negras Negotiating Situation Comedy

Memory is a selection of images, some elusive, others im-
printed indelibly on the brain.
                                              —*Eve's Bayou*

Now That's Black!
                                                    —BET

Remember *The Brady Bunch,* the *Partridge Family,* and *Happy Days* from their
original airings? If so, consider yourself rare. With their new lives in syndication heaven, their current runs forge a whole new set of ideas and memories
that cloud their entrance into our lives—at least for me. Nevertheless, it seems
that back then, they anchored our maturation. The scenarios, mishaps, and
songs filled children's play—normalizing the disconnection in living experience that they fostered. For me, however, these programs' familiarity and comfort level paled in comparison to the feelings I experienced after watching the
first episode of *The Cosby Show.*[1] As first-year students at Clark College, my dorm
mates and I sat glued to our sets.[2] Once the episode ended, Black women,
without plan or cue, came chattering into the hallway about it. We all felt
pleased and affirmed. Identifying with that life we then aspired to, we young,
Black, college women saw the future spoils of our higher education. The venue
of that view gave us something wanted yet unfulfilled.

In 1970 Gil Scott-Heron prophesied: "The revolution will not be right back
after a message about white tornado, white lightning or white people. . . .
The revolution will not be televised."[3] We (one year shy of being baby boom-
ers and at the elder end of Generation X) had watched nonrevolutionary Blacks
on television via shows such as *Good Times, The Jeffersons,* and *Sanford and Son.*
Yet we, even in 1984, were not far enough beyond the newness of Negro visual representation *not* to make calls when a particular or a preponderance of
Blacks appeared. Therefore a program like *The Cosby Show* had assurances that
Black communities would watch.

Up to that moment most prime-time television programs were comedies—
comedies that supported the idea that Black fictionalized lives functioned only

to distinguish White (light) ones from the background—leaving Blacks as shadow. African-Americans supported them because no alternatives for visualizing ourselves existed. In its generic form the situation comedy was predisposed to exoticize and, in essence, to make living blackness funny. Thus, contradictions in our spectatorship came partially from the form. It is the form, then, that I turn to in interrogating how Black women factor into situation comedy.

SITUATION COMEDY: THE REAL DEAL

Television scholar Patricia Mellencamp says, "Given U.S. TV's . . . reliance on parody, an internal referentiality to itself and other media's forms, styles, and characters . . . TV history . . . is remarkably consistent—or, better, fashionable."[4] From its beginning, and unlike radio, television programming foregrounded capitalism, decisions based along the profit margin as dictated by consumer demand (or demand created for the consumer). Yet simultaneously, television, as an integral part of society, drives the cultural milieu it seeks to emulate and receive profit from. Because of its inability (or rather lack of desire) to extricate itself from this environment, television emits and constructs racialized, gendered, sexualized, and generational tropes. One of the ways it has done this most successfully is through genre, and the most successful genre has been the situation comedy.

Television comedy endures as a recognized dramatic form that uses humor and ends happily. Despite perpetual berating for its racist, sexist, homophobic, and inane articulations and presumed influences, the sitcom maintains financial and cultural viability nationwide.[5] The American situation comedy is a complex system that encompasses advertisers, networks, and production companies that "continuously negotiat[e] problems of textual dissent while [keeping] the audience . . . at arm's length."[6] The genre's development and economic potency have always coexisted with problematic notions of race, sex, and the American ideal. Because of, and perhaps in spite of, these constants of profit and set definitions, television comedy has generated voluminous popular and social critique.

Ethnic humor is one of the sitcom's original and most stable aspects. It exists in comedy "as a function of social class feelings of superiority and white racial antagonisms."[7] Extending itself particularly from minstrelsy, ethnic humor allows racialized hierarchical positioning to institute itself without commitment. In other words, ethnic humor reigns often at the expense of objectified Others—those defined as minorities, women, homosexual, poor. So when one begins to talk about African-American women in television, one is in essence privileging the butt of television humor.

Like all visual representation in narrative form, the television comedy has a formula and a recognizable rhythm, providing viewers with a working knowledge of its proceedings. Successful sitcoms possess memorable and strong (perhaps larger than life) characters, certain predetermined and presumed elements of humor (jokes, puns, malapropisms, plays on words, monologues), and a stabilizing, comforting element, one that often surfaces as racialized (or normalized in the case of whiteness). Minus the canned laughter and the music that separates scenes, almost all other sound is diegetic. For the audience, the sitcom genre provides a familiar, comfortable, and contained friend/entertainment vehicle/information venue/light source. Yet despite its economic and popular success, the comedy genre continues to provoke debate among visual scholars, practitioners, and activists.

SITCOM THEORY AND HISTORY

Horace Newcomb sees the sitcom as "providing a simple and reassuring problem/solution formula." He believes that as the most basic of television genres, it is most distant from real problems, creating a reality gap that causes discomfort.[8] Others approach this television genre from its relationship to the family. Darrell Hamamoto suggests that "[a]lthough sometimes absent in its conventional nuclear form, the family has served as the model of all social formations short of political organization in the television situation comedy. . . . The television situation comedy, even as it promulgates dominant social ideologies, exposes the failure of liberal democratic society to argue conclusively the case for its long-term legitimacy."[9] It seems to me, however, that although the idea of home in the sitcom maintains patriarchal, White, heterosexual norms, this same idea simultaneously addresses, includes, and subsumes difference. Therefore, sitcoms *legitimize* the democratic familial circle by consistently altering and incorporating societal changes—always reauthorizing and authenticating a common notion of home.

Theorizing television through a feminized frame of reference became popular in the 1980s largely because of the role television played in the suburban household of the 1950s and 1960s. As we know, home occupies a special, desired, and safe place in the public imagination—like its dominant element, mother. Yet within this domestic milieu television was seen as usurping patriarchal authority in the home. Nina Leibman has argued that sans laugh track, situation comedies exhibit melodramatic forms that centralize the nuclear family—and, thus, women. Men controlled viewing upon returning from work, but women ruled during the day.

Very quickly these women became the target of television's funders, the advertisers. Lynn Spigel contends that this "family circle" of women and television "threatened to make men into female spectators."[10] Yet controlling the purse strings of the medium, particularly production and distribution, prevented this from occurring. And like the apparatus itself, scholarly television discourses privilege male voices and are male centered. As Lynne Joyrich has argued: "[W]hile television spectatorship may be figured as generically feminine, . . . cultural differences are overlooked [such as] the historical split between consumption and production (in which women *are* the primary consumers while men largely control television production)."[11] Male televisual positioning prefigured women's representations.

More specifically, either through vehicles created for Black male stars—for example, *The Cosby Show* (1984–1992), *Fresh Prince of Bel-Air* (1990–1996), *The Sinbad Show* (1993–1994), *Martin* (1992–1997), *Hangin' with Mr. Cooper* (1992–1997), *The Wayans Brothers* (1995–1999), *The Jamie Foxx Show* (1996–2001), or *The Steve Harvey Show* (1996–present)—or those turned into male vehicles, such as *Family Matters* (1989–1998), Black sitcoms, in particular, became (pre)-occupied with men. These male-dominated spaces lead to and address Joyrich's contention that television possesses a tension of "culturally constituted notions of the feminine and the masculine." As television addresses male viewers, it simultaneously elevates the "infantile [which offers and then denies] the feminine conventionally associated with television. . . . A common strategy is thus to construct a violent hypermasculinity—an excess of 'maleness' that acts as a shield."[12]

In *Fresh Prince of Bel-Air, Martin, The Steve Harvey Show, The Jamie Foxx Show, The Wayans Brothers,* and *Malcolm and Eddie* (1996–2000) this hypermasculinity surfaces—partially because these shows are built around male characters. However, racial constructions and historical positioning also play a role. In these contexts male virility usurps what Kathleen Rowe deems the unruly woman's ability to create a disruptive spectacle for herself and forwards the notion of a singular, Black male identity.[13]

Robin Means Coleman has investigated this coupling of race and gender, self-image, and representation. In her ethnographies of African-American responses to situation comedy, many of the *women* rejected "distorted characters who possess some deficiency—the socially powerless—opting instead to accept only the powerful part of the images."[14] Coleman interprets her findings to mean that the positive "must be carved [out] of imagery of exaggeration and ridicule."[15] The findings indicate also that much more activism and research are needed in this area.

Scholars have analyzed the relationship between American women's self-image and reception of television representations of them predominately via class structures.[16] Characterizing images as feminist—pre or post—Andrea Press examined women's work, television empowerment via resistance, and women in the family. Although she, like Ella Taylor, used the character Clair Huxtable (Phylicia Rashad) from *The Cosby Show* quite liberally, the racial component of Rashad's fictionalized identity rarely surfaced in deference to class analysis.

As it stands, very few Black women hold lead roles in television comedy or in all of television.[17] Women in general serve primarily as supporting characters. They wear roles—mothers, wives, harlots. Their biological sex confines and defines their activities, their thoughts, their movement, their world. Lucille Ball's *I Love Lucy* (1951–1961) appeared as pioneering because it allowed a woman to direct the narrative and to be its focal point. Although Lucy occupied a conventional space as an at-home wife and mother for most of the series, her antics beyond laughter strove for insertion into the patriarchal frame of fame, fortune, and subjectivity. Yet other programs featuring women of the late 1960s and early 1970s lacked the same punch. Programs such as *Bewitched* (1964–1972), *I Dream of Jeannie* (1965–1970), and *The Flying Nun* (1967–1970) offered examples of White women's proper place and modes of behavior— Black women remained in theirs too, the kitchen.

Over a short decade, however, program popularity became defined by the eighteen-to-forty-nine-year-old urban market, which transformed the sitcom of the 1970s and 1980s. This phenomenon forced television to become much more serialized, more open to social issues of the time. MTM (*Mary Tyler Moore, Bob Newhart,* and *Rhoda*) and Norman Lear's Tandem productions (*All in the Family, Maude, Good Times,* and *The Jeffersons*) led the way. The Lear sitcoms influenced a shift in the terrain of the country's broader conceptual dilemmas—race, gender, class—whereas the MTM sitcoms helped alter the conception of character—feminist, independent, single, working.[18] In many ways MTM women possessed a complexity previously unknown to the genre of situation comedy. The television space had been so completely male dominated that the 1970s and 1980s erupted as decades making room for women.[19]

This rupturing helped change conventional modes of presentation within the genre. For example, in early television only soap operas engaged in character replacement and, then, with only minimal attention devoted to it. However, as part of a new spectator inclusion, character replacement began to occur regularly in sitcoms. This action not only openly acknowledged character replacement but parodied it. It broke the illusion so carefully constructed in film and television but also, I believe, encouraged people to think of the image as reality—something more indelible to our hearts by owning up to the falsity of the apparatus. In the 1990s, prime-time network sitcoms *Roseanne, Married with Children,* and *Fresh Prince of Bel-Air* all replaced permanent ensemble characters. Those actions, coupled with more in-your-face slapstick self-referentiality than had been previously seen, changed the situation comedy form. They helped renew the palatability of Negro minstrelsy and dramatically increased its presence. Even infrequently used strategies such as direct address became more significant aspects of narrative structures.

Look at an example of how overt television acknowledgment adds the final comedic twist to an episode of *Martin*. In Gina's (Tisha Campbell-Martin) absence her pregnant friend goes into labor with only Tommy (Thomas Mikal Ford), Cole (Carl Anthony Payne II), and Martin (Martin Lawrence) present to help. After a series of over-the-top comedic ploys, the baby—a plastic, brown doll—shoots from the woman's womb area into the hands of medical-assistant-turned-running-back Martin. The character/actor Tommy shouts, "Wait, wait, wait! Hold on man. Martin, where's the umbilical cord?" In close-up the actor/character Martin replies, "Damn it, Tommy. We don't need umbilical cords." In a cut to an extreme close-up he jibes, "This is TV!"[20] Updated and expanded modes of presentation like these offered a modicum of inclusiveness for the audience—a wink that endeared the program to the spectator. And in this case it provided reassurance to the few non-Colored audience members accustomed to equating African-Americans with idiocy and procreation that this behavior still existed.

Moving beyond programs like *Father Knows Best*, where the father dominates the program, and Lucy's beloved "waa" to the television camera, the structural devices employed within contemporary sitcoms beckon the spectator further inside. The seamlessness of the narrative is traded for insider knowledge. This intrusion into the viewer's personal sphere has propelled Black access into prime time. With producers' and writers' increased confession of television artificiality, they have encouraged Black role expansion. Somehow, it seems, the more the apparatus widens, the more "real" representations appear—a reality that ultimately collapses into racialized and gendered essentialism.

Cultural critics Ella Shohat and Robert Stam attack these cues toward reality in visual culture. They maintain that representation illustrates a refraction—claiming that "artistic discourse constitutes a refraction of a refraction; that is, a mediated version of an already textualized and 'discursivized' socio-ideological world."[21] Further, Andy Medhurst suggests that comedy exists primarily as a controlling force. It functions, he believes, to police and guard the "ideological boundaries of a culture,"[22] checking the space between dominant and subordinate. This helps to keep laughter's power in the hands of the dominant.

I concur both with the notion of refraction and the controlling, manipulative forces of comedy but also recognize that these refractions provide clearer examples of Black lives than aforementioned invisible references (à la the women of *Amos 'n' Andy*). Perhaps, any colorized representation of Negro life makes the refraction seem more tangible to those it represents—those so

FIGURE 2

"Florida's Problem."
Episode 118 of *Maude*
(original airdate
February 13, 1973).
Left to right: John Amos,
Bill Macy, Bea Arthur,
Esther Rolle.

accustomed to the White-washing of their lives.[23] Plus, as suggested by Coleman earlier, Black women often pick and choose what to embrace.

Medhurst suggests further that "because comedy is nothing if not contradictory, humour can also be disruptive to the social order, a full-blown challenge or a persistent sniping from the margins, a force for the advocacy of social change, ridiculing power rather than reinforcing it."[24] In the 1970s, comedies such as *All in the Family* (1971–1983) and *Maude* (1972–1978) attempted to redress certain racialized and gendered constructions embodied in the White psyche, albeit in-your-face.[25] By humorously addressing the sociopolitical issues of the time—race, women's work, and war—while grappling with how these issues affected White America, these Lear series challenged societal norms and changes while still returning a profit—an American, capitalistic success.

For example, in the episode "Florida's Problem" on *Maude* (1973), Florida's (Esther Rolle) husband (John Amos) demands that she quit her job as the Finleys' maid (fig. 2). She refuses. This causes a battle of gendered wills and racialized debates of marital relationships between Florida and her employer, Maude Finley (Bea Arthur). This type of open discussion provided an innovative and progressive approach to normalizing perceived social differences. However, not many others followed in that vein and none, except *Frank's Place* and *Roc*, have been Black-cast comedies.

America's progressive view of difference has come not from altruistic feelings and urges for equality but from a transforming American look, sound, and especially count. As illustrated with the civil rights and women's movements, the results of the Vietnam War, the professional faces of affirmative action, and the beginning of a new deregulatory economic era, America has changed. And television comedy has transformed itself along with it (despite some periodic television and societal resistance as shown in the popularity of *Happy Days* (1974–1984), *Laverne and Shirley* (1976–1983), and *The Waltons* (1972–1981).[26]

Although wearing the proper skin, however, Black women failed to benefit substantially from the colorized onslaught of 1990s comedies. David Atkin commented: "In spite of . . . apparent progress, it is striking that the criterion offerings involving minority females lagged far behind those featuring white females. Single minority women, who represent something of a double minority to producers and audiences, remain culturally unfamiliar entities."[27] On the surface this unfamiliarity seems antithetical to the claims of postmodernism, which not only allows and encourages the margins to speak (Toni Morrison, Maya Angelou, bell hooks) but suggests that others will be receptive to their voices. But it looks as if taking into account the extenuating circumstances of real Black women's lives bars and perhaps confines them to reel, "unfamiliar entities." Therefore, interrogating the television comedy form unveils many roadblocks to Black women's participation. Whether talking about its articulations as reality, its ability to parody itself, its location as uniquely feminine, or its commonsense understanding in our daily lives, television comedy proves a critical battleground for women—even Black ones.

WHITENESS AND TELEVISION COMEDY

I suggest that whiteness, television, and representation connect intimately. Whiteness frames television, thus impacting representation. Acknowledging the propensity of whiteness in the postmodern era, scholars began to address this spotlight—this unacknowledged whiteness—in the fields of cultural and ethnic studies.

The term *whiteness* itself takes shape and form through overlapping and sometimes contentious definitions of its presence and normality. Ruth Frankenberg insists that "the term 'whiteness' signals the production and reproduction of dominance rather than subordination, normativity rather than marginality, and privilege rather than disadvantage."[28] John Fiske calls it a "strategic deployment of power."[29] Toni Morrison asserts, "Even, and especially when American texts are not 'about' Africanist presences or characters or narrative or idiom, the shadow hovers in implication, in sign, in line of demarcation."[30] Carol Boyce Davies believes that even in its unacknowledged state whiteness provokes blackness.[31] As discussed here, whiteness reigns as a controlling, dominating, patriarchal, standard-bearing ideology that regulates visual production, influences viewer consumption, and exists without notice or name. In its invisibility whiteness, along with blackness, supplies an overarching context and meaning to television representation—especially comedy.

However, analogous to Jean-François Lyotard's postmodern impulse, Nick

Browne's notion of the television "supertext" argues against discussing television within a theoretical framing—like whiteness—that does not specifically address commodity control. Browne insists that a more effective method of investigating television comes via its production and presentation. In fact, he suggests that the television schedule—the supertext—must be investigated before addressing the commodity—program—supported within the schedule.[32] While this theory serves as a useful tool in television studies, it does not consider the impact and effect of whiteness discourses.

I believe that the supertext of whiteness functions beyond the schedule. It is the funding source, the production head, the distribution line, and largely the exhibition ward. The only element of the television food chain that escapes the direct control of white ideology is the individual viewer's ability to turn the television on or off—making its viability as a theoretical and actual application, beyond the schedule supertext, a mandatory consideration. Additionally, the schedule holds increasingly limited connection to television texts in this postmodern era. With the VCR, syndication, frequent schedule changes, remote control, satellites, Internet, and digital options, television viewing differs for contemporary audiences not only because of external factors but, more important, because of internal ones.[33] As distilled and configured, whiteness operates as a constructed, immaterial, largely untenable entity, yet its pervasiveness causes material and tangible visual effects on those it provides for, as well as on those it excludes. Whiteness defines American situation comedy and, consequently, the stake Black women have in it.

Further, over the entire past century, scholars from W.E.B. Du Bois to Trinh T. Minh-ha have documented various types of historic nonpresence, nonhumanity for Colored women as shown initially in films ranging from *Gone with the Wind* (1939) to *Pulp Fiction* (1994) to *Mission Impossible II* (2000). Said representations often coincide with the expected filmic role of Colored servants or extras to be seen but not heard. For example, the Black maid Mavis (Verna O. Hobson) serves literally as part of the mise-en-scène in Woody Allen's *Hannah and Her Sisters* (1986). She cooks, serves, cleans, and functions in the neurotic Thanksgiving world of the others but in silence and without notice. Her presence in the opening and closing of the film, coupled with her lack of sound, encourages whiteness and blackness—the neurosis of it in this case—to establish their circularity, normality, and hierarchical placement.[34] Trinh asserts that "silence can only be subversive when it frees itself from the male-defined context of absence, lack, and fear as feminine territories."[35]

The corollary to Hobson's fictional depiction, as Jeanne Noble reminds us, is that "[m]ost black domestics see their work as unattractive. Reflecting the feelings of their society, they look upon their job as requiring little skill, and they believe that nobody would do this work if they could do anything else."[36]

Images visually confirm the legitimacy of those feelings. Black women in their historic servitude and physical appearance assume a certain uncomfortable present absence within White visual culture. Moreover, Black women *must* negotiate this whiteness, this presumption, if they are to acquire any agency.

In real-life, introduced settings Black women receive acknowledgment by Whites. But once outside that arena, often their entire beings melt into a sea of colored bodies that move across the pathways of "regular" Americans. They remain unrecognized until the next time they occupy their proper place. With fewer Black domestics in Hollywood film and television narratives, their embodiment comes through the roles of the assistant (not secretary nor receptionist), the fast-food worker (not the manager), the middle-management executive of human resources (not of finance), and the mystic/Tarot card reader.[37]

With majority Americans so accustomed to seeing colored faces with their "inner eyes," Negras easily assume anonymity and obscurity by virtue of their physical location.[38] In television one example occurs in a 1990 episode of the cop/law drama *Law and Order.* Detectives Greevey (George Dzundza) and Logan (Christopher Noth) investigate an apartment in a Black tenement. Inside they walk toward the camera and pass a Black child on the steps. The shot cuts to the child watching them pass without their noticing her presence. She calls out, "Are you the man?"—eyes and voice pleading to be recognized. Without returning her look or motioning with his head Greevey replies, "We sure are."[39] In other television dramas Grace (Jonelle Allen) of *Dr. Quinn, Medicine Woman,* Rhonda (Vanessa Williams) of *Melrose Place,* and Guinan (Whoopi Goldberg) of *Star Trek: The Next Generation* all achieved subjectivity only when occupying their predetermined spaces.[40] These examples imply that within American cultural capital, if Colored women fail to appear in a Black-cast program, namely comedy, actualization and therefore subjectivity become improbable.

THIS IS COSBY'S HOUSE!

After the cancellation of *Amos 'n' Andy* and *Beulah* no other sitcoms concerning African-Americans appeared on prime time for fifteen years. Consequently, from the late 1950s until the end of the 1960s the narrative of situation comedy was thoroughly dominated by professional, college-educated WASPs.[41] This television dearth would later reverse itself following Vanessa Williams's winning of the Miss America crown and the explosion of male-dominated Black cinema. But one decisive development convinced network television executives that "going Black" once again could create substantial profits: the phenomenal success of *The Cosby Show.*

Reminiscent of earlier cinema and sitcoms, the greater preponderance of 1980s and 1990s Black comedies pictured happy, smiling faces of those still deemed the nation's "problem people." In his book's title, *Toms, Coons, Mulattoes, Mammies, and Bucks,* Donald Bogle captured the projected types of African-American images that prevailed in television. Some, like those Clark College freshwomen, thought that *The Cosby Show* was different.

In 1984 *The Cosby Show* introduced the ideal American family that just happened to be Black. An unprecedented success, the program aired for eight years, reigning in the number one spot for five of those years. For the first time on television a Black, professional, upper-middle-class, two-parent family appeared with an obvious orientation toward Afrocentric cultural specificities.[42] From their artwork to their clothing to their nonverbal modes of communication, a recognizable Negro context emanated from the program. African-Americans recognized this and watched faithfully. Other spectators tapped into the universality and humanity of the show's messages and tuned in faithfully, too.

The program began, functioned, and ended with a solid nuclear (American) family. David Marc called it "a kind of upside-down *Amos 'n' Andy,* offering a vision of a well-to-do inner-city black family living a life utterly compatible with the values and goals of the suburban middle classes."[43] Despite the condescending and racially charged flippancy of his assessment, *The Cosby Show* did mirror mainstream White situation comedies where the home-social sphere was dominated by men (or one man) but populated by women.

Both parents are white-collar professionals. Cliff Huxtable (Bill Cosby) operates a medical practice, and his wife, Clair (Phylicia Rashad), is a partner in a law firm. Whereas Cliff's office exists as an extension of the house (and consequently of himself), we rarely see Clair working or discussing her work at home. This lack of attention to her profession provokes Taylor to remark that "the celebration of the opening up of women's roles in the 1970s shows becomes, in the 1980s, at best a rehearsal of the costs of careerism for women, at worst an outright reproof for women who seek challenging work."[44]

Bill Cosby created believable, stable, and progressive Black women who held their own, although he always retained control. The Cosby women were eclectic and attractive. Their moral center revolved around Cosby himself. Plus, along with Clair, he guided the daughters and son, Theo, through dilemmas and decisions that reflected his values of hard work, modesty, and prosperity. Although it was refreshing at that time to see a multiplicity of Black women, their roles remained subordinate to the magnitude of Cosby. In fact, Mike Budd and Clay Steinman argue that the show could critique sexism partly because it largely ignored racism.[45]

Most television products featuring marginalized and disenfranchised subjects were "outsider creations" that attempted to tell the majority population about the minority. *The Cosby Show* was an "insider creation" (or as inside as possible, with no mode of physical production and distribution), designed, says Dates, "for the minority group to contribute its own culture and identity and to allow it to express its unique worldview"[46]—all within the confines of a television sitcom.

Yet despite its unconventional emphasis on a culturally specific context, the series harkened to 1950s sitcoms such as *Ozzie and Harriet* and *Leave It to Beaver* and 1960s fare such as *The Brady Bunch*. In these worlds no shortages, crime, or drugs existed. Fredric Jameson considers this nostalgia for an earlier era of *nonexistent* family coherence a striving for a type of realism, one encapsulated by the past and fearful of the uncontrollable and Colored present.[47] Sut Jhally and Justin Lewis characterize *The Cosby Show* as a form of enlightened racism.[48] Herman Gray contends that the program "constructed and enabled new ways of representing African Americans' lives . . . [but] within black cultural politics of difference . . . [it confined] black diversity [to] the limited sphere of domesticity and upper-middle-class affluence."[49] Whatever one's position, progressive or reactionary, no one can dismiss the fact that *The Cosby Show* spawned a host of other programs featuring Black families, for example, *Charlie and Co* (1985–1986), *A Different World* (1987–1993), *Family Matters* (1989–1998), *The Parent 'Hood* (1995–1999), *The Hughleys* (1998–present), and *My Wife and Kids* (2001–present).[50] It introduced a model for Black representation on national television beyond the realm of news and music videos. Unfortunately, its thrust, although duplicated, has yet to be sustained. The veracity of this statement comes through looking at an example of Black comedy's first prolific home—the Fox Television network.

THE RISE OF FOX

On the backs of African-Americans Fox Broadcasting emerged as the fourth "major network." In 1987 it began airing comedies that other networks had passed on, shows such as *Married with Children* (1987–1997), *Duet* (1987–1989), and *Tracey Ullman* (1987–1990). Trying to differentiate itself from the other networks, Fox decided to take chances with its programming. According to Kristal Brent Zook, Fox "wanted to be the rebel network."[51] Besides differing its subject matter and genre, this gamble involved targeting an underserved and younger audience while offering Black faces in bulk. Its Generation X target demographic included African-Americans, but the network also aimed for White, hip-hop young adults eighteen to forty-nine years old—by way of the racialized bodies of Blacks.[52]

According to Zook, "[b]y 1993, the fourth network was airing the largest single crop of Black-produced shows in television history. And by 1995 black Americans . . . were a striking 25 percent of Fox's market."[53] With Fox's and cable elevation, viewership at the other networks "declined by a corporation-wrecking 25 percent."[54] John Caldwell suggests that this "hemorrhaging of viewership" may seem ironic given the fact that extreme forms of stylization and spectator-binding visual imagery also emerged during the very same years.[55] Yet corporate desperation necessitated a shift in programming, as feelings of angst filled young Whites with a sense of the collapsing job market and the recognition that "trickling down" did not necessarily mean trickling down to them.[56] Consequently, programs such as *COPS* (1989–present), *The Simpsons* (1987–present), and *Married with Children* (1987–1997) excelled because of their (1) harkening to a previous, profitable time, (2) sarcasm, and (3) response to the darkening economic and television horizon.

Fox programs in the 1990s featured African-Americans *In Living Color* on *The Sinbad Show*. They were *Living Single* mostly in a *New York Undercover*–type of situation while constantly being placed between a *Roc* and *Martin*. Puns aside, these shows presented lighthearted, and in some respects, safe comedies. Zook argues that these Black-produced shows embraced autobiography, improvisation, aesthetics, and a certain pride in Black visual signifiers.[57] Yet most lacked the edge of *The Simpsons* or the irreverence of *Married with Children*, the exception being *In Living Color*.

In Living Color's (1990–1994) creator, Keenan Ivory Wayans, developed a skit-driven, satirical comedy show that creatively commented on Black and other cultures. Central to *In Living Color*'s humor, according to Herman Gray, was its framing of race and forays into the construction of whiteness. Gray maintains that "[w]hether in relation to liberal guilt, assumptions about (white) feminine beauty, or the normalization of racist absurdities, whiteness is a consistent object of ridicule, satire, and commentary."[58] In 1992, however, because of creative differences with the show's White producers, Wayans departed acrimoniously, followed by several other Black cast members. The show turned into a watered-down, ethnic slugfest as the cast became more than half White. The loss of Black visionary and actual control resulted in not much more than well-worn stereotypical offerings of ethnics.[59]

Beyond this, the Black Fox programs received a vastly different marketing thrust than their network cohorts. Widely acclaimed *Roc* (1991–1994), for example, lasted only three years before it was canceled. Although declining viewer numbers were cited as the reason for its cancellation, capitalism and the NFL contract with Fox provided more of the rationale for its and other sitcoms' demises. The other less socially conscious series, however, survived longer.

Thus, in the late 1980s and early 1990s Rupert Murdoch (CEO of News Corporation, Fox's parent) "found ways to profit from the cultural production and consumption practices of African-Americans . . . [and] also manipulated, to the collective detriment of black people, governmental infrastructures designed to balance the racially distorted playing field of media ownership. When such infrastructures threatened to limit Murdoch's monopolistic domination, . . . he simply had them removed."[60] This included Black faces that might bar his ascendancy to the fourth network position. By 2000 no Black-cast comedy existed on the Fox network. They migrated, or were otherwise exiled, to the UPN and WB upstarts that were busy trying to emulate Fox's success via Black programming. With all of this corporate maneuvering, 1990s comedies developed a peculiarity of their own.

CONTEMPORARY BLACK SITUATION COMEDY

At the threshold of a new millennium, television programming possessed a decidedly ethnic flavor. Whether through advertisement or as part of program content, Black urban youth culture framed the aesthetic. Those same youth suffered from the commodification of their culture. Labeled hip-hop, it dominated mainstream America. Yet instead of producing dramatically different ideological and representational landscapes, as forecasted by scholars such as Jean-François Lyotard and J. Fred MacDonald, television at large looked substantially unchanged. The same types of family coherence *(The Cosby Show, Family Ties, The Parent 'Hood)*, modicum of slapstick *(The Simpsons, Saved by the Bell, Martin)*, and incredulity *(Alf, 3rd Rock from the Sun, Homeboys in Outer Space)* were offered—achieved provisionally (and alas, the difference) in Black and sometimes brown.[61]

With television demands for quick ratings' successes, the representation of Black culture in sitcoms became grounded less in statistical, historical, or cultural actualities and more within barely researched and undocumented social imaginaries—mythologies sustained by producers and writers who operated on the capitalistic principle of supply and demand. Consistently, White and Black *creatives*, if you will, visioned African-American life in the singular. This depiction, they hedged, would advance a sustained and lucrative way of representing Black people.

Cultural critic Stuart Hall posits that the definition of cultural identity adopted and utilized in visual culture consists of a shared, collective, and common self—one based on historical experience. According to Hall identity forms "stable, unchanging and continuous frames of reference and meaning, beneath the shifting divisions and vicissitudes of our actual history."[62] This collective cultural naming and claiming serves as the de facto guide of most image-producing industries. White supremacist patriarchy that dominates visual culture does not stand alone, however, in its use of collective cultural identity as a foundation. Almost all U.S.-based movements and many postcolonial struggles have coalesced on the precept of an essentialized identity, almost always predicated on race. Thus, racialized visioning rests on a long and extended history that includes Black characterizations, sitcoms, and the few Black women within the two.

Black screenwriter Franklyn Ajaye contends that the main problem of representation resides with the control of image production. He laments that "[i]t's absurd to let white television executives and producers have sullen ghetto hip-hoppers and lascivious buffoons set the cultural agenda for African-Americans."[63] This agenda setting, however, is not a new phenomenon. Blacks' and other marginalized groups' roles in television comedy endure routine characterization by what Nina Leibman calls ethnic repression, ethnic inferiority, or ethnic exotica. She asserts that early in television history "all ethnic groups were reassured that proper consuming habits and esteem for puritanical ethics would situate them along an axis of potential (although ultimately unattainable) assimilation."[64] But like the promises and possibilities of *Brown v. the Board of Education*, Jesse Jackson's bid for the presidency, and enterprise zones, the cultural identity marked and produced for Coloreds provided minimal and confined spaces for Black performers and often contentious ones.

Ideological positions mapped themselves onto the bodies of African-American characters and labeled their identity. In the 1970s, for example, Michael Evans (Ralph Carter, *Good Times*) wore Black cultural consciousness and academic achievement like a badge of honor. The two complemented each other. His 1990s counterpart, however, acquiesced to narrative and cultural stereotypes of Black men and their connection to education. Steve Urkel (Jaleel White, *Family Matters*) signified the contemporary consequence of educated Black boys—effeminacy, underdevelopment, and nerdishness.[65] Postmodern cultural identity for American Negroes remained simply humorous. Moreover, a telling contradiction existed between these popular depictions and the number of marginalized people shown.

Despite the rumblings about a Black programming inundation, the actual numbers remained low and were confined to one arena. In more than four hundred new network and cable sitcoms aired in prime time between 1980 and 2000, nearly seventy carried predominantly Black casts. Almost half of them, however, lasted for less than one year. Additionally, according to a study conducted between 1981 and 1991, of more than nineteen thousand speaking roles on prime-time television, people of color spoke only thirteen percent of them—that includes all people of color.[66] By 2001 the numbers reflected improvement, but they also reflected a television world overwhelmed by "able-bodied, single, heterosexual, white, male adults under 40."[67] This perceived abundance, but actual lack, heightened with Black women's representation.[68]

I focus on the *Fresh Prince of Bel-Air, Martin, Living Single,* and *Moesha* because they represent not only the legacy of *The Cosby Show* but also twenty-first-century projections of African-American women in terms of work roles, characterization, class, and identity.[69] Plus, 1990s series introduced often-neglected class disparities among African-Americans—from the Bel-Air community to the poverty-stricken, amorphous South-Central L.A.

These series offered fascinating and unique yet problematic constructions of Black womanhood, propelled and extended from earlier representations. Speaking specifically of *A Different World* (1987–1993), for example, Herman Gray suggests that contemporary Negroes were wrapped in a culture-specific blackness. These Black bodies were "routinely adorned with hairstyles and draped in clothing that clearly signaled the rich repertoire and vernacular of black youth culture. In this way the show integrated the looks, styles, and feels of black youth culture without seeming artificial or forced."[70]

In these updated sitcoms Black women's experiences still appeared marginalized within the narrative, the mise-en-scène, the modes of production, and the fiduciary structure. The racialized framing left limited room for the gendered construction imposed upon them. Yet African-American women's hyphenated and unacknowledged structuring increasingly impacted television comedy. At the crossroads of gender, race, class, and generation, womanism and Black women's representations stood poised for action. The 1990s comedies, therefore, exemplified the tension that remained and was proffered by, with, and through the hyphens of Blackness, Americanness, and womanhood. With this television background I turn to *Fresh Prince of Bel-Air, Martin, Living Single,* and *Moesha* to excavate contemporary meanings offered by and derived from Black women's representation in situation comedy.

FRESH PRINCE OF BEL-AIR

Begun in 1990, *Fresh Prince of Bel-Air (FPBA)* emerged as a vehicle for the rapper Fresh Prince, aka Will Smith. It was the comedic version of coproducer Benny Medina's real life.[71] In the tradition of early television characters like *Good Times'* J. J., *Diff'rent Strokes'* Arnold, and *Family Matters'* Urkel, Smith plays a charming coon—in this case a boy from urban (Black) west Philadelphia—uprooted from his "dangerous" community to a life of safety and wealth with relatives in the hills of Bel-Air, California. The supporting cast exists as narrative foil to the Fresh Prince (fig. 3).

This functioning nuclear family (in other words, mom and dad at home) includes the Fresh Prince's aunt, Vivian Banks (Janet Hubert-Whitten 1990–1993, Daphne Maxwell Reid 1993–1996); her husband, Judge Philip Banks (James Avery); their children Hilary (Karyn Parsons), Carlton (Alfonso Ribeiro), Ashley (Tatyana M. Ali), and, later, Nicky (Ross Bagley). Also included

FIGURE 3

Cast of *Fresh Prince of Bel-Air* (NBC). *Back row, left to right:* Janet Hubert-Whitten, Joseph Marcell, Alfonso Ribeiro, Tatyana M. Ali, Karyn Parsons. *Center:* James Avery. *Foreground:* Will Smith.

(Courtesy of Jerry Ohlinger's Movie Material Store)

in this family unit is Black British butler Geoffrey (Joseph Marcell)—a sort of irreverent Mr. Belvedere, Mr. French, and Benson (from *Soap*) all rolled up in one.[72] The women of the series either take care of, depend on, or worship Smith—in direct correspondence to their age. Ashley solicits advice, Hilary needs protection, and Vivian depends on him to help with the others.

The narrative of *FPBA* operates in predictable sitcom fashion, with Smith moving from one mishap to another. As described by NBC's press, "Will (Smith) charms, disarms and alarms members of his adoptive uppercrust family with his streetwise ways."[73] The Fresh Prince is the Captain Kirk or Mack of Bel Air, and beautiful, young Black women want him.

The siblings' WASP-y names, Hilary, Carlton, and Ashley, forecast their hierarchical positioning and the potential reversal of class structures faced with the real blackness embodied in Will. In fact, the comedic tension of class created by Will's presence drives the story. Moralistic in tone, the program allowed Smith to evolve from a young, irresponsible teenager into a successful university student by series end. Although the women matured also, they failed to substantially evolve. The same type of class tension forwarded the romantic comedy *Martin*.

MARTIN

The series *Martin* brought to life the 1943 musings of Zora Neale Hurston, who talked in her essay "The 'Pet' Negro System" about Colored people's positioning: "when everything is discounted, it still remains true that white people North and South have promoted Negroes—usually *in the capacity of 'representing The Negro'*—with little thought of the ability of the person promoted but in line with the 'pet' system."[74] Hurston's pet system, in an updated form, exemplifies the character Martin Payne in the series of the same name, which began August 27, 1992. The show's creators, Andy and Susan Borowitz, previously helped pen the aforementioned *Fresh Prince of Bel-Air*. When the show premiered, mixed popular reviews appeared. *Time* magazine called *Martin* a "post-Cosby show farce, a show for the I-am-not-a-role-model Age of Charles Barkley, a comic romp that puts the 'id' back in video."[75] In other words, *Time* claimed that the show reintroduced Afrocentric clowns. However, similar to other romantic comedies, *Martin* possessed the "evolution and intransigence" of romantic coupling—that is, according to television scholar Bambi Haggins, "the logistics . . . banter and the unwavering adherence to the [romantic comedy] formula and to the autonomy embedded within it."[76]

Haggins maintains that the success of this form of comedy comes through the audience's ability to accept two things: the construction of a happy ending

FIGURE 4

Cast of *Martin* (Fox). *Left to right:* Tisha Campbell-Martin, Martin Lawrence, Carl Anthony Payne II, Tichina Arnold, and Thomas Mikal Ford.
(Courtesy of Jerry Ohlinger's Movie Material Store)

and banter—"the witty, rapid-fire repartee, replete with sexual innuendo, double entendre and lots of sexual tension that inflects the dialogue."[77] Like White cinema predecessors and even television series such as *Mork and Mindy* (1978–1982), the coupling in *Martin* revolved around and hinged on the male protagonist and his love interest (fig. 4).

Martin postured himself as a tough, macho (sexist) man. Yet for all of this machismo, this hypermasculinity, he remained devoted to and controlled by Gina Waters (Tisha Campbell-Martin). Several friends stayed (almost literally) in their lives: Gina's best friend, Pamela 'Pam' James (Tichina Arnold), and Martin's partners, Tommy Strong (Thomas Mikal Ford) and Cole Brown (Carl Anthony Payne II). Beyond these permanent cast members, Lawrence impersonated several other recurring characters: Otis, an ancient security guard; Jerome, a 1970s throwback player; and Roscoe, a delinquent child neighbor of Gina's. More germane to this study, Lawrence transformed himself into two Black women—his mother, Evelyn Payne, and his b-girl neighbor, Sheneneh Jenkins.

Over the course of the series Gina, Martin, and their sidekicks traversed contemporary and commonplace relationship drama until series end, when they moved to California for continued Buppie mobility. Via humor their staying power turned on Martin's capitulation to love despite class disparities.

LIVING SINGLE

The women of *Living Single (LS)* forwarded a classless agenda similar to that of *Martin* without wading through the same class minefields. In *Living Single* middle-class success is already solidified. Touted by some as "the first voice of the self-sufficient Black woman," *Living Single* centered on the lives of four Black, single, young, urban women (fig. 5).[78] Three of the women lived together while the other stayed there most of the time. All were professional, confidant, attractive, and in American capitalistic terms, successful. Played by veteran young performers, the women composed a family unit—in an extended Black family context. The program was built around rap artist Queen Latifah (aka Dana Owens), who played Khadijah James. In the show she publishes a hip-hop magazine called *Flavor*. Kim Fields (Tootie, from *Facts of Life* fame) played Regine Hunter, an ingenue. Erika Alexander portrayed high-powered lawyer Maxine Shaw, and comedienne Kim Coles appeared as Synclaire James, the simple cousin/secretary to Khadijah. These Black women offered a unique twist to Generation X, Black America by introducing the commodified hip-hop aesthetic but grounded in the vernacular and style of a gendered, mainstream African-America. The cast completed itself with their upstairs neighbors/lovers/male counterparts Kyle Barker (T. C. Carson) and Overton Wakefield Jones (John Henton).

The producer and creator of the show, Yvette Lee Bowser (a young, Black sistah herself), envisioned the program as an extension of herself and her friends.[79] During the series run we see Black women's lives unfold across various dilemmas—many peculiar to Black women and women in general. As

FIGURE 5

Cast of *Living Single* (Fox). *Left to right:* Queen Latifah, Kim Fields, Erika Alexander, and Kim Coles.

(Courtesy of Jerry Ohlinger's Movie Material Store)

will be explored later, the series moved from its inordinate focus on women's problems with men to address such topics as breast reduction surgery, lesbianism, maternity, and general human frailties. With its twofold series end, we watched the women moving in different directions but remaining family nevertheless.[80] The young adult demographic of this program and its hip-hop foundation paved the way for the final sitcom I will examine here, *Moesha*.

MOESHA

Created in the mid-1990s, *Moesha* (1995–2001) capitalized on the sugar-sweet, pop-culture singing sensation Brandy Norwood and courted the teen-aged market. Played by Norwood, *Moesha* tries to humorously illustrate the struggles of growing up young, Black, and female in Los Angeles. The character is surrounded by a TV-typical nuclear family that includes veteran stage and television actress Sheryl Lee Ralph as Moesha's stepmother, Dee Mitchell; William Allen Young as Moesha's father, Frank; and Marcus T. Paulk as the little brother, Myles. In 1997 Norwood's actual brother, Willie Norwood Jr., debuted as Moesha's cousin/brother.

Typical to the centering of a character, Moesha has several friends that explore the angst of coming of age in a Black, middle-class context. They include childhood friend turned love interest Hakeem (Lamont Bentley), girlfriend Niecy Jackson (Shar Jackson), and Kim Parker (Countess Vaughn). Of all the series I present here, *Moesha* most embodies the broadening of Black American culture for larger mainstream consumption. With its placement in Leimert Park, Los Angeles (a revitalizing middle-class Black community), *Moesha*'s positioning addresses poignantly the complexities of affirmative action gains and assimilation for young Black Americans, particularly in a place where "No color lines" and "Can't we all just get along" are city mantras.[81] Yet her gendered lead opens up spaces for the ensemble cast to flourish (fig. 6). Further, it allows for social issues to become better articulated.

The series focused on serious issues but allowed Moesha to discuss them from a teenager's point of view. Frequently, the comedy ends in a lesson learned rather than in a return to normalcy. Every episode concludes with Moesha reflecting on the show's twenty-two-minute dilemma. This program particularly reflects the complexities of teen life in the twenty-first century.

SO IT BEGINS . . .

All of these programs' opening credits enunciated the battle between African-American women's objectification and their agency. *FPBA* quite explicitly announced its agenda toward Black women in its series opening—none appear.[82]

FIGURE 6

Cast of *Moesha* (UPN). *Left to right:* Ray J, Shar Jackson, Marcus T. Paulk, Brandy, Lamont Bently, Yvette Wilson, William Allen Young, and Sheryl Lee Ralph. *Courtesy of UPN Media.*

In this opening Fresh Prince raps about his coming to Bel Air and, in cartoon fashion, illustrates the words. Similar to the tempo and style of a song that popularized him in 1988, "Parents Just Don't Understand," Smith anchored the narrative, an accurate preview of what happens in the program.

Martin's opening credits introduced the show's narrative conflicts and the victor of each: male over female, poor over rich, Black over White, light over dark. Movement, as part of various spatial and temporal discourses that are often overlooked, gave the opening an overall characterization not articulated by any of the opening's other formal structures. Rudolf Arnheim has suggested that "it is the task of the actors and the director to emphasize the expressive qualities of motion and thereby to define the character of the entire film as well as that of the single scene and the single shot."[83] *Martin*'s opening adhered to this filmic theory. It provided the context for gendered, classist, and sexualized relationships that direct the series.

Specifically, in the first two seasons the show's title font pieces itself together through animation. A musical background with a strong bass beat paces the women's voices singing the name *Martin*. Intermittently, testimonials are heard from a deeper, presumably (his) masculine voice. For example, one says, "I'm the man." The image of Lawrence, the actor, appears next to his name (blurring the boundaries of the real and the fictional) and jump-cuts into several shots of himself along with his two female-impersonated characters. Lawrence's Sheneneh appears, twisting her shorted hips. Clearly the hips are an important part, as they are severed from the rest of her/his body, are in the foreground, and occupy central framing—a signal of this "woman's" and other women's "physical" importance to the narrative. The mother character is shown also in a sweater, white wig, and skirt (plus a moustache).

In a medium shot Gina, the character, appears beside the actresses' name and then in relation to other elements. One of these elements is Lawrence's head, enlarged and overshadowing her body. The scene cuts to the two kissing in long shot and then to an extreme close-up. The opening includes Cole, Tommy, and then Pam (the compositioning of which changes slightly in the 1994–1995 season). In her brief appearance Pam looms larger than the two men, according her some power. However, she is the only character shown lying down. Unlike the men and Gina, Pam receives only a one-second shot alone before being thrust with all the other characters. Even in her brief frame with Gina, "her girl," she receives lesser status.

In that instance Pam appears smaller. Gina is in the foreground with her enlarged head as the focus of the frame. She glances in Pam's direction but fails to look directly at her. Pam, on the other hand, looks directly at Gina. Although her whole upper body is shown, Pam's positioning denies her subjectivity. In other words, she factors as the quintessential visual prop frequently offered in music video. She leans back to point at Gina. In Black kinetic vernacular, she gives Gina the "it's all about you girl" sign—in some ways conceding her own power. This gesture and her placement not only signify her minor importance to the series but introduce problematic color considerations plaguing Black communities. Binaries like these illuminate and define the series.

Living Single's opening credits give quite a different view of "today's Black woman." Queen Latifah, in voice-over, raps over a sound track of women singing "We are living, single." Originally, the series opened with multiple shots of Manhattan, brownstones, and a young Black woman (Big Les) hip-hop dancing in silhouette on the rooftop of an apartment building, as white sheets blow on a clothesline. The scene then cuts to cast members lined up as the camera pans across their dancing bodies. In both versions individual headshots materialize as colorfully framed pictures with fonts of the actors' names. Big Les dances alongside each character as the song exclaims, "I'm glad I got my girl." With the rap sustained throughout, this scene is intercut with shots of lipsticks in a store window and Regine in full diva regalia plastered against the elevator door of Khadijah's *Flavor* magazine. The other three women snap their heads to look at her. In the version that concluded the series, singing introduced the show, the lipsticks disappeared, the rap was shortened, and Regine's drama disappeared.

Bambi Haggins believes that the white sheets blowing on the clothesline particularly define the text of *LS*. She associates them with the KKK and racist oppression. The sheets, she maintains, symbolize washing by "thousands of African-American women who worked as domestics in White households," and, I add, the White world of network television. Haggins suggests that in each instance "the fly-girl triumphant dance ends in front of the sheets, within sight of the sheets. The trauma, the history, the stereotypes condensed in the image of the sheets are 'always there' during the fly-girls—even when it is not visible within the frame."[84] This constant negotiation brings us back to the way whiteness frames television in general and situation comedy in particular. Yet not until *Moesha* does the full-blown visual realization of Black women's successful negotiation become manifest.

The opening of *Moesha* combined the progressive tendencies of *Living Single* with the sensibilities of urban youth, squarely centering the singer turned actress. In the legacy of *Julia, Thea,* and *Mary Tyler Moore,* the *Moesha* opening fostered a sense of independence and womanist coming of age. Frequently, episodes began with a teaser before the narrative actually began—a technique reintroduced in 1990s prime-time television. Moesha's voice-over monologues introduced sociopolitical and/or cultural dilemmas to be covered in the upcoming episode. But her actions often foreground youth privilege and entitlement rampant in contemporary culture.

As Norwood, stylishly clad, dances and lip-synchs her own voice, the show's other characters move behind her on a cyclorama-like visual wheel. She sings "I gotta do what I gotta do. I gotta move," alerting the viewer that this Generation X girl truly reflects the gains of the 1980s. She expects the backing of her family but will go on her own to achieve what she wants. Creators Ralph Farquhar, Sara Finney, and Vida Spears saw to that. Says Spears, "We wanted *Moesha* to be someone who reflected who we were as teenagers and someone who not just young African-American girls, but all girls, could relate to."[85]

Having contextualized these series' trajectory and how they introduced themselves to the television audience, I turn to four intertwined elements in television comedy that define and give meaning to Black women's representation there: work roles, characterization, class, and identity.

THE SUIT MAKES THE WOMAN?

As is well known, American capitalist culture frequently defines who you are by what you do. This ideology, however, flies in the face of traditional African-American culture—where work/status presumed nothing about your character or ability. What complicates this conundrum further is that situation comedy offers only rare glimpses of characters actually working, even when the site of humor is the workplace.

In Caucasian-dominated comedies such as *The John Larroquette Show, Wings, Nurses,* and *NewsRadio,* invisible buses arrived and departed, passengers bought tickets, planes flew sans pilots, and patients only sporadically existed. Of course, exceptions existed to this comedic nonwork ethic in series such as *Murphy Brown, M*A*S*H, Ally McBeal,* and *Cheers* (*Cheers* only because the work involved drinking and everyone participated).[86] But added to this television oddity, many television comedies position their characters in occupations that necessitate creative expression—spaces where most real-life Americans *don't* work.

For example, in the romantic comedy *Mad about You,* Paul (Paul Reiser) was a documentary filmmaker and his wife, Jamie (Helen Hunt), a public relations executive. In *Friends* Monica (Courtney Cox) worked as an assistant chef, and in *Designing Women* the women all designed stuff (or served as beautiful P.R., as in the case of Suzanne). This pattern existed in Black-cast comedies too. In *Martin* (as in *Newsradio*) the radio program aired frequently without a technician. Martin was its disc jockey. In *FPBA* Hilary became a weather anchor, and Ashley began a singing career. And in *LS* Khadijah ran a magazine with Synclaire's assistance, and Regine worked in fashion. Only one of the series featured, *Moesha,* positioned characters in jobs found in mainstream working culture. Dee Mitchell worked as a high school vice principal. Moesha and her girl friends were students, and Andell (Yvette Wilson) ran a cafe. Creative occupations work well within White comedies because the quantity of sitcoms on television allows for many varied examples of work to appear. However, the occurrence has regressive ramifications with representations of African-Americans, especially Black women.

Because disproportionate numbers of Colored women characters work in occupations that involve performance or the creative/emotional side of human existence, they fail to achieve validation inside capitalism. Very few Black doctors, factory workers, lawyers, administrative assistants, teachers, or scientists are shown—and seldom are they Black women.[87] Many of these occupations require college degrees, vision, and/or an ability to thrive, not just survive. The lack of Black women shown in variant nonperformative occupations negates the actual look of the United States and suggests an erasure of gains made by this population.

Further, most of these work roles equated Black women's work with entertainment. Ashley's singing career, Patti LaBelle's jazz bar *(Out All Night)*, and Hilary as weather girl illustrated the most overt examples of this. But subtle work
roles like Jackee Harry *(227)* and Regine Hunter *(LS)* as pseudofashion divas,
discredit actual nurses, fast-food workers, teachers, and child-care providers
who work for their families. In other words, the work created for Black women
in television comedy reflects mainstream's proclivity to position them in servitude or performance (or both, as in the case of Nell on *Gimme a Break*). It leads
to simplistic designations for how and what African-American women should
and can be.

WHO IS THIS YOU SAY I AM?

Donald Bogle suggests that essentially two roles exist for Colored women
in visual culture: the mammy and the tragic mulatto. Filmmaker Marlon Riggs
added the role of the pickaninny. And Gloria Naylor invites spectators to
imagine African-American women's, "Nutmeg arms leaned over window sills,
gnarled ebony legs carr[ying] groceries up double flights of steps, and saffron
hands strung out on back-yard lines."[88] In other words, historic visual knowledge of Black women confines them to work that cleans, cooks, suffers, or
entertains.

The importance of talking about specific characters harkens back to chapter 1 and the dearth of representation on television. When one's frame of reference of others comes predominantly from the media (television, film, radio,
the Internet), that image becomes the reality of unfamiliar people. Despite
protests to the contrary, such as "I know this is a stereotype but . . . ," characterizations say something quite specific about African-American women—this
group in particular because of its paucity in visual culture. Consequently, situated somewhere between Jean-Paul Sartre's objectifying gaze and spectator
viewing that can confer agency (mostly in the Black imagination) live the
Black women of *Fresh Prince of Bel-Air, Martin, Living Single,* and *Moesha.*

The commonalities of these televisual Black women marked their differences. Sixteen sustained representatives of African-American womanhood
were provided in these television programs.[89] Minus Vivian, Mother Payne,
Dee, and Andell, all played under forty. They maintained a certain sense of
style—wearing clothes that complemented their weight, their skin tone, and
their own particular personas (or male interpretations thereof, especially in the
case of Sheneneh). Their homes reflected an Afrocentric perspective through
art, artifacts, and music. Many real-life middle-class, educated Blacks (remember those Clark College freshwomen?) appreciated these women because they

represented notions of themselves—intelligent (beyond Hilary and Synclaire), multiple skin shades, ambitious, and successful. Others laughed at and with their search for love, their conflicts with self, their maturation, and Lawrence's ascription of them. Like those Arizona women Savannah, Gloria, Bernadine, and Robin, most of these characters awaited the exhaling moment.[90] And still other spectators wondered why such bourgeois, superficial, and trivial ascriptions of African-American life continue(d).[91]

Differences emerged through their characterizations too. Banal, one-dimensional characterizations came through in the performances of Ashley and Vivian Banks. As an American child turned teenager, Ali's role (like the other women's on *FPBA*) was to provide support for the Fresh Prince. Over time she matured. She dated, worked, and sang and was included in family decisions. But her status and, in some way, her gender relegated her to the periphery. In the "Bundle of Joy" episode, which focuses on Nicky's impending birth, Ashley, feeling excluded and a bit jealous, "acts out"—as the old folks say. She fantasizes about her invisibility, complains about being displaced, and insists that no one hears her. Throughout the episode, the family assures her that she is not only loved but is also an important member of the family unit. Even so, in the final scene they drive off for dinner without her.[92]

Although scenarios like these awarded the actor Ali with lines, they sustained her objectification. She functioned as Will's "yes-(wo)man" and as a beautifying fixture on the set. Nothing in Ali's acting, attire, or the narratives surrounding her marked her as a particularly progressive woman, or as Black for that matter (if one subscribes to Black monikers). She occupied the space of an American (White) teenaged television family member. Her name even helped identify her class (and in some ways racial) positioning. Further, her placement gave additional commentary on the class structure of the comedy, as well as on contemporary Los Angeles culture.

Mother, Vivian Banks, another one-dimensional character, proved noteworthy not so much for the role but because of her interaction with the television operating system itself. As noted earlier, this role was occupied by different actresses, an uncommon, although not unheard of, phenomenon in situation comedy. According to the entertainment press, the mood swings of the then real-life pregnant Janet Hubert-Whitten conflicted with the producers and star, Will Smith.[93] After three seasons they replaced her but also demoted the character within the series. Not only does the new Vivian (Daphne Maxwell-Reid) carry fewer lines but forwards the narrative even less in the series than the prior character. This Vivian became a virtual living prop. Although the narrative change may have stemmed from the network's desire to avoid a recurrence of the previous scenario, I believe that the replacement choice sought to silence Black women who talk too much—who call attention to themselves and away from the main male character. In addition, the replacement choice itself added to Negro intraethnic color conflicts—ideas I will explore further momentarily.

Another interesting character, Kim Parker of *Moesha*, evolved as the legacy of *Martin*'s Sheneneh. Loud, round, and clueless, she steals scenes with her audacious, self-centered, and inane ruminations without signs of development. Yet she and her mother's antics proved showstopping enough to warrant a spin-off series of their own. *The Parkers* debuted on the UPN network during the 1999–2000 season. Kim and her mother, Nikki (Mo'Nique), are Kathleen Rowe's unruly women. Their sexuality oozes through anti–Ally McBeal bodies. They recognize popular-culture limitations but move beyond them. They make themselves spectacles because the narrative allows for it, which proves exceptionally gratifying to Black audiences.[94]

For similar reasons, the character Regine Hunter of *LS* deserves attention; in fact, she demands it. Producers promoted Regine as "a beautiful social climber in search of self and a man."[95] This rather simplistic and trite description of Regine evokes stereotypes of Black women (and women in general) who need a man, any man, to complete themselves. Yet Regine, unlike Suzanne Sugarbaker of *Designing Women*, maintained the historic film and television topography that labels Black women money grabbers, connivers, and vamps. Figures such as Nina Mae McKinney in *Hallelujah* (1929), the prostitute in *Car Wash* (1976), or Sondra of *227* illustrate that legacy. In one episode of *LS*, for example, a White feminist therapist/entrepreneur calls Regine an Olympian—a woman who "go[es] for the gold but not [her] own because [she's] too afraid to compete. [A woman who wants] a man to run [her] race for [her]."[96] Much of Regine's figure typified the characterization of Black woman as gold digger—at least partially.

Yet despite their generally static and flat genre characters, these comedies provide progressive representations of Black womanhood that espouse a certain womanist nod. *Living Single* contained two characters that personified this ethos frequently. As I stated earlier, Khadijah (Queen Latifah) owned a business. Tall, big, young, and outspoken, this character challenged male (sans racial consideration) depictions of the successful woman. Those who follow rap (and even those who don't) recognized Queen Latifah's longtime engagement with feminism. More recently, she reached mainstream audiences with her film appearances and daytime talk show. Ironically, her strong Black woman stance and visual strangeness married her to the rumor of lesbianism.

Because of rumors' ability to disrupt and destroy, *LS* attempted to distance Queen Latifah from a lesbian aesthetic. Although homosexuality received a degree of attention in 1990s prime-time drama, early situation comedy rarely touched it. Only in irreverent sitcoms such as *Roseanne, Married with Children, In Living Color,* and *Ellen* was the subject even broached.[97]

Completely taboo in Negro communities, issues of homosexuality aired only in jest or as heterosexual quips on Black-cast comedies (particularly in *Martin*). Lesbianism was rarely addressed.[98] Over time the producers softened Khadijah's look through hair styling, clothing, and makeup—making her more feminine. She became more than the foundation of the series. She usurped Synclaire's space as the conciliator. Khadijah soothed contentious situations while retaining her own determined way of getting results. This feminization worked as part of the absence of and in tandem with the whitening of African-American women despite the sistah (Bowser) at the helm. It helped keep Latifah from becoming a lesbian Antichrist in the Black community.

Competing for the title of best Black feminist, and unlike any of the other women characters of these series, Maxine Shaw (Erika Alexander) was unique. Toned, contemporary, and razor sharp, Max wore sex like a DK tank top. Her sexuality coupled with her quick wit defied containment. She not only harbored feminist articulations but extended them to their logical conclusion—the woman handled things. Similar to Betty Lovejoy in Tina McElroy Ansa's *Ugly Ways* (1993), Max refused pigeonholing or confinement by men. And unlike Nola Darling (Tracy Camilla Johns) in *She's Gotta Have It* (Lee, 1986), Max refused to concede except on her own terms and through her own definition.

Maxine spoke hip-hop's womanist idea that women can do anything men can. Young women rappers grappled with this legacy in both their lyrics and their visual representations. Max possessed a voracious appetite—both for food and for sexual conquest. A series-long affair with Kyle opens her vulnerable side. In the end Bowser writes a long-term coupling with a baby due.[99] A stereotyped and completely objectified Maxine could never move much beyond banter and condescending innuendo (such as Pam with Martin), nor could she establish the credibility that Sheneneh also lacked. This freedom allowed her to shatter the whitening silence that normally quells Black women's sexuality and humanity.

People called *Living Single* a *Designing Women* in black. Despite the disparities in age, region, and context (not to mention the lack of an upper-class White sensibility), the two shows shared certain attributes. Both series possessed their own unruly women. Although *Designing Women* (1986–1993) contended with Julia's (Dixie Carter) mouth and Suzanne (Delta Burke) in every other way, *LS's* Max swaggered with sex and language. She seized opportunities to become an unruly woman—taking over the conventionally male-occupied space of aggressor—in order to usurp male potency and claim a space of her own. Describing *Designing Women,* Jeremy Butler remarks that these women "do belong to an unruly sisterhood of TV women who have disrupted the discourse of patriarchy, who have dared to become subjects in a medium and a culture that thrives on the objectification of women."[100] *LS* follows in that same tradition.

The characters Gina in *Martin* and Moesha of *Moesha* may be the most mainstream American women in this group of comedies. Although Gina's willingness and desire to date a man like Martin stretched the humor, the character worked because she provided stability. Gina created a nurturing context and emblematized everything that Martin desired—her skin, her dress, her job, her outlook—but purported to hate—education, money, and upper-class material success. Gina complemented Martin. And although she often physically stood between Pam and Martin, she theoretically represented an opposition to Pam and Sheneneh as an example of what femininity and real Black women should look and act like.

Moesha, on the other hand, emerged from the generation of widespread Black consumption. Born in the age of hip-hop, Moesha moves through life with a sense of entitlement and righteous desire to get paid. For example, when her father gives her a new Saturn for graduation, she returns it because it does not reflect her desire or her vision of herself. However, Moesha bubbles with Judeo-Christian morality. She always takes the high road and strives to set a good example—so much so that early on many teenagers labeled the program (and Norwood's image) sellouts. Further, her moralizing fell on many deaf ears. Says Bill Stephney, "By the nineties, you have the kids of the sixties generation, who know how to make money, but who don't have the sociopolitical orientation their predecessors had"[101]—nor the desire to change the world. Nevertheless, the majority of the teen market began to embrace the program, and it served as the anchor of UPN's programming.

The more unusual characters of these series were those dizzy Black women—Hilary, Synclaire, and Niecy. As a trope, idiocy taps historical roots as far back as *Gone with the Wind* (1939). Butterfly McQueen's Prissy became famous for her high-pitched, frantic mantra "I don't know nuthin' 'bout birthin' no babies."[102] Bogle believes that the Prissy characterization represents "carefully controlled and modulated mayhem."[103] Nevertheless, that modulation failed to transfer to early television. Sitcom antecedents to 1990s roles included Jenny Willis (Berlinda Tolbert) in *The Jeffersons*, Thelma Fry (Anna Marie Horsford) in *Amen*, and Denise Huxtable (Lisa Bonet) in *The Cosby Show* and *A Different World*. *A Different World*'s Freddi (Cree Summer) often took leave of her senses also. Ironically though, once she claimed her black parentage, sensibility returned. Despite objectifying characterizations that come with this stereotype, womanist recuperation appeared possible for those actresses and spectators who moved beyond the confines of dizzydom.

Hilary of *FPBA* met this challenge. Besides her ability to cleverly deliver a

FIGURE 7

A grieving Hilary (Karyn Parsons) of *Fresh Prince of Bel-Air* and her "second" mom (Daphne Maxwell-Reid).

punch line, Parsons claimed humor by becoming the brunt of her own jokes. *Variety* described the character as a "brat-pack wannabe . . . who steals the show with just a few lines." [104] For example, in a rare dramatic scene, Hilary laments not having said good-bye to Treavor, her fiancé, before his bungee-jumping accident (fig. 7). In monologue she looks to heaven, says good-bye to him, and tearfully turns to go into the house, whereby she smacks into a glass door, breaking all illusion of her emotional depth and reinscribing her lunacy.[105] Of course, we must question whether slapstick empowers or shackles. Although certain aspects of the scene relegate her to the domain of idiocy, Hilary rules the space by controlling the laughter. The audience laughs not only at her but also with her. Thus, in this case slapstick empowers.

The character Synclaire of *LS*, on the other hand, tended to be less effective. As a dizzy blonde (in Black), she woo-wooed everyone into feeling better—the quintessential feminine duty and being. Her romantic coupling with Overton, the goofy but quaint upstairs handyman, supplied most of her occasion for dialogue. Kim Coles played Synclaire safe—not too far left of center but enough to indicate something was askew. Thankfully, this character evolved. As the series progressed, she developed goals, desires, and ambition. Even in Synclaire's stupidity, spectators could recognize her maturity.

Finally, the character Niecy functions a bit differently from the other two. Whereas the character Kim Parker on *Moesha* is clearly clueless, Niecy exhibits only periodic sense lapses. Clearly, Niecy has book intelligence, having received a college scholarship. She studies and places her goals first, always. For example, when Moesha becomes her roommate, Niecy's commitment to her studies triumphs over her desire for fun and friendship. She evicts Moesha from the room because, in part, of Moesha's lack of study habits. These three characters—Hilary, Synclaire, and Niecy—moved Negras' representation beyond the confining space of strong Black women. Even with Hilary's shallowness, Synclaire's domesticity, and Niecy's dizziness, they helped show that, like others, Black women make mistakes, are multifaceted, and sometimes surprisingly soft.

CLASS

In American culture class functions as the silent perpetuator of difference. And in Black communities it continues to sever historic, political, educational, and economic linkages. The Bankses of the *Fresh Prince of Bel-Air* belonged to the upper middle class with Will as their lower-class flavor. The *Living Single* crew represented upwardly mobile college-graduates' aspirations, and the characters of *Martin* formed a hybrid of middle- to lower-middle-class economic social positioning. The Mitchell family of *Moesha* reflected the most middle of the middle class—with Hakeem lending a blue-collar working-class vibe.

Romance served as one example of how class functioned in these sitcoms. Heterosexual romantic coupling between people of different classes is not a new cultural, cinematic, or television occurrence. In fact, it has served as a popular and well-worn device to forward narrative—often the coupling founds the story. In television the unexplored tension between Tony Danza and Judith Light in *Who's the Boss?* (1984–1992) kept the series running for eight years— a tension built on their role reversals and class positioning. In Black women's literature and film Terry McMillan's *Disappearing Acts* (1989) and Showtime's adaptation of the novel (2000) dramatize the relationship between a music teacher and a construction worker. Many of J. California Cooper's short stories cover similar ground. Cross-class couples also exist in such Black films as *Bustin' Loose* (Scott, 1981), *New Jack City* (Van Peebles, 1991), *Strictly Business* (Hooks, 1991), *Sugar Hill* (Ichaso, 1994), and *Set It Off* (Gray, 1996). More often than not, however, the bulk of this type of coupling remains in the province of drama and whiteness. In a quite problematic way, however, *Martin* proved an exception.

Reflective of the underacknowledged class disparities rampant in Black communities and the larger American society, Gina earned more, came from an upper-middle-class family, held a college degree, and maintained a professional career, whereas, at the beginning of the series, Martin barely earned enough to pay rent, came from a lower-middle-class background, and received a G.E.D. Over the course of the series the two melded their class disparities. The story suggested that because love conquers all, their differences blended and in some way eventually dissolved. Although this is a plausible explanation, I submit that over time Martin usurped the space occupied by Gina.

Beyond haute couture cravings, her bourgeois tastes became his; her desires were articulated as his own; and her work promotion was only recognized through his. As will surface again in television news, Frantz Fanon's theory of blackness desiring whiteness manifests itself in the cross-class coupling of Gina and Martin. This is neither to deny nor denigrate African-Americans' attainment of accoutrements via capitalism; their expression of them in *Martin*, however, reflected the ongoing debate in Black communities of whether certain successes, certain types of desire, imply a selling out. Martin intimated this about Gina and her family while coveting their class positioning. In espousing a certain "real" blackness (validated from his socioeconomic background), while wrapping himself in accusations of her whiteness, Martin dominated and controlled the cultural landscape. Gina stood as the metaphor by which his American dream was realized.

The most in-your-face example occurred within the early "Break Up" trilogy episodes.[106] Gina gives Martin a sculpture of buttocks for Valentine's Day. This leads to a vitriolic verbalization of their class differences, with his friends fueling the flames. Cole goads Martin that Gina is changing him. Martin complains, "Why does Gina give me that ole bougie stuff?" The first of three parts, Gina and Martin eventually realize that their romance can conquer anything, meaning, Gina relinquishes her upper-class sensibilities to live with her true love. She gains real blackness through Martin.

Dress, house, car—all of these represent the American dream. In *LS* Bowser surrounded her Black women with Afrocentric markers—similar to such fare in *The Cosby Show*. Physically, they inhabited a modern apartment with Black-specific artwork. They chilled in art-house cafes, kept up with citywide cultural occurrences, and knew the latest dances, forms of speech, and fashion trends. For the dream to work, however, access, responsibility, elevation, and parity must be available.

Because that has often not been the case in Colored communities, Black women have bought into and claimed the tangible aspects of the dream—at least as shown on television. Watching Gina sport a tailored business suit, Hilary show off the newest Mizrahi, and Regine track a man by his designer cologne, the spectator realizes the importance of a first, or material, impression to these characters. Material success functioned as the most central component and the distinguishing feature of the Colored women characters in these series. In *227, Family Matters, Hangin' with Mr. Cooper,* and *Amen* the familial setting restrained dress and its outward expression to predetermined appropriateness for the setting. But engagement with hip-hop and youth offered and forwarded a different sense of style.

The class sensibility of creators Bowser on the series *Living Single* and Farquhar et al. on *Moesha* was obvious. Within the *LS* apartment the ladies wore robes, rollers, and sweats. But when they stepped out of that brownstone, they were fly! Period. Moesha, too, donned trendy clothing that reflected the 1970s chic of 1990s teens. Class consciousness grounded every Black sitcom I have examined. This consciousness, however, failed to consistently address abuses and desires that privilege brings.

IDENTITY 1: TALKING THE TALK

Finally, we turn to identity in the discussion of Black women's representations in sitcoms. How Black women identify and are identified has become acutely important in contemporary debates about representation. Frequently, it generates the most commentary. Early in the 1970s, Afro-American speech patterns on television became a focal point in the larger discussion of Black English. One study concluded that the result of African-American assimilation into larger society was its linguistic patterning of majority culture. The study suggested that in situation comedy "[t]he language heard . . . is a homogenized version of the dialect which gives the impression of speakers in transition *between* speech communities. . . . Consequently, not just race, but class and political position, are becoming increasingly significant predictors of [Black English] use." [107] In other words, speech on these situation comedies presented a Black dialect in correlation to class positioning. The dialect used was applied only to assert difference—difference in socioeconomic positioning, in perceived desirability, and in presumed intelligence. [108]

In the 1990s wars raged on the veracity of Black language patterns. Yet in situation comedies standard English reigned supreme for Black women. [109] Rarely did Negras in comedy speak anything but standard American English. Characters such as Pam, Sheneneh, Pam Tucker (Erika Alexander) on *The Cosby Show*, and Lavita *(The Steve Harvey Show)* proffered an affinity for slang and the vernacular of Black, urban youth speech. Yet the misuse of verbs (especially *be*), malapropisms, and cursing in large measure remained absent from their talk and the province of Black men.

Offering dialect/slang helped authenticate the fictional sitcom world. Shohat and Stam have insisted that "inscribed within the play of power, language becomes caught up in the cultural hierarchies of Eurocentrism." [110] Standard English usage weds Black women to whiteness, whereas Black men achieve both elevation and empowerment with their black talk. Further, this push toward authentication surfaced in sitcom monologues that were, with the exception of *Moesha*, written for Black men.

David Marc likens sitcom monologue to a sermon, saying that it "asks the anonymous members of the assembly to spontaneously merge into a single emotional organism capable of reacting uniformly to the metaphor, wisdom, and worldview of one appointed personality." [111] *Martin*'s program teaser, for example, introduced his character in monologue (at least in the first two seasons). In Martin Payne's view the world was constructed as both Black and male. In a monologue during the 1992–1993 season Martin talked to his radio audience about the problem with the sexes. In essence, he maintained, women do not know their place. His commentary teased and goaded the audience into accepting and laughing at the ramifications of this sexist commentary. Moesha Mitchell, on the other hand, used monologue not to talk directly to the viewer per se but to allow spectators inside her reflections on and motivation in life. Via womanish diary writing, Moesha emotionally bookends the narrative in order to shape it. By these types of monologue Black women earn subjectivity within speech.

Another interesting aspect of speech is offered in these sitcoms. Throughout *Martin,* Lawrence peppered his male character's speech with expletives, often within even longer diatribes against women. Would women gain power through this ability to curse? In some ways, I believe, yes. Free speech gives equality potential existence. However, the cursing itself does not make what women say heard or progressive. It simply demands attention. African-American women in television comedy suffered not only from a lack of roles and narrative lines but also from containment and contradiction in appropriate speech. The mantra that "good girls don't say things like that" silences grown women. As Carol Boyce Davies affirms, "It's not everything you can talk." [112]

Beyond talking, *LS*'s creator, Bowser (or, more accurately, the actresses themselves), captured the common nuances of African diasporic peoples—a neglected part of the Ebonics debate. For example in the episode "My Funny Valentine," as the whole ensemble relax in their coffee spot, they banter easily and freely about Kyle and Overton entering the open-mike contest. Kyle refuses to participate until Overton reveals that the first-place prize is three hundred dollars. Kyle then mocks an earlier White performer's dramatic rendition of the *Love Boat* theme song. Members of the ensemble break into laughter—not obligatory, contained, or obnoxious but sincere, loud, and familiar. No culture-defining, over-the-head high-fives surfaced. But through the clapping of the hands, the gripping of palms, and the sort of rock that all employed, an aspect of Black culture and spirit absent from many representations came forth. [113]

IDENTITY 2: A QUESTION OF COLOR

The paper-bag theory and its slave-rape history continue to plague Colored communities and their representations in visual culture. As April Sinclair's Stevie reflects: "I'm not saying I look like homemade sin or anything. . . . I had dimples and my features seemed right for my face. My straightened hair was long enough to make a pony-tail. My skin was the color of Cracker Jacks. But most negroes don't get excited over folks who were darker than a paper bag."[114] In many instances, the shade of skin serves as yet another objectifying criterion. As the 1980s and 1990s celebrated and hoisted up Colored-girl difference, cover girls Naomi Campbell, Tyra Banks, Halle Berry, Brandy, Alek Wek, and Mary J. Blige graced products and runways. Vanessa Williams, Suzette Charles, Debbye Turner, Marjorie Vincent, and Kimberly Aiken all won the Miss America crown. Janet Jackson, Whitney Houston, T.L.C., and Lauryn Hill smashed record sales as some singin', cross-over-achievin' sistahs. Black women from the darkest ebony to the color of divinity held the forefront of public visibility. Despite these successes, however, beauty was articulated by essentially one shade.

According to *The Color Complex: The Politics of Skin Color among African Americans*, "[i]t is apparently an inviolate rule in Hollywood that Black actresses . . . are always lighter than their Black leading men."[115] Television, the writers suggest, makes color less of an issue than does Hollywood filmmaking. However, that presupposition, coupled with the fact that women surface largely in supporting roles, goes against the actualities of television programs and the viability of Black women's progressive representations across color lines.

Herman Gray cites *A Different World* (1987–1993) as an example of programming that reflected the vast spectrum of Black women's coloring. Yet one of its central characters, Whitley (Jasmine Guy), maintained the tragic mulatto stereotype. Historically this character type emerged from the progeny of raped Black women slaves and their masters (unless you buy into the Jeffersonian idea of a slave mistress and consent or reference New Orleans's *placage*). Wealthy, spoiled, and selfish, Whitley elicited contempt but compassion from the audience as she endured her often superficial hardships. In the 1989 "For She's Only a Bird in a Gilded Cage" episode, for example, the "impoverished" college student Whitley makes a dress from her living room curtains. She needs this new dress because her bourgeois mother is coming to visit. This hardly seems like a place for laudatory positioning.

Further, big Black women on television comedy occupied the historic roles of either mammy or sapphire. Fiercely independent, these prototypes ruled their households with their cantankerous personalities and prodigious selves. These women exemplified society's aversion to women deemed fat or loose. Kathleen Rowe suggests that "[f]at females are stigmatized as unfeminine, rebellious, and sexually deviant (under- or over-sexed). Women who are too fat or move too loosely appropriate too much space, and femininity is gauged by how little space women take up."[116] Similar stigmatizing characterizes dark-skinned women. Dark complexion, weight, and morally unacceptable behavior all burdened the bodies of Negras. Rarely does television "do fat." And in the case of Black women, dark skin often substituted for this fat. Consider, for example, Nell Harper in *Gimme a Break,* Veronica Washington (Anna Marie Horsford) in *Rhythm and Blues,* Kim Reese in *A Different World,* Vivian Banks (the first one) in *Fresh Prince of Bel-Air,* Thea Turrell (Thea Vidale) in *Thea,* and Nikki Parker in *The Parkers.* Through their size and/or skin tone, all supported and served as confidants, or quite literally mothers, to the characters of their respective programs—even if the program was their own star vehicle, as was the case with *Gimme a Break, Thea,* and *The Parkers.*

Chelsea Paige *(Out All Night)* mothered not only her daughter Charisse (Vivica A. Fox) but also her tenants (Morris Chestnut and Duane Martin). And although efforts were apparently made to draw these women as independent, intelligent, and appealing, Black women's concerns, ambitions, attractiveness, and sexuality consistently failed to materialize. Kathe Sandler addressed the fractious issue of color in the Black community in *A Question of Color* (1989). She contends that the colorizations caused by "master['s romp] in the slave house"—as Me'Shell NdegéOcello called it—continued to damage and plague the psyche of African-Americans.[117] Over the course of this writing, friends and colleagues agonized over the representations of Black women's skin tones. The women, normally falling along shade lines, questioned, "Why does Martin always get on Pam?" or "Why can't the characters be pretty because of their darkness instead of in spite of it?" Others just stated, "Black women don't act like that," referring to Hilary and, in some way, her skin.

As a former model and a modeling agent, Bethann Hardison has stated that color is simply "a fashion." She says, "Sometimes when a company desires a clear visual difference in their ad, they'll ask for a Black model who is definitely Black looking."[118] But similar to Stoney's (Jada Pinkett Smith) survival in *Set It Off* (1996), unfortunately, the characters Gina, Whitley, and Hilary symbolized what the American dream looked like in Black. Whiteness and the institutional mechanisms of race refuse to work simply. It may seem odd to link the two—fatness and blackness—but contemporary sitcoms and images suggest a direct correlation. Further, the genes that produce color also impact women's crowning glory.

IDENTITY 3: IT'S A HAIR THING, YOU WOULDN'T UNDERSTAND

See what I'm getting at is, if we still have to tell these ten-a-year hair stories to satisfy our license requirements, let's at least tell them differently. Let's tell them from another point of view so we'll stop thinking they are simply harmless female bonding lessons, and see them for the self-hate horror stories that they really are.

—Pearl Cleage

In women's communities, particularly Black ones, hair incites concern, discussion, and humor. Continually negotiating the standards of beauty as articulated within Anglo mainstream culture, Black women struggle to find their political and cultural voice within chemically relaxed, braided, and natural hair care/wear. Consequently, hair issues form a central part of *Living Single, Martin,* and *Moesha.* In *LS* the topic took center space perhaps in response to the actualized woman's space. But more likely, the stereotyped gendered associations with women and their hair made it a cogent recurring topic and a potentially profitable one for hair-care advertisers.

Hair served as fodder for Martin and Pam's incessant bickering in *Martin.* And in *Moesha* the young women needed the right hairstyle to maintain a certain status. Pam served as the brunt of Martin's humor directed at her perceived unmanageable and unattractive ethnic mass. Regine's constant changes in hair designs made her the topic of conversation and, frequently, ridicule. Scholars have taken up the Black woman and her hair as an ongoing sociological/cultural phenomenon.

Cultural critic Kobena Mercer attacks Blacks whose cultural capital involves demeaning women with straightened hair. He argues that "[t]hrough aesthetic stylization each black hairstyle seeks to *revalorize* the ethnic signifier, and the political significance of each re-articulation of value and meaning depends on the historical conditions under which each style emerges."[119] Valid. Nevertheless, Black hairstyles received frequent definition against a Euro-American aesthetic. The 1980s reclamation of Black nationalistic power came through the words of Malcolm X, African-inspired attire, the infusion of rap, and the frustration of disempowered working groups. This climate allowed for hairstyles sans chemical alteration to receive value. Black women reclaimed and expanded African braiding traditions and the wearing of natural hair textures, cuts, and styles.

Yet during this same renaissance (especially in the 1990s) corporations, U.S. governmental divisions, the South, and many Blacks themselves contested this new ethnic look. The return to kinks even spawned litigation in several instances. For example, several Hyatt Hotel employees filed discrimination suits because they were forbidden to wear their hair in braids.[120] Yet this tension of Black women's hair culture provided humorous fodder for the sitcom arena.

Hair jokes abounded in all Black comedies but were particularly prominent in *Living Single* and *Martin,* with the characters Regine and Pam. Regine's attitude came via her wigs. From the first episode of *Living Single* Regine sported long, short, slicked-back, and bobbed wigs. Jokes abounded about her hair politics, primarily among the female characters. Yet Regine's hair transformations, often in a single episode, helped reassert a certain right, a certain style (fig. 8).

Through her variant Black hair Regine formed a quasi resistance to the

FIGURE 8

Regine and her hair.
Living Single.

monolithic, homogenous identity imposed by White culture. So despite her limited character dimensions, Fields's comedic timing and style—more specifically, her hair—contributed to progressive Black women's representation beyond stereotype. In Regine's case hair was not only fashionable; it was political.

On the other hand, with Pam, in *Martin,* hair visioning came through Western condemnations of the African continent. Martin Payne took a monolithic and pejorative view of the wave pattern of African descendants' hair. He nicknamed Pam "Bedebe" (a reference to naturally tight curled, kinky, nappy, or portions of Negro hair outgrowing a chemical process). Pam's hair (which looked similar to Gina's in its texture) elicited denigration continuously. Numerous African-American women possess this "bad hair." This makes negotiating with an American sense of beauty necessary. Achieving physical self-satisfaction, against the constant barrage of bad hair jokes and self-hatred hurled in the sitcom world, required constant vigilance.

In her ethnographies of Black women of various ages, hair type, and socioeconomic positioning, Ingrid Banks concluded that hair matters on various psychological, social, political, and cultural levels. In the lives of Black women hair constitutes a critical territory in contests of beauty, ability, and self-esteem. Says Banks, "Attitude and emotion are placed on the site of one's head as opposed to inside one's head."[121]

All of the aforementioned identifying characteristics are relevant as Black women in television culture and in real life negotiate the superwoman mythology. They must look good, be good, act good, always. This directive comes in response to paternalistic imperatives and the media's assault on their donned behavior. The 1970s Charlie fragrance commercial applied most aptly to Black women.

Before the White women's rights movement Colored women brought home the bacon, fried it up, and supported their men and families. They were not allowed to forget. The stylization of Black characters in contemporary sitcoms added to their popularity and made the discrepancies that surfaced even more difficult to reconcile. Language, skin tone, and hair—significant identifying markers for African-American women—ran with and counter to the prevailing and ever-changing notions of race and class.

COMEDIC CONTEXTS: GENDER AND SEXUALITY

Only a man knows how a woman is supposed to act.

—*M. Butterfly*

Finally, attention to gender in sitcoms came through feminized attributes I have described above and through tensions caused through blackness and class. As I mentioned earlier, one of the most disturbing aspects of womanhood's construction surfaced through Martin Lawrence's impersonation of the b-girl type, Sheneneh Jenkins. Not unique to comedy, male impersonation has often produced laughter. This time, however, it came at the expense of a specified segment, the Black, urban young woman. When *The Flip Wilson Show* aired, from 1970 to 1974, White comics had long been impersonating women. Although Wilson's comedy/variety show received high ratings, its portrayals of Black culture created dissension in Negro communities resulting in part from the life of Flip's female alter ego, Miss Geraldine Jones (fig. 9).[122]

Geraldine was a woman of the world. Her claim that "the devil made me do it" became a mainstay within the American cultural psyche. Extremely sarcastic, she delivered her lines verbally but always punctuated the point with her body. She would often erupt with, "I got it together, honey," snapping her fingers and tossing her blonde wig in punctuation. But, says Dates, "For creating this character, Wilson was accused of encouraging effeminacy in young black males who, some believed, would use him as a role model."[123] Some scholars have suggested that contemporary female impersonation originated with minstrelsy. Robert Toll maintains that "women, like Negroes, provided one of the few stable 'inferiors' that assured white men of their status."[124] Beyond expressing fear that Wilson's character may encourage homosexuality among boys, however, few have commented on Wilson's version/vision of Black womanhood.

In many ways Geraldine was an early feminist. Always stylishly clad, the character exuded femininity while still occupying and recuperating maleness —the presumed power—within. For example in one skit she sought counseling from a therapist because her boyfriend, Killer, refused to make wedding plans. Dressed in a short pink dress with pink pantyhose and shoes to match, she walked in and announced, "I'm not crazy." And even in her highly sexualized poses and motions, she cautioned the doctor, "Don't push me!"[125] These admonishments seemed necessary to preserve control and respect as assertive Black women find themselves frequently disrespected and described as controlling and/or crazy. In the case of *Martin*'s Sheneneh, however, womanhood's power reversed itself.

One drag queen remarked that cross-dressing is "ninety-five percent illusion and five percent substance."[126] With Lawrence's representation, however, no illusion existed. Lawrence made an unattractive and barely believable woman. Presented physically bigger than Lawrence himself, the body of Sheneneh represented Black class disparities and anxieties displaced across a gendered body. She disrupted the narrative with her loud dress; her broad voice, body, and articulations; and her insistent demands for attention (fig. 10).

FIGURE 9

Flip Wilson *(left)* as Miss Geraldine Jones (with O. J. Simpson) in *The Flip Wilson Show.*
(Courtesy Jerry Ohlinger's Movie Material Store)

FIGURE 10

Martin Lawrence as
Sheneneh Jenkins in
Martin.

Further, Sheneneh encouraged continued perceptions of Black women's inability to get along with one another. F. Michael Moore believes that "drag performers convey important truths about perception, gender roles, and sexuality. . . . [M]uch of what we call gender is based on perception alone."[127] In *Martin*, Sheneneh, Pam, and Gina were consistently at odds. Pam and Sheneneh (as the lower-class ones) constantly threatened physical violence toward each other as the leading way to resolve their differences. An earlier nonfictional interpretation of this character is found in Shirley Clarke's 1967 film *A Portrait of Jason*. This non-dragged queen displayed the difficulties of Black men who claim a woman's view in a world that does not validate either the gender or the color in which he/she is wrapped. Sheneneh served as an important figure to the television representations of Black women because her presence overtly illustrated that existing tensions of class, race, and gender lie right below the surface of Negro and American life.

THE CULTURAL LOGIC OF BLACK WOMEN'S OBJECTIFICATION WITHIN LAUGHTER, OR, STILL LAUGHING OUT LOUD

The situation comedies that aired in the latter half of the twentieth century gave Black women more freedoms through the narrative, style, and diegetic work roles than ever before. When Jackie (Tyra Banks) and Will argued, word for word they appeared equitable—in height, in frame, in stature, in power. The cultural shorthand for Black women's empowerment came through the markers of dress, hair, roles, and skin, as well as through those binaries that announced societal angst. Yet they forwarded examples of Black women's communication systems beyond the classroom of *A Different World*.[128]

Television creators remained committed to creating Black-cast comedies. In the fall of 1994, for example, another Lear show, *704 Hauser*, appeared on CBS as a spin-off of *All in the Family*—the twist: a Black family occupied the house. It aired for less than one month. *The Hughleys* (1998–present) took its place. Programs such as *Girlfriends* (2000–present) provided a watered-down version of more explicit cable offerings (in this case *Sex and the City*). But, with its housing on UPN, *Girlfriends* exhibited only limited signs of advancing Black women in humor. Other programs appeared and disappeared quickly. *Thea* (1993–1994), *South Central* (April–June 1994), and *Under One Roof* (March–April 1995) promised a difference but were eliminated too quickly to make one.[129] Because of this, ascribing meaning to these series continues to be both difficult and disturbing. Ironically, the Screen Actors Guild released a study that maintained that African-American lead characters were actually *overrepresented* in 2000 prime-time television, in some ways perhaps suggesting the mind-set of the future.[130]

The Black women presented in these comedies explored roles and ideologies heretofore rarely seen. They were indeed funny in many cases. But, once again, the greater proportion of Black women's representations remained in supporting, mammyfied, and one-dimensional capacities. Beyond blackness, these sitcoms excavated stereotypes of White women and superimposed them on Black ones.

Womanist theory does not suggest nor advocate that televised or real-life Black women forgo their tendencies to provide comfort and support. It does, however, call for opportunity, recognition, and subjecthood—in other words, African-American women's centering in sitcom narratives. The comedies I have examined authorized that ability only in small quantities and sometimes only as a token. Thus, for Black women in situation comedy the struggle continues for recognition, value, and sustained ability to share in the laughter while laughing out loud.

3

I GOT YOUR BITCH!

Colored Women, Music Videos,
and Punnany Commodity

> . . . n all the time i'm thinkin of the videos
> you know / where the brotha's in the beat up car / drivin
> real slow / he got money [. . .]
> cuz it's kinda in style for lil honeys
> to be all over somebody big who look like
> somethin white people call the police on
> cuz they jus look wrong / n honeys be all over them in like
> twos n threes
> sometimes / in the videos / i know you seen them /
> so what i'm sayin is it's kinda in style to be kissin
> n huggin n rubbin on somebody
> who knock you out in a minute / but still give you money to
> get ya nails done /
> it's hip you know / in style n shit /
> n I'm not one who don't like style
> cuz i'm lookin kinda fly
> in my knee green boots and
> black raiders jacket /
> but you know style ain't what you see on tv.
> —Ruth Forman, "Green Boots n Lil Honeys"

This excerpt from "Green Boots n Lil Honeys" captures the dialogue between contemporary Black women dubbed "video hoes" in music video and spectator assessment of them.[1] In "Booting Booti Off the Box" Helen Kolawole wondered aloud, "What's behind the female flesh cavorting around swimming pools in the endless stream of rap and r&b videos?"[2] What indeed? As shown previously, Afro-American women's representations in television culture defy neat definition, stability, or totalization. The genre of music video intensified and capitalized on this instability, largely through its presentation and format. As advertisements themselves, music videos virtually erase the distinction between commercial and program—Pat Aufderheide coding them "nonstop sequences of discontinuous episodes."[3] This blurring of product and promotion surfaced in many contemporary media (infomercials, film, print advertisement, morning news). Yet in music video Black women negotiated a more insidious denigration and empowerment dance while simultaneously participating in transforming relationships between themselves, Black men, and spectators.

Despite condemnation by Tipper Gore's Parents' Music Resource Center, academic Sut Jhally, and some musicians themselves, music videos have prevailed and excelled since their introduction in the early 1980s. Early record company budgets for this marketing tool amounted to no more than fifty thousand dollars per video. By 1994 budgets extended into the millions. As the only medium discussed with an announced intentionality, music videos introduce, expose, and usher consumers toward and situate them before a particular artist, predominantly within the comforts of home.[4]

Initially, record companies produced music videos and gave them to video national outlets like BET, MTV, The Box, and hundreds of local outlets, gratis. Now they charge a fee. Video presence has become an integral part of the marketing mix of musical artists. And regardless of content or audience demographics, the omniscient principle of sales guides music video production. Producing videos that appeal to male gazes, stereotype cultural institutions and norms, and/or poignantly objectify women, marketers examine and directly target mechanisms that fuel human desire for goods, belonging, and escape, emotions that lead to consumption.

Within situation comedy Black women's ability to achieve agency occurs infrequently because of the genre's inscription in whiteness and its mechanical form. In the music video market, however, the potential for profit drives innovation and risk-taking in ways that sitcoms refuse to attempt—increasing potential for women's subjectivity.[5] Beyond this risk-taking proclivity, the production costs for music video are considerably less than television comedy. These costs and risk differences provide an opportunity for female artists to introduce and claim some parity with their male counterparts. Despite its regressive, capitalist agenda, music videos' unrecuperated gaps allow Black women to voice and visualize themselves differently. And because the gaps forge a space for agency, the analysis of music video must dwell there.

MUSIC VIDEO INDUSTRIALIZED

The Reagan-Bush years encouraged deregulation and corporate mergers. Media companies seized the opportunity to expand. After 1980, Capital Cities bought ABC, which was then purchased by Disney; NBC became the province of General Electric; CBS was usurped by Lawrence Tisch and then bought by Westinghouse and later sold to Viacom; Sony bought Columbia Pictures from Coca-Cola; Time, Inc., merged with Warner Brothers Studios and then with Turner Broadcasting; Matsushita Electric bought MCA, but MCA was then bought by Seagram and renamed Universal Studios; the *New York Times* bought Affiliated Publishers (parent of the *Boston Globe*); Viacom (which already owned HBO, Showtime, MTV, Infinity Broadcasting, Nickelodeon, UPN, TNN, CMT, and VH-1) bought Paramount Communication and then merged with Block-buster Video and AOL, and later with Time Warner. Viacom also owns publishing giant Simon and Schuster. Further, telecommunications corporations such as Verizon joined with Telecommunications, Inc., to control viewing along multiple lines of communication.[6] And, continually, the urge to merge refused satiation.

Some contend that by the end of 2000 essentially ten media conglomerates controlled 95 percent of all film, television, video rental, cable, and Internet output.[7] Although originally Black-owned BET moved toward becoming the premier deliverer of the African-American audience, Blacks and other ethnics played only a virtual role in these refashioned media alliances.[8] In other words, representations of Coloreds rested only limitedly in Colored people's control. Consequently, narrowed cultural/corporate producers presented similar material—culturally already familiar material.

Patricia Mellencamp contends that in this climate "the same artifact is marketed cross-culturally as a book, a film, a food product, a song, a toy, and a costume."[9] This strategy became particularly evident in the marketing of Black culture. By the mid-1990s a certain Black style defined television, a culture-specific style that, Americanized and whitewashed, remained unacknowledged in its Black heritage. I turn to BET for a fuller exploration of its role in Black music video dissemination.

BLACK ENTERTAINMENT TELEVISION

Beginning with only six hours of airtime, BET concentrated most of its initial programming on music videos. These videos gave new access to Black musicians and singers unwelcome on MTV. Advertisers such as Oldsmobile and McDonald's utilized the channel because it reached the growing Negro middle class. Nike and Coca-Cola bought ads because they delivered the twelve-to-thirty-four-year-old consumer at half the cost of MTV.[10] Beyond Michael Jackson's and Prince's videos (the first videos by Black artists to receive airtime on MTV in 1983), Colored audiences saw Atlantic Starr, Vanity-6 ("Nasty Girls" in nasty lingerie), and Midnight Star on BET, artists who had limited crossover appeal but whom Negro audiences enjoyed and, more significantly, bought.[11] This selling aspect intrigued BET's owner. Similar to his yuppie counterparts and allowing for the nature of television, Robert Johnson conceived of BET as a "business opportunity that had been ignored."[12]

Black Entertainment Television is the nation's first and only cable channel devoted to and targeting African-Americans.[13] Available as part of basic cable packages, BET was founded by Robert Johnson, a former National Cable Television Association lobbyist in 1980. The network's initial funding came from three major corporations: TCI, Taft Broadcasting Company, and Home Box Office, which gave it room to develop and protection from early losses. In his 1980 promotional tape to cable companies and advertisers Johnson claimed that the networks had failed to promote significant offerings to the Black audience. This audience watched more television than any other group and earned about $70 billion annually. BET promised to deliver this unaddressed capital opportunity. Thus, Black Entertainment Television qualified itself as a blue-chip investment.[14] It went public in 1991 but private again several years later.[15]

BET delivers public affairs programming, dramatic and comedic series, and music videos that showcase Black characters and Black themes not shown on other cable channels or network television. However, the greater proportion of its programming is music videos. Further, several elements hamper its ability to effectively serve its target audience. First, because BET belongs to cable, its audience must be wired, have the channel within the franchise that serves their area, and, by extension, pay for the service.[16] Second, with much of its programming coming from off the networks, the offerings reflect the same one-dimensional notions of Blackness and gender that networks already employ. And third, despite BET's Black-business status, African-American communities receive little tangible benefit from supporting it.

In her study of BET and the Black audience Felecia Jones concluded that most people watched BET to view a certain type of program and to learn about Black people. The responses to her survey suggested that younger respondents and those with a higher racial orientation appeared less critical of BET's programming than were older and lower racially oriented people. Her study suggests that "the affinity of racial/ethnic groups toward programming . . . reflects their concerns."[17] In other words, African-Americans want to see their reflection but are ambivalent about the programming reflected there.

During the mid-1990s, Black Entertainment Television began developing into a multimedia conglomerate. In its 1993 annual report BET touted that it could now deliver the Black audience to underwriters through its cable, publishing, pay-per-view, direct marketing, and radio arms. BET aimed to be the premier vehicle for selling the African-American audience to advertisers. Systematically, it mimics the networks with no apparent move from selling the audience. Says Deborah Jaramillo, "Rather, their alleged ability to sell the Black audience seems to be a point of pride. It's almost a mediated slave trade validated under the rubric of multiculturalism or Black pride."[18] BET's major drawback rests with its limited movement beyond previous presentations of Blacks. While achieving quantity, it lacks depth and in some respects, scope. Despite its limitations, however, BET's appearance paved the way for other "watching-while-Black" opportunities.

In November 2000, for example, Viacom bought BET holdings for $2.5 billion in stock and assumed over $500 million in debt. Mel Karmazin, Viacom chair, believed that BET was a valuable vehicle for a conglomerate to reach Black consumers. He reasoned that (1) as a market Black consumers were growing faster than the rest of the country's consumer markets, (2) Black household income was growing faster than the rest of the country's, (3) Black consumers used more media than the general market, and (4) ad spending for African-American consumers was growing faster than the rest of the country's, although advertisers paid less to get their advertising product.[19]

With those trends in mind Robert Johnson suggested that "the time is now where strong African-American brands with tremendous value should put themselves in league with strong general market brands that can add even greater value. . . . I see this as a positive development . . . and I hope one day there'll be other African-American companies that create the kind of value created at BET."[20] Although the veracity of Johnson's statement remains untested, BET (at least at the turn of the century) provided the preponderance of Black imagery on television.

Cable proliferation allowed music video to evolve. In 1980 Cox Communications established cable operations in my hometown, Omaha, Nebraska. The following year Music Television (MTV) was launched. Yet despite MTV's introduction as first, BET looms in my remembrance of early music videos. Perhaps this strong recollection resounds so powerfully because of the network's dedication to portrayals of familiar and similar faces. These memories returned full force while I was reading E. Ann Kaplan and wincing as she struggled to position herself in this contemporary, generation-specific milieu. Although not part of my childhood, watching music videos was a viable element of my teenage years. My cheerleading squad, like others nationwide, incorporated Michael Jackson's *"Beat It"* choreography into our routines.[21] This proximity made it difficult to discern the dramatic changes produced by the arrival of music videos—historical specificity coming largely through reexamination of visual texts, critical research, student discussions, and self-reflection. Nevertheless, although I do not claim a superiority in intimacy to the text, I suggest that experience and familiarity help negotiate the nuances, contours, and specificities of music video and the oft-forgot music they promote. This closeness forges a unique context for the music video realm's original and continued circulation.

Kaplan believes that, like the new Colored texts of situation comedy, "MTV appears [as a symptom] of Reagan's America in its unquestioning materialism."[22] In this America music video pushed forward with a redirected focus on popular culture, the economic realities for record companies shifted, and cablers realized music video's permanence. In fact, as the business of television and music continued to morph with the promise of the information superhighway, the five-hundred-channel environment, two-way interaction, and MP3.com, music videos provided new ground for communicating with consumers. Despite their phenomenal impact, however, they remained for a long period on the fringe of television critical studies—already the fringe of filmic discourse.

MUSIC VIDEO CRITICAL STUDIES

Early studies of music video covered critical ground similar to that of film narrative analysis. Thomas Johansson linked music video to youth culture and postmodernism. Blaine Allan fused connections between music video and musical cinema. Issues of sustained narrative, authorship, direct address, and artistic merit guaranteed publication. The body also became a central theoretical debate, more to the point, the disembodied female. Spectacle theories of music video breathed new life into sound and star texts. Yet music videos' brevity, commercial ties, incestuous relationship to the musician as actor, and television home continued to be overlooked, as was the music itself.

E. Ann Kaplan was one of the first theorists to critically engage music video. In 1987 *Rocking around the Clock: Music Television, Postmodernism, and Consumer Culture* appeared as a case study on the company Music Television and the larger music world of television. She discussed the notion of a twenty-four-hour continuous flow of postmodernist discourses.[23] Like Marsha Kinder, Kaplan spoke largely through the vocabulary of psychoanalysis, suggesting that more than any other television network or genre before it, MTV exists as a vehicle of consumption. It induces a hypnotic trance of sorts. This trance forces spectators into a perpetually unsatisfied state of leisure as they abide "under the illusion of imminent satisfaction through some kind of purchase."[24] Although linking the industrial with the visual proved extremely useful in examinations of the text, Kaplan's focus on MTV virtually excluded racialized constructions and their impact on music production, articulation, and the MTV flow. Kaplan focused instead on the trope of gender exclusively. Yet, as Dan Rubey notes, music's marriage to visual imagery foregrounds issues not only of gender but also of race.[25]

In "Music Videos: The Look of the Sound" Patricia Aufderheide examined music video history and its ability to engage a youth audience through consumerism. Believing that music videos provide an alternative to social life, she proposed the dream structure as a metaphor for music video: "Dreams . . . create gestalts, in which sensations build and dissolve. And so they nicely match the promise and threat of consumer-constructed identity, endlessly flexible, depending on income and taste."[26] For this theory to work, therefore, Freud's dream theory must be evident not only through the production and industrial framework but within the texts of videos themselves. Granted, artists used dissolves, fog, and mirrors to create dreamlike or daydream musical fantasies, as, for example, in SOS Band's *"Tell Me If You Still Care"* (1983). But when appropriating this dream prism as a theoretical model, critics rarely moved beyond the theory to ascribe broader sociological, cultural, or historical explanations or implications.

Following Kaplan's lead, Lisa Lewis furthered the scholarly study of music video and gender through her book *Gender Politics and MTV: Voicing the Difference* and her other publications. Lewis provides a system for analyzing music videos along two axes. She argues that in female rock video, control of image making gives female musicians the ability to create women-identifiable images and fosters female authorship.[27]

She classifies videos as either access or discovery signs. Access signs emerge when women appropriate male spaces and claim parity with them. Discovery signs celebrate traditional female spaces devalued by patriarchy. Lewis argues that through the intersection of these signs, "girls in the audience are encouraged to understand that access to the privileged realm of male cultural experience and representation is partly a matter of discovering their own cultural legacy."[28] Again, however, African-American cultural production's profound influence on the 1980s and 1990s musical landscape receives only limited consideration within Lewis's work.

In her book Lewis examines the lyric and video texts of Negro artists Michael Jackson and Tina Turner. Yet their relevance to *Gender Politics* comes through their gender and their ability to be raceless. For example, Lewis believes that Jackson's *"Beat It"* appropriates White male-adolescent discourse for Black males, while leaving the discourse's gender bias intact. The lyrics, she maintains, "invoke the many issues of power and powerlessness, authority and lack of authority, blackness and whiteness, and maleness and femaleness."[29] In essence, Jackson's figure represents middle ground—Americana. Yet in order to elevate gender, Lewis had to discount and minimize Jackson's racialized presence and musical aptitude.

Against the vein of postmodernism and, in some ways, feminism, Andrew Goodwin's *Dancing in the Distraction Factory* attempts to culturally assess the world of music television in an industrial, visual, and music-centered context. Within a larger British (world) culture Goodwin claims that the problem with theories that link postmodernism with music video (Kaplan, Robin Roberts, Marsha Kinder) is the inversion of chronology and the hierarchical ordering of video to music. This practice, he contends, leads to an exaggeration of the importance of music video, which negates the fact that visual spectacles have constantly worked in tandem with the music itself. Goodwin asserts that "academic theorists frequently relate this iconography to . . . categories without taking account of its more prosaic intention—that of evoking the excitement of a live pop performance." [30] These theories also exclude the possibility that "music television might resemble music." [31] In other words, the lack of understanding of music itself and consistent inattention to it undercuts critical analysis of the music video form. Goodwin's notions find support in John Caldwell's assertion that the discipline of critical studies often overlooks the actual television text and the complexity of viewing "in lieu of a dominant concern with master interpretive allegories, verbal content, or social meanings and effects." [32]

Goodwin's own critique fails, however, to adequately account for the role music video plays in contemporary culture. As a marketing tool and a substantial part of an artist's image, videos are often conceived in tandem with the music and lyrics. Neither artist nor record company creates or imagines the music alone. Some Generation Xers would assert that music video has even replaced live performance. Consumers look to those musical vignettes to illustrate the prowess, acumen, and creative dexterity of their favorite artists. Further, in many racialized communities, live performance does not necessarily exist as the defining interactive moment by which the listener engages with the music and the artist. Performance is watched, music lived.

In terms of women, Goodwin found nothing particularly redemptive about music video, a lack that feminist scholars and music practitioners dispute. Both Lisa Lewis and Robin Roberts not only laud the music video as a site for feminist reinvention but also forward the medium as a necessary field of inquiry. Ignoring Goodwin's warnings, Roberts explored "feminist videos" through varied musical genres—country, rap, and rock. [33] And as a theoretical tool, she deconstructed certain videos for their use-value in advancing a feminist discourse.

Roberts insisted on the marriage of postmodernism and feminism as practice. But painfully, almost the entire text of *Ladies First: Women in Music Videos* confines itself to a feminist framework couched specifically in White feminist concerns. Although she utilized examples from an array of Black women performers—from Aretha Franklin, En Vogue, and Janet Jackson to Me'Shell NdegéOcello, Queen Latifah, and Salt-N-Pepa—race, class, and generation only factored tangentially in her analysis of feminism for the masses. She elevated rap as a recuperative, feminist site in many of her examples and devoted two full chapters to genre and textual analysis of Queen Latifah's *"Ladies First."* In paying these homages, however, she still neglected the cultural context of rap, the racialized discourses proffered through it, and what produces the material. [34]

The aforementioned scholars engage music video in a way that moves beyond simplistic binaries. However, in their expressed or perfunctory lack of attention to the functioning of racialized, generational, classist, and in some way industrial discourses, they neglect a broader assessment of the impact and contributions of African-Americans and particularly Black women to both music and video (even as some usurp their urgency and agency à la Roberts's Queen Latifah). Similar to the trappings of situation comedy, the theoretical framing of music video perpetuates patriarchy and a hierarchy of whiteness as it claims to decenter it.

Given this critical overview, questions must be asked that speak to the discontinuities in theory, form, and representation. How does the medium's commercialism shape video and the spectator's reception of it? What impact do performance, style, and womanist discourses make on the video and the career of the performer? In a highly stylized and commercialized entertainment vehicle, how (or can) Black women claim subjecthood? And finally, if music video is an example of an ideal postmodernism, in what capacity do Black women appear in this futuristic landscape? To address these questions, I turn to a brief history of music performance, music television, and their encounter with the -isms of music video.

MUSIC PERFORMANCE ON TELEVISION

Contrary to popular belief, television *did* present music makers pre–music video. From the late 1940s and early 1950s programs such as *The Toast of the Town* (later *The Ed Sullivan Show*) and Steve Allen's *Tonight Show* featured performers like Sarah Vaughan, Ella Fitzgerald, and Carmen McRae.[35] One of the first African-Americans to host a network television program was singer Nat King Cole.[36] Although appearing for only one year because of lack of national sponsorship and poor ratings, *The Nat King Cole Show* highlighted Black musical artists unable to cross over to White audiences.

These early music television performances led to programs that focused solely on music performance: *American Bandstand* (1957–1987), *The Midnight Special* (1973–1981), and, more germane to this study, 1970's *Soul Train. The Midnight Special* featured mostly rock musicians but sometimes hosted other performers, such as Diana Ross and LaBelle (Patti LaBelle's early group). These acts performed their hit songs "in concert" with revolving guest hosts. The other two series (sanitized, with one for Whites, the other for Blacks) appealed to teenagers by showing new dances and featuring popular performers lip-synching their songs.[37]

As of 2001 *Soul Train* continued to survive amid a deluge of music programs but in an elevated position. The program has become an icon in Black America, and artists pay homage by appearing on it.[38] *Soul Train* creator Don Cornelius maintains that "'Soul Train' is the longest-running, uninterrupted, first-run syndication TV show in history. That says a lot for soul music. The show and its franchise will last as long as soul music thrives."[39] Because *Soul Train* now competes with many similar programs, however, the show lacks its earlier relevance in providing consumers/spectators a privileged view into the sight and sound of Black music. Beyond these programs, bands from the 1970s recorded concert footage and made rudimentary video stories. Early Black groups in this format included the Hughes Corporation ("Rock the Boat"), LaBelle, and the Jacksons ("Enjoy Yourself").

Music video, as ushered in by MTV and as a cultural and commercial phenomenon, reigns as a viable artistic and increasingly necessary avenue for the marketing of musical artists, especially African-American ones. In 2000 MTV reached 340 million households in 139 territories. It, along with its corporate mate VH-1, produced enough product to virtually go anywhere monitors lived. MTV prevailed despite its duplicitous nature. Further, Internet development made music videos accessible to anyone with a modem. Music videos were promoted as forums where diversity flourished. Yet they also provided a platform for the perpetuation of debased and essentialist ideologies endemic to American society. This duality became acutely exemplified in the videos of rock, hip-hop, and rap—where gender, race, and class often coexist in a contentious state.

Recognizing the potential buying power of and demand by the African-American audience for rap music, MTV introduced *Yo, MTV Raps!* in August of 1988.[40] Despite the network's problematic history with Black artists, *Yo, MTV Raps!* became one of the most watched programs on the channel. This program and its counterparts on BET's *Rap City* and The Box featured the music of popular and emerging rap artists. Many critics argue that these artists produced the most interesting and innovative music of the twentieth century. Their music propelled American and world culture into a definitively darker look. Like J. Fred MacDonald's assessment of television evolution in general, some thought that music video held the potential to eradicate racism and sexism.

THE MUSIC BEAT

The scholarly positioning of music video gives Andrew Goodwin's argument of videos' privilege over music credence. But understanding music and its context is necessary to comprehensively engage visual performance. African-Americans, as largely West African descendants, elevate the placement of music in life. For example, John Miller Chernoff writes that "[t]he tradition of using songs to express philosophical, ethical, or satirical themes is so much a part of African musical idioms that it has continued, along with many rhythmic characteristics, within the development of Afro-American styles."[41] Yet these rhythms and styles receive only limited critical attention when juxtaposed with the visual allure of music video. The visible focus restricts investigations and ignores the visceral, where music reaches its consumers. This critical lack helps to keep misconceptions about Blacks and their relationship to music alive.

This notwithstanding, music intimately contributes to many African-American life experiences—not as a tangential observation but as a palpable part. Yet not all Negroes buy music, listen to the radio, or attend concerts. And certainly African-Americans, like all sentient beings, possess divergent musical tastes. Many of these lives, however, are not bereft of music. Music engages numerous African diasporic people as the background of neighborhoods, within the humming of church selections, through the opening of a civic organization meeting, or during the introduction to the local high school's basketball team. I remember, for example, awaking at my best friend's house to the mellow and soothing tune of George Benson's "This Masquerade," a favorite of her mother's. Remembering artists such as Benson, along with day-to-day engagements with the sights and sounds of Black America, intimately ties people to soul music. This tie goes beyond visual studies into an ongoing, pragmatic, lived experience. These reflections reinforce the importance of including the music itself in the analysis of the visual—regardless of one's relationship to the text.

BLACK MUSIC VIDEO

Despite this need, the preponderance of critical work on music video centers on the visual. Studies encourage an identification of the video with the artist and, consequently, with the spectator. Music videos combine elements of performance, narrative, and visual presentation in overlapping and integrative ways.[42] The images contain certain semiotic codes for consumers to decode and use. Some of these "markers," according to Dan Rubey, include the "music and its level of emotional arousal, song lyrics, the accompanying narrative . . . choreography and performance style, musical style and genre, costume and fashion, physical characteristics of the actor/performers . . . mise-en-scène . . . camera work . . . and editing techniques.[43] Music video has helped transform mainstream acceptance and appropriation of rap and r&b artists—making transgression of the musical veil more fluid.

Armond White believes that although music videos have failed to precisely depict African-American daily life, they recognize "the fashion, psychology and lifestyles that mainstream cinema might prefer to ignore. . . . These images and poses may reflect the singers' backgrounds or simply the way they want to be seen."[44] White contends that music video's expansiveness has helped define the culture that propels Black popular culture beyond its ghetto stereotypes.[45] That may be, as evidenced by the growth and glam of programs like *Total Request Live* on MTV, where musical genres converge to illustrate an anything-goes culture. Yet apparently White missed (or refused to acknowledge) videos such as Poison Clan's *"Check Out the Avenue,"* in which an urban, blighted neighborhood triumphs and becomes glorified in said stereotypes, or Too Short's *"More Freaky Tales,"* which elevates misogynist bravado. It recognizes Black women (literally and figuratively) as a nation of freaks. In spite of music video's progressiveness (in terms of quantity and perceived quality), many rap and r&b artists visually and lyrically only revisit ongoing American ascriptions to Black misogyny, violence, and self-hate.[46]

Some researchers have theorized that an "impression management" strategy exists that guides this Black video making. They define *impression management* as "the strategies and tactics individuals use to control the images they project to and the impressions they make upon others."[47] Another theory, "situated identities," suggests that individuals present a variety of selves for different situations. Sonja Peterson-Lewis and Shirley Chennault submit that Black artists combine these strategies to facilitate their appearances on mainstream video outlets (namely, MTV). Through the tactics of accumulating new associations, denying associations (or neutering), and disassociating from previous contacts, artists work to position themselves in the lucrative video market. However, this attempt to gain a certain type of agency and control is not always, or even usually, made manifest because artists generally (and genderly) possess limited control over the image-making process.[48]

In the past A&R (artist and repertoire) agents acquired undiscovered talents and fashioned them to the music company's need and vision for a particular commodity fit. What they do currently, according to VH-1 editorial director Bill Flanagan, is try to find the next hit wonder.[49] Discussed extensively by scholars and the media, rap artists, for example, often perpetuate and articulate a persona antithetical to their particular life experiences. Often an impoverished, gang-bangin, criminal existence becomes the artist's popular persona, sometimes in direct opposition to a working-class existence he or she led prerecording contract or that the artist maintains post–platinum success. Moving away from this persona, even when success affords vastly different living situations, nets cries of "selling out" and not "keeping it real." And unlike actors in situation comedy, recording artists, particularly in rap and rock, assert a synonymous bond to their performance image.

Performing one's self, or construction thereof, makes the lines and distinctions of image and artist actuality extremely tenuous. Indeed, the perception of a "reality factor" helps sell music.[50] In this male-dominated musical real world, most women occupy the traditional artistic role of sex object. Hip-hop's legacy of objectification comes from music videos' initial interaction with the larger music world's hierarchical placement of women within other types of music, namely rock.

Media critics agree that the most blatant sexist and masochistic images of women appeared in early heavy metal videos. In them, groped, beaten, and posed women visually implied not only consensual actions but also desired ones. Sut Jhally's documentary *Dreamworlds II* (1991) likened music video to aestheticized violence—disturbingly illustrating this point by juxtaposing a cinematic rape scene with several music videos. In this documentary Jhally described the multiple ways in which male-oriented and -dominated music video simply reflected adolescent male fantasy. For example, many early rock videos displayed women in cages.

Mim Udovitch reminisces that "time was—in the early 80s—all you ever saw were women in bathing suits in cages. Nowadays, you're much more likely to see women in bathing suits in or near water."[51] This she sarcastically considers progress. In addressing women artists' videos she adds: "For the female body, whether it's Annie Lennox in the grip of an eyelash curler or the future Mrs. Warrant getting hosed down in *Cherry Pie*, being the masochistic object is practically de rigueur. . . . Like it or not, women's bodies are (and have been for centuries) so intensely visually fetishized that there's not much they do that doesn't look like a male fantasy."[52] Twenty years past their introduction, these pubescent male dreams thrive despite the browning and feminizing of the teenagers watching music video. Some argue, like Janice Faye Hutchinson, that the hip-hop generation just wants to have fun and are not afraid to say so. Unlike the 1960s hippie free-love movement, today "young people are living a free love devoid of the political rhetoric, sometimes pretensions, of the 1960s."[53]

Regardless of the forum, (r&b, rap, reggae, pop, or rock), male videos offer a surfeit of women—in excess of the performing male artist(s). More often than not, the same standards of beauty articulated in cinema and situation comedy and reified in the Miss America contest reign in this genre. In an industry where image and style impact and determine success, a certain "look" is a valuable commodity. Therefore, the basic requirements for Negras (women extras, or "video hoes," as termed by music video practitioners) to decorate the set are light skin, long hair (real, processed, or weaved), curvaceous bodies, and nice teeth. Dance or lip-synch ability is optional. Given these physical requirements and allowing for racial convergence, White women "stand-ins" appear as the basis for inclusion.

For example, highly successful musical artists/actors Janet Jackson and Vanessa L. Williams fulfill these visual obligations. Although underdiscussed, their skin tone played a crucial role in their success. Dan Rubey suggests that Janet Jackson's light skin and facial features "locate her in the marginal area between black and white, the culturally loaded space of the mulatto."[54] In U.S.

FIGURE 11

Queen Latifah in
"I Can't Understand"

culture mulatto translates as acceptable enough for White America and better than Black. And in Williams's case the shade of her skin helped secure the
Miss America crown. Likewise, it assisted in her entertainment success subsequent to her dethroning. In Black male videos—regardless of genre—the
heroines, objects of desire, and love interests were usually epitomized by
lighter-skinned Black women or Latinas.

Artist Me'Shell NdegéOcello addressed this phenomenon on her *Plantation
Lullabies* (1993) CD. In the song "Soul On Ice" she admonishes Black men by
decrying "Visions of her virginal white beauty dancin' in your head. You let
your sisters go by. Your souls on ice. . . . You no longer burn for the mother-
land brown skin. You want blonde-haired, blue-eyed soul. Snow white passion
without the hot comb."[55] As it had for the sistahs in situation comedy, skin
color maintained its visually loaded symbol of oppression and acceptance in
music video.

K. C. Arceneaux argues that Black music videos exist in a matrix of others—the presentation of which combine "a complex visual imagery that can
be surrealistic, narrative, collaged, and thematically violent, seductive, nostal-
gic, historical, and political."[56] An example of its surrealist possibility can be
found in Queen Latifah's *"I Can't Understand"* (1993). Special effects of the artist image—on a dolly, in split image, and with various lenses—create a surrealistic worldview while Queen Latifah raps about life's crazy complexities
(fig. 11).[57] The song/video begins with the lyrics played backward; they then
reverse themselves so that we see/hear Latifah saying, "I can't understand . . .
things are going crazy." This relatively simple narrative becomes more complex as visual narratives help release Black women from the all-knowing, all-
doing trope of Black superwomen.[58] This Colored woman becomes fragmented
and disillusioned, as well as simultaneously distanced and up-close. In the end
she fails to achieve closure. This example empowers Black women because it

allows for humanity to prevail, in this case, characteristics of vulnerability and doubt. It appeared, however, on an album that generated only marginal sales.

In fact, most video imagery failed to support subversive or powerful lyrics. For example, in Karyn White's double platinum recording "I'm Not Your Super-woman" (1988) the lyrics make a stand for Black women's recognition and vulnerability. The video, however, subscribes to traditional, fictionalized narra-tive techniques, which keep women begging for acceptance and recognition on their men's terms. So more poignantly, although one could walk around the streets of various communities and find multiethnic women singing proudly, "I'm not your superwoman!", on their television screens at home a visual check offered a bleak alternative.

No doubt, music videos are tailored—made like a pair of tight jeans but manufactured mostly by male producers and directors. Consequently, struc-tural discontinuities exist between women's visual representations and their articulations.[59] Many scholars and journalists have focused on the preponder-ance of women's videos constructed for the male gaze, as exemplified by the aforementioned critical study. However, examples exist that offer subjectivity and choice for African-American women within and outside of the video nar-rative. In these videos the artists' walk and talk achieve consistency.

In contemporary culture, rap and a few uncategorizable music genres have provided the greatest area of musical contest. Their visual articulations reflect this propensity. However, pitfalls surface when ascribing feminist discourses across women's visualized bodies within these realms. These pitfalls come, in part, through the moving body itself. Highly energized forms of dancing pre-sented in many videos (as popularized and promoted by MC Hammer, his en-tourage, and the 1992 *Too Legit to Quit*" video) have polarized discussions of female agency potential.

Rudolph Arnheim theorized that five factors influence how viewers expe-rience motion: movement of the object, impact of perspective and the distance between the camera and object, effect of the moving camera, synthesis of in-dividual scenes to create an overall composition of motion, and interaction of movements as situated next to each other through montage.[60] Associations of motion shape spectators' engagement with Black women. For example, Dan Rubey applauds Hammer's *Too Legit to Quit*" as an example of Black women's movements progressing beyond pure sexuality: "The female dancers are sexy and attractive, but the energy and skill of their dancing combined with the athleticism and fleshy muscularity of their bodies present them as women en-joying and displaying their own bodies, not passive objects of a victimizing male gaze."[61] Whether this idea bears itself out becomes clearer as we begin to further examine works by prominent and successful female artists. Neverthe-less, Black women's moving bodies have become a site for confrontation.

Some of the most requested videos on *T.R.L.* and the now defunct The Box are (were) ones that feature(d) a preponderance of "rump shakin," "bumpin n grindin," and "booty callin." Andrew Ross believes that what lies behind all this "butt action" is the tradition of a "black esthetic based on the erogenous display of the female buttocks": "Often maligned and distorted by the white appetite for black spectacle, rump-shaking has nonetheless long been the motor force in black popular dance and performance traditions, not to mention the theater of daily life. As a result of such traditions, the female butt can signify as a source of authority, if not power, in black culture. By contrast, for a bossy white girl like Madonna, the pussy is the place of power."[62] Skirting the validity of Ross's power of the booty mantra, dance and performance do have a historic legacy in Negro communities. The confluence of television with the potency of dance and the body propelled the imagery of African-American women into a distinct, sexualized category. Music forms the nexus of these categories—particularly the genre of rhythm and blues—and, consequently, is where this work turns.

R&B

Prior to the 1980s rhythm and blues evolved steadily as a musical force. Gaining mainstream (that is, Caucasian) acceptance, it laid the groundwork for disco and rap. Although r&b has retained its status as a Black cultural form and forum, commercialism and music video gave this formerly fairly insulated genre a prominence and audience infusion unknown prior to it. John Caldwell suggests that commercials, more than any other 1980s and 1990s form, "exploit[ed] the discursive and emotive power of hyperactive and excessive visual style."[63] Blacks, already equated with style, served well in this new visual excess.

Increasingly, corporations employed the Motown sound to hawk their wares. For example, artists such as Ray Charles, with Pepsi's "Right thing, baby" and his rendition of "Georgia" for *Designing Women;* Aretha Franklin singing about Clairol's "Natural Woman"; and Natalie Cole's "This Will Be," which introduced NBC's *Three Sisters,* catapulted Blacks into mainstream sight and sound.[64] Although this embracing of Colored culture elevated a select few, some critics argue that the r&b Black arts movement derailed as the mainstream pilfered its ranks. Marvin Gladney asserts that "the existence of dominant commercial concerns has meant that mainstream successes have almost invariably lacked hip-hop's [and r&b's] political, racial, and social consciousness, as well as being insensitive to many of the aesthetic principles such as vivid metaphors."[65]

It is within this climate that Black women such as Janet Jackson, Vanessa L. Williams, Whitney Houston, and Gladys Knight have taken center stage. They were among the few Black women singers accepted early on within the music

FIGURE 12

Early 1980s Janet Jackson.
(Courtesy Jerry Ohlinger's Movie Material Store)

video format (appearing first on BET). In particular, Janet Jackson profited as the baby of a successful musical family. With her sibling Michael blazing the path, the youngest Jackson tested many venues of performance—acting and some singing—before finally claiming her own space as a recording artist/ actor (fig. 12).

FIGURE 13

The 1990s Janet Jackson
in *"Love Will Never Do."*

With five enormously successful recordings and more than thirty music videos, Jackson has produced a large volume of lyrical and video work. Rubey reads her early *"Nasty"* release as "a feminist film theorist's programmatic deconstruction of the male gaze." [66] Robin Roberts agrees. Others have situated "Control," "Love Will Never Do," and "What Have You Done for Me Lately?" songs and videos similarly.

Jackson's impact on the music video sphere came largely through music sales successes, which afforded her more visual liberties and control. This assuming of control directly impacted the look and content of her music videos, giving Jackson an agency not assumed by many other artists—male or female, Black or White. Some argue, however, that her continually slimmer body, facial surgeries, and skin lightening move her away from a womanist subjectivity and toward pleasuring male, White-defined objectivity (fig. 13). Plus, her increased direction toward highly sexualized material (both lyrically and visually), although relishing her own sexuality secretly, make that sexuality seem almost dirty—private beyond the point of what could be considered liberatory.

Christened with animalistic tendencies, debased by rape, and constantly visioning rapes by White slave owners (as seen in the various shades that characterize Black folks), African-Americans in general and black women in particular project a physical appearance constantly at odds with White America. The sexual body appears to be particularly problematic—the butt, breast, and the heralded and feared penis. This historic tension has translated into the schizophrenic actions and beliefs of Negroes regarding their own physical beings.

On Jackson's single "If" (1993), for example, the lyrics on the jacket provide the only context for knowing what the hell she's saying. On this *janet* CD Jackson talks about oral sex, intercourse, and exhibitionism but avoids the

"Parental Warning" label by obscuring the consumer's ability to understand it. The lyrics suggest an empowerment for Black women by voicing sexual needs and somewhat acting them out in the video. But the lyric-visual deception capitulates to puritanical mantras that position the Black woman as both whore and ice queen. In this "light" perhaps Mim Udovitch is right.[67]

Like Jackson's, the star texts of Whitney Houston occupy a unique space in music history. As winner of several Grammys and numerous other awards, Houston radically altered the music horizon for Black women, particularly for their crossover possibilities. As a prodigy of a successful singer, Houston possessed the talent, style, Afro/Euro beauty, and contacts to become what seemed an overnight sensation. Because of her immediate crossover appeal, she avoided certain blockades to MTV and the fights over image control. Marla Shelton posits that her iconic figure served as a "visual and musical strand by which to trace the 'integration' pattern of Black popular culture during the 1980s to the present."[68]

Houston's performance in the film *The Bodyguard* (Jackson, 1992) exemplified the status, cultural capital, and disparities she occupied within Negro and the larger American culture. The film allowed her to exchange her blackness for popularity but prefigured it as a portion of a biracial romantic coupling. This coupling alienated portions of Afro-American as well as Caucasian communities. Yet within the film and beyond the music video *"Queen of the Night"* Houston's status as a successful recording artist freed her to cross musical genres and maintain props in multiple listening communities, at least through the early 1990s. Her pop-rock song-video and clips from the film were intercut with Houston's performance—scenes reminiscent of rock concerts. The popularity of this song and video made En Vogue's subsequent *"Free Your Mind"* video/song possible and popular.

En Vogue emerged as a recording ladies' quartet in 1991. "Free Your Mind" appeared on their *Funky Divas* (1992) recording. The lyrics urge people to free their minds from prejudice, specifically along racial and gender lines. The video opens on a zoom-in of a dark, Negro woman with baby locks. She is surrounded by bald, shirtless White men. All look in different directions. Only she possesses a gaze, looking directly, albeit sheepishly, into the camera. A woman's voice on top of the image queries: "Prejudice, wrote a song about it. Like to hear it? Here it go."[69] After this pronouncement, the group En Vogue sings out "free your mind." The shot cuts to a wide shot of a poster drawing of a White caricatured male head shot in business attire with his mouth agape and a stuffed monkey in the foreground. It seems to indicate that Orwell's Big Brother watches. The bass offers a strong acoustic line, reminiscent of rock music. Visually, a line of multiracial, multiethnic men and women walk arm-locked and in slow motion toward the camera.

The setting is a fashion show/concert with En Vogue as the models/performers. Photographers snap pictures and onlookers dance around the outskirts of the auditorium. Dressed in all black, the four women parade the look of dominatrix, similar to Madonna's look in *"Justify My Love."* But in this visual display the women deal only superficially with sexual politics (although some would argue that their dress connotes a certain eroticism that foregrounds discussions of sexuality). John Leland suggests that En Vogue, like the group Salt-N-Pepa, "play sex as sex, but also as politics. At a time when popular music is particularly hostile to women, theirs is a celebration of female sexual control."[70] Evidence of this control can be assessed both within the lyrics and this video.

As the group members individually walk the runway, each has a specific commentary on looking relations—particularly those relationships that objectify Colored women. Each member lip-synchs one stanza:

> I wear tight clothing, high heel shoes. It doesn't mean that I'm a prostitute. No, no.
> I like rap music, wear hip-hop clothes. That doesn't mean that I'm out sellin' dope. No, no, no.
> Oh Lord forgive me for having straight hair. It doesn't mean there's another blood in my heirs.
> I might date another race or color. It doesn't mean I don't like, my strong Black brothers.

In this first stanza the group wonder aloud why society indulges in shallow preconceptions. What made this video and text particularly compelling was their juxtaposition of uniquely Colored women's encounters with society and the visual illustration of the problem.

In the second verse, the women sing:

> So I'm a sista. Buy things with cash. That really doesn't mean that all my credit is bad.
> So why dispute me and waste my time because you really think the price is too high, for me.
> I can't look, without being watched. No. You rang my buy before I made up my mind.

After the last line Terry Ellis thrusts her pelvis forward and strikes the overused pose women assume in male videos—legs agape in a V (fig. 14). The expression "Ow" is heard in voice-over. In male videos the camera or the male singer himself would then move through the opening of the unidentified woman's legs. In En Vogue's case, however, Ellis kicks, crosses, turns, and walks away (figs. 15, 16). She subverts and denies traditional male view and access.

The lyrics continue:

> Oh now attitude. Why even bother?
> I can't change your mind. You can't change my color.

FIGURES 14, 15, 16

Terry Ellis in En Vogue video *"Free Your Mind."* She v's, closes the gap, and struts away.

During the next two musical bridges, the video shows a Black male torso with white hands caressing it from the back while overhead shots display White men with their mouths agape. Additionally, a White (presumed) punk rocker jumps into the crowd, conjuring scenes of a grunge/rock concert. The young Black woman who appeared at the beginning of the video now sits smiling as the men turn their gaze toward her and massage her shoulders. The final segment of the song features a guitar solo that recalls Jimi Hendrix. This again reinforces the mantra to free your mind through replication of certain freedoms called for, especially in this case, during the sixties and seventies.

Robin Roberts erroneously critiqued the video as a central visual text for gendered empowerment. She claims, for example, that the line "I can't look without being watched" is an indictment of male gazes and is directed toward all women. Although the gaze may be a male one, the look that En Vogue refers to is frequently a more racialized one—one directed at Coloreds in stores where proprietors/sales clerks ascribe a propensity for stealing to Colored bodies. This look comes from both males and females. Thus, the visualization of *"Free Your Mind"* not only calls for an outside action, but it examines specific oppressions. In this heightened fashion world, Black women could find voice lyrically and visually by confronting taboos (Black-White coupling) and mechanical (camera) objectification. This video powerfully indicts both race and gender discrimination; however, it fails to address one other pervasive prejudice in music video, ageism.

Endemic to visual and lived American culture, music videos have treated badly those aging and older artists who have dared to enter its r&b purview. Attempting to reinvent or update themselves, many formerly popular artists embraced the visual practices of incessant dancing, lip-synching, and sexiness as defined by youthful, naked bodies. Artists such as Aretha Franklin, Patti LaBelle, Tina Turner, Diana Ross, and Gladys Knight—all musical divas—began altering their sound and image, largely shown through the music video. Some of their crossover attempts were successful (fig. 17). Others withered in this new visual world.

In Franklin's music video *"Freeway of Love"* (1985), for example, Franklin surrounds herself with young, thin, multicultural women and men. As they dance around her, she sings and two-steps to the beat—yet synchronously and visually out of place and time. Her changed, more grainy voice and expanded figure highlight her difference and ineptitude in this Generation X music video realm. Yet ironically, in part because of the forum, this became her biggest selling record in twelve years, earning her two Grammy awards.[71]

Likewise, when Diana Ross departed from her haute couture to contemporary culture, she faltered. In her 1982 *"Muscles"* video for example, Ross's aged body contrasts noticeably with the young, buffed men surrounding her. She

FIGURE 17

Gladys Knight exemplifies deft negotiation of the music video realm in *"I Don't Want to Know."*

looks tired and old—a danger in the commodification of music, where only men possess the ability to transcend age visually. When women do appear on television middle-aged, the difference, as Patricia Mellencamp says, is that "women must not look it—yet another double bind or simulation—chronology disavowal."[72] Beyond her participation within music video from the beginning, this "not looking it" may be why Madonna (as she enters middle age) continues to prosper. For others, however, instead of creating an example of progressive spaces for older women in music video, Ross's imagery in *"Muscles"* provided fodder for their exclusion.

However, when she returned to her Motown musical heritage, she recaptured the vitality of her visual past performances. In the 1984 video *"Missing You,"* a song dedicated to Marvin Gaye, quintessential Diana Ross flows through the video in two outfits: a full-length, white sequined gown and a sleek, black sheath. Photographs and footage of Marvin, her days with him, and past performances with the Supremes fill the video. Toward the end of the video she ascends stairs as a silhouette of red and blue lights shine through her gown. This lighting accentuates her figure, and the finale captures the former grace, glamour, and aura of Motown's Diana Ross and the Supremes.[73] Plus, it allows Ross to enter the music video realm on her own terms. The same visual success follows Aretha Franklin in her 1998 release *"A Rose Is Still a Rose."* Written by Lauryn Hill, the video situates Franklin as a part of the narrative but not as antithetical to the Queen of Soul legacy she embodies. And because I've mentioned twenty-first-century-hip-hop-guru Lauryn Hill, I turn now to the most expansive genre iteration of Black women's musical trajectory and visualness, rap.

RAP MUSIC AND THE HIP-HOP COMMUNITY

Rap as a musical form began in the 1970s in New York City's South Bronx. However, its marketing emerged in the 1980s. With its poor and marginalized roots the music became a perennial "cash cow" for the record industry. Dan Rubey suggests that "[i]f heavy metal is the music of tribal identity for young whites, rap music serves a similar function for young blacks."[74] Beyond negotiating royalty compensation for sampling, the cost of producing rap groups was relatively low initially, at least compared to other music forms. The bulk of the profits went to (and remains with) the record company. Tricia Rose says that rap music emerged in a music system historically steeped in the exploitation of artists. This industry compensates its artists with small flat fees and signs them to rigid and lengthy production contracts.[75]

Rapping comes from the traditions of Black oral culture—a favorable nod toward Black talk blended with pastiche, if you will. Following the parameters of Fredric Jameson's assertions, this pastiche produced a "neutral practice of . . . mimicry . . . without that still latent feeling that there exists something normal."[76] Rap fused gospel rhetoric, r&b, and the language acumen of specific Black youth artists. Unlike other musical forums, this genre belonged almost exclusively to young people—specifically young Black men. Some have argued that hip-hop and its rap component help negotiate African-American and Caribbean-American youth history, identity, and community. Further, Rose claims a tension for this product between "the cultural fractures produced by postindustrial oppression and the binding ties of black cultural expressivity that sets the critical frame for the development of hip hop."[77] Under the rubric of testosterone, rap became heralded as the cultural agenda and tone-setter for all of Black America.

Violent, misogynistic, and self-hating articulations of many rap lyrics came from what producer and former Motown executive Andre Harrell called "Reaganomic rap groups." He based this assessment on absences found in urban Black communities, remarking that "Reaganomics took away after-school programs, took away summer jobs, took away student loans. So you got a whole generation of rappers who've grown up under the auspices of Generation X. Who grew up with no hope and all they see is pain."[78] Similar to U.S./World Bank/IMF policies regarding structural adjustment, the trickle-down theory translated into slashed jobs for youth, slashed welfare, slashed educational opportunities, and slashed physical outlets. In other words, the trickle dried up before it hit the hood.[79] In music this pain translated into profits. Thus, many women in the rap industry fought to capitalize on this lucrative, anger-for-profit, male-centered market.

One of rap's early and sustained entrepreneurs, Russell Simmons, offered a view of women that defines their participation. In the rapumentary *The Show* (Robbins, 1995), Simmons discussed his clothesline Phat Farm and how women piqued his interest in fashion. Yet it was his rationale for attending fashion functions, besides "some tall bitch," that revealed his thought and business trajectory of and for women. He explained his own commentary: "I didn't mean bitch, I mean worldly sophisticated, independent, bad-ass bitch. You know. The kinda hoes every man wanna marry. . . . I mean bad bitch. Super bitch. Super powerful, independent, successful, bitch. Not like, no, necessarily, not at all derogatory. No way. Cuz, I love women. I can't sympathize with all the rappers be talkin they hate the hoes. I love girls."[80] This rambling received confirmation and exclamation as the film's next shot shows Simmons on the phone with a group of young girls surrounding him. They say in unison, "Thank you daddy," and laugh, foreshadowing scenes in which prostitutes praise their pimp in *Pimps Up, Hoes Down* (1998). Unfortunately, this "bitch aesthetic"—this demonization of women—not only surfaced within male speech, attitude, and business vision, but also through many women's own lyrics and music videos.

WHO YOU CALLIN A BITCH?!

Like other professional sistahs, "lil honeys" in the rap music industry came into their own during the late 1980s and 1990s. From rapper/business owner/actress/talk show host Queen Latifah to money guru Lil' Kim to producer extraordinaire Missy "Misdemeanor" Elliott, female rappers commanded the microphone to preach and teach on topics ranging from love to shooting up the neighborhood. These rapping young women asserted that they would not sit on the sidelines as their male counterparts identified, defined, and denigrated them as bitches, hoes, and hoochies. In their music many attacked not only those who produced this type of characterization but also the system that perpetuated it. They captured an audience for their views on sex, work, Black consciousness, and equal rights. Both their message and their marketing directed their focus. Yet initially they failed to sell.

In 1995 Danyel Smith maintained, "Women hip-hoppers can't sell as many records as their male counterparts. Salt-N-Pepa, MC Lyte, and one-hit wonders J. J. Fad are the only women who have ever had a single or album certified gold (sales of 500,000). No one else has reached that plateau—not Yo-Yo, not Boss, not even Queen Latifah."[81] This was before T.L.C. sold four million copies of their release *Crazysexycool* (1994) and Da Brat reached platinum with her *Funkdafied* CD (1994).

Many women rappers claimed feminist stances although, historically, aggressive Afro-American women have been perceived as threatening. Their actions challenged White patriarchal definitions of femininity. This challenge brought cries of foul by Black community leaders and young men in the rap game. Yet Patricia Hill Collins suggests that "[t]o ridicule assertive women . . . reflects an effort to put *all* women in their place."[82] The implication of this relegation may be that music videos empower women artists only enough to obtain the correct demographic (males aged twelve to thirty-four). Consequently, women rappers' music videos have not been immune to subversion by male visioning. Further, women rappers have had to negotiate the difficult terrain of White feminist thought against racial realities. Nevertheless, some female-driven videos provide laudatory spaces for female artist and spectator articulation, subjectification, and empowerment. In fact, cultural scholar Valerie Smith contends that all performance has contestable potential. She argues that just because music videos often play into hegemonic discourses, this fact does not make their contestable moments moot.[83]

Considered part of the "old school," Queen Latifah, MC Lyte, Roxanne Shante, Yo-Yo, and Salt-N-Pepa all began rapping in the mid-1980s. Noted initially for their masculinized hardness, these women "dissed and dismissed" males' characterizations of their gender while still visually appearing as one of the fellas. Issues that female audiences related to and/or that had a distinct female orientation, such as BWP's "Cotex," Latifah's "Ladies First," and Salt-N-Pepa's "I'll Take Your Man," made them popular. However, unlike their White, gendered sisters (women rockers), Afro-American women rappers did not exclude men entirely from their lyrical purview.

Robin Roberts has argued quite correctly that rap music particularly suits feminist agendas. She believes that because "rappers endemically focus on themselves, [if] the performer is female, she can use this self-promotion without altering the musical form. Rap's emphasis on lyrics also tailors it to a political agenda, for listening to the words requires thoughtful attention."[84] Similar to her role in *Living Single,* Queen Latifah's rap image softened over time.[85] In music video she blended both her image as a hard-core rapper with more feminized looks in terms of attire, hairstyles, and makeup. Yet in the 1993 recording *Black Reign* Queen Latifah rehardened her sound and image. She sought fans' approval, saying, "'Yo, Latifah back, dropping knowledge,' not dropping some rinky-dink party record."[86] This followed only marginal sales of her 1991 release *Nature of a Sista'.*

Addressing the "bitch aesthetic" that began in the 1980s but flourished in the 1990s, Latifah recognized the denigration and insidiousness of her own recuperation of the term *bitch*. In an interview she remarked that she found even herself using it. On checking that behavior, however, she realized that the term may not be emancipatory at all. Men never carried the bitch moniker except if being condemned for "womanly" characteristics. Therefore, by examining her *"Unity"* video (more commonly recognized by its hook, "Who You Callin a Bitch?") we see an example of how Queen Latifah visually reframed this terminology.

The video opens with Latifah fired up. She is angry about men denigrating women by calling them bitches. The rap suggests that verbal, physical, and self-abuse are partially a result of women's allowing for and embracing of disparaging terminology. As she walks past a group of males, one grabs her behind. When Latifah turns around to confront him, the guilty party responds, "Yeah, me bitch," and laughs. She continues:

> Since he was with his boys, he tried to break fly.
> I punched him dead in his eye. Who you callin' a bitch?

These words come with a corresponding action taking place visually. Therefore, she physically illustrates the harmful effects of the term *bitch* and urges Black women to rally against the term's use.

Numerous critics have argued that female rappers recuperate messages offered by their male counterparts and subvert them. Patricia Hill Collins suggests that this type of self-definition becomes important and necessary for African-American women, who are consistently and systematically objectified. She considers these acts a series of negotiations that "aim to reconcile the contradictions separating our own internally defined images of self as African-American women with our objectification as the Other."[87] These artists' confrontational style actually reprises the anger of Negras in 1970s blaxploitation films.

I pointed out in chapter 1 that cinema's angry Black women served as precursors to Black women on television comedy and drama. They shot into blaxploitation stardom in films described by Ed Guerrero as a "series of cheap ghetto action adventures that in almost every count replicated the values, visual style, and exaggerated sex and violence of their male-focused counterparts."[88] Yet as quickly as these films and roles emerged, they disappeared. Consequently, the limited power realized by these gendered and racialized figures was effectively silenced, leaving only the rearticulation and redemption of male-proclaimed bitches.

Despite the aesthetic nod and Madonna's notions, bitch remained bitch. Even with popularization, redefinition, and stylization, mainstream and even hip-hop culture recognized *bitch* to mean female dog—unworthy, unattractive, and inhuman. Yet artists continue to try and refashion it. For example, Missy Elliott tries to subvert the term in her "She's a Bitch" (1999) by explaining in the hook:

> She's a bitch
> When you say my name
> Talk mo' junk but won't look my way
> She's a bitch
> See I got more cheese
> So back on up while I roll up my sleeves.

Elliott attempts to reinterpret *bitch* as defiance based on monetary wealth. Earlier attempts at this revisioning came from artists such as Boss and Bytches with Problems. U.S. pop culture in the 1990s applied the term to women so liberally that it began crossing radio and television airways in programming that would earlier have edited the term out. But patriarchy's validation of this feminized denigration fails to make women's usage of it transgressive, especially if we consider disparities in income, housing, and accessibility.[89]

BY ANY MEANS? . . .

Emerging in 1986, the group Salt-N-Pepa (Cheryl James, Sandy Denton, DeeDee Roper) blended hard-core lyrics with sexuality. On the wings of their surprise recording success "Push It," they produced a video that featured choreographed dances with male dance backups. In it they wear black satin unitards, red boots, and big biker jackets. This dress allows them a stance simultaneously tough and sexy. Their five albums/CDs to date address relationships (both platonic and romantic), women's needs and desires, and various social concerns such as AIDS. Early in their careers they proclaimed themselves feminists. Says Salt in an interview, "We're doing something that only guys are expected to do and doin' it right!"[90]

Very Necessary (1993) was the group's first LP produced and written by the group's members. In the videos for this album they celebrated this achievement and their new physiques that accompanied it. These women wanted to *Shoop* (code word for sex) and directly, visually alert men to that desire. They do this by exemplifying Lisa Lewis's theory of access signs. The video presents typically male spaces (the basketball court, the beach, and the Girlie Club) and inverts the social interactions that are typically perceived to take place there. S-N-P sit as voyeurs while skimpily clad men parade through, strip for them, and generally entertain them. The group transgresses these boundaries especially in the Girlie Club, where the ladies' night provides women with all the rights, privileges, and responsibilities therein.

At the beach Pepa identifies the object of her desire and pursues it. She explains to the others—the intertextual and extratextual female spectators—

I'm not shy so I asked for the digits.
A hoe? No, that don't make me.
See what I want slip slide to it swiftly.

Later in the video the ladies assert themselves fully. Male guest rapper Otwane "Big Twane Lov-Her" Roberts enters the scene wearing his patriarchy like sex and announcing:

I hit the skins for the hell of it;
Not just the yell I get.
Ooh, ooh, ooh, for the smell of it.

FIGURE 18

Pepa giving Big Twan
a whiff in *"Shoop."*

Pepa lifts her leg to give him a whiff of vaginal secretions and commands, "Smell it" (fig. 18).

In a similar scenario T.L.C.'s *"Ain't 2 Proud 2 Beg"* (1992) attempts the same inversion of male space. Nataki Goodall argues that in T.L.C.'s "demand for sexual fulfillment, the group shows that women need not (indeed, cannot) claim the higher moral ground on the field of sexual desire. Nor, the group reminds us, do men have a monopoly on desire. These are women who see sexual fulfillment as natural and good, and, above all, their right."[91] In their visual articulations Salt-N-Pepa celebrate Black women and exhibit these women's diversity in the selection of backup dancers. The same applies to the men who literally decorate the video.

Although feminist women rappers' examination of social issues generally commanded a "take no prisoners" stance on the road to equality, these women became interestingly self-reflexive. At the juncture of music performance and production some acquired the rewards of capitalist consumption, produced within sexist and racist structures. K. C. Arceneaux examines how these tensions became visible by comparing videos of Queen Latifah with those of Big Daddy Kane. Arceneaux asserts that gender opposition exists within the videos, but placed side by side, "they exist together paradoxically. . . . [T]heir two varying positions are not resolved by their collision."[92]

Addressing this conundrum, others like bell hooks believe that consumers, and Black women especially, must guard their representations. Otherwise, these representations may be "appropriated and exploited in white supremacist capitalist patriarchy, [and] we may find ourselves falling into traps set by the dominant culture."[93] In other words, if women rappers claim to stand in the gap for women's progress, they need consistency and integrity of lyrics and

FIGURE 19

MC Lyte with her
"Ruffnecks."

imagery. But like mainstream male video, many stray from feminist agendas. A special example of the difficulties encountered is made evident in an early work of artist MC Lyte.

MC Lyte (Lana Moorer) began rapping at age sixteen. Self-characterized as a tomboy, Moorer achieved initial popularity through rapping and by looking and acting like the fellas around the way. Her first recording, *Lyte as a Rock* (1988), accorded her recognition and respect from the music industry, as well as from her male colleagues. By her third recording effort, *Act Like You Know* (1991), she, like Queen Latifah, had softened her style, espoused more socially conscious ideas, incorporated diverse rhythms that she liked, and feminized her look. For these actions her sales fell dramatically. Consequently, in her release *Ain't No Other* (1993) Lyte returned to her hard-core roots.

In the single "Ruffneck" Lyte tolerates lies against her and a dearth of affection as necessary and endemic to her hard-core, interpersonal relationships. She chants, I "hit 'em wit a bit of skins and he's outta here," as she visually compares a departing plane to sexual exchange. MC Lyte realizes that in acquiescing to an inverted misogynistic rap diatribe with this recording, she compromised herself.[94] But more than that, her particular dilemma shows that imagery can be not only defining but confining.

In the *"Ruffneck"* video Lyte feminizes her look through obvious makeup. The musical refrain, "Gotta watch out, gotta get a ruffneck" finds her in a coordinated black and white pants ensemble (one that hides all aspects of bodily dimension).[95] Further, her accessories include a matching skull cap, which aligns her with her male contemporaries. Although surrounded by tough-looking young men, she appears to control them and the situation (fig. 19):

Acting like he don't care, but all I got to do is beep him
9-1-1 and he'll be there.

The video exposes and glorifies the beauty and lifestyles of Black, marginalized young men. Lyte's female posse gives consent to her preference for rough-necks by listening and videotaping men who are "rough and right." The women tape the men for their own visual pleasure.

Lyte suggests that the roughnecks' attitude masks the inner workings of the "authentic" man. However, this masking more accurately reflects what she herself did. MC Lyte veiled a fuller representation of what *woman* could mean in order to sell music. She herself attests that "it seems to be working."[96] The positions MC Lyte took validate women rappers' limiting so-called feminine representations in lieu of a harder, visual style. The image she assumed trapped her in a male construct where fear of failure motivated further pro-ductivity. As the Wu Tang Clan so aptly articulated, contemporary images cen-tered the idea of C.R.E.A.M. (Cash Rules Everything Around Me).

GANGSTA BITCH

In a different way Boss (Lichelle Laws) exemplified the legacy of womanist gains. Laws grew up in a Catholic-school, middle-class-Detroit environment. The artist Boss, in contrast, was a gangster girl from the streets. Cursing was her main means of communication, and Boss toted guns and ammunition, with an articulated proclivity toward using them indiscriminately.[97] The con-trast between Laws and Boss made her figure especially disturbing. Her pro-ducers and Sony created an image for mass (male) consumption from a proclaimed reality of which the artist was virtually ignorant. She became Milli Vanilli gone gangster (or Vanilla Ice cross-gendered). Boss dubbed herself a new, self-styled woman: "I'm both a gangster and a smart business person. I know what I'm doing, and I know how to make it in this business."[98] Her vid-eos gave clues to the tension created between real and reel Negras and the rhetoric employed.

Boss's *"Run, Catch, and Kill"* illustrated how the process of image making turned rhetorical.[99] In the video Boss pretends to be a gang member watching a film about women becoming part of gang life. The video exists as part of the promotion for Allison Anders's film *Mi Vida Loca* (1994). In the video and through her lyrics Boss maintains that the film characters act as if gangster-hood is a game. But for real-life gang members such as herself, gang member-ship is serious and life-threatening. Reminiscent of Julie Dash's technique in *Illusions* (1983), the video's lyrics and imagery get at the heart of Boss's irony. The rap authenticates her gang membership in a fictional music video that promotes a real fictional film about the actresses in the film fronting about gang life. This commodified layering, this hyper hyperreality, takes Lichelle

Laws all the way to the bank while confusing and debasing the image of African-American women.

The first female rapper signed to Dr. Dre's label, Boss initially received wide acceptance from male audiences, the rappers' community, and young Black women. Her deep and edgy voice coupled with cornrowed hair and intermittent skullcaps gave her a masculine aesthetic. In *"Run, Catch, and Kill"* Negras (and Latinas in the film) throw signs, smoke crack (presumably), fight, and live the cinematic male gang life. Some critics such as Tricia Rose have argued that women use this form of imaging strategically. They present and promote women's presences masked (once again) or as Mary Ann Doane suggests, masquerading, in order to distance themselves from their own self-image. Women assume this stance in order to achieve palatability within dominant (male) culture. It opens a space for women's voices to be heard.[100] Yet, as should be obvious, with such extensive image manipulation, duplicity reigns.

Boss's image resembled what Carol Clover suggests about women in horror films. An angry woman, says Clover, "can be imagined as a credible perpetrator . . . of the kind of violence on which, in the low-mythic universe, the status of full protagonist rests."[101] Boss represents this angry woman. Audre Lorde suggests that Black women *can* use anger "to help define and fashion a world where all our sisters can grow."[102] Yet venting in service to patriarchy and capitalism diffuses this wrath's potential. Boss's video failed to channel or even address Lorde's recommendation (or to encourage women who endure abuse). Even as Boss pretends to advise young women against gangs, the demonstration of her war wound and her tough fighting facade all glorify the life she castigates. Despite her early success, by 2000 Boss had virtually disappeared from the hip-hop scene. However, her introduction and popularity made palatable (and profitable) Da Brat—another "tough bitch."

In Black entertainment culture there have always been raunchy women. These women resided in the Black psyche and belonged to the community. For example, Millie Jackson's 1989 album cover, *Back to the S__!*, featured her in black feathers, leather, and lace lingerie while sitting on the toilet. With one black pump on and the other in her hand, Jackson's facial expression tells the story. She's in mid-dump. The most successful release from this recording, "Hot, Wild Unrestricted! Crazy Love!," left little to the imagination.

Thus when Da Brat (Shawntae Harris) released her third album, *Unrestricted*, in 2000, she followed the legacy of Boss, Millie Jackson, and others (fig. 20). For this appearance she traded in her quintessential big shirts, baggy jeans, and braids for a more mature, curvaceous, and commercial sexiness (defined by fleshy parts in loosely sewn clothes). Says the artist, "You've gotta show people you've grown. You can't come with the same type of sh*t and think just 'cause you look good you don't have to work as hard. It's still all about the

FIGURE 20

Da Brat showing some skin.
(Courtesy of Jerry Ohlinger's Movie Material Store)

music. It's all about the whole package, lookin' good, smellin' good, tastin' good. But can't nobody f**k with me on the lyrics, not any females."[103] Yet Da Brat's liberal use of profanity (digitized in music video) and her self-embraced negative denotation ushered in another type of problematic video.

DAMN RIGHT SEX SELLS!

In the latter part of the twentieth century probably the most controversial and daunting mainstream artist for Black communities was Lil' Kim (Kimberly Jones). The performer Lil' Kim, like Smooth et al. before her, equated her independence and strength with material parity. In many ways she represented the fruits of womanist/feminist agitation, the right to define oneself. The problem? Kim embraced objectification as a career choice.

The conflictedness of mainstream feminism receives voice in a testifying moment of character Ling Woo (Lucy Liu) of *Ally McBeal* (1997–present). Ling charges the contemporary discourse of "women as object" with hypocrisy:

> Every woman wants to be thought of as desirable. . . . The women there [in her mud wrestling club] make nearly 100,000 dollars a year. How? These drunken Neanderthals hurl money at them. Go into that club, you'll come out with a lower opinion of men. . . . Sex is a weapon. We all use it. We tease. We tantalize. We withhold it, something we do in almost every walk of life be it marriage, business. . . . Women are exploited by the high-heel shoe. Women are exploited by the idea that we have to paint our eyelashes every day just to go to work. . . . Pharmaceutical companies spend billions of dollars convincing the world that cellulite is evil. Is that to empower a woman? What world do you live in?[104]

In this context Kim's stance makes sense. Her professional position suggests that, if sex sells, why shouldn't I get mine?

Lil' Kim emerged as the only female member of the Notorious B.I.G.'s Junior M.A.F.I.A. in 1995. She contributed to several male rap artists' work before releasing her own first album *Hard Core* in 1996. Writing all of her own lyrics, Lil' Kim discussed sex candidly and explicitly in this release. Sean "Puffy" Combs produced the CD with bumpin' riffs and rhythms. This album appeared at the same time that Foxy Brown, another hard-core sexualized female, was making waves. Record companies' marketers insinuated a mock competition between the two. But by 2000 Kim had extended her success to multiple avenues of popular consumption. In fact, says Akissi Britton, "Corporate America's response has been a stream of endorsement offers—from Iceberg Jeans and Candi's shoes to M.A.C.'s Viva Glam III lipstick. In the past year alone, the fashion icon has graced the covers and pages of such magazines as *The Source, XXL, Vibe, Out, Honey, Vogue* and *Harper's Bazaar*. In *Interview* she appeared wearing only head-to-toe Louis Vuitton body tattoos."[105]

Lil' Kim disturbed everyone, especially Black women. In many minds she reified the ugly history of Black women's sexuality. Lil' Kim forced the collective consciousness of Black women's feminist articulations to grapple with not-so-deeply buried feelings about their bodies and ongoing negotiations with sexuality. She flaunted her ability to attract men with her body and expected some type of financial reciprocation for their appreciation. For example, during the 1999 MTV Music Video Awards she wore a pastie over her left nipple. On the stage Diana Ross twirled the tassle on the end of it.

Many argue that Lil' Kim allowed the media to use her despite her admonishment that "you can't pimp this" (one of Smooth's key refrains).[106] However, Lil' Kim's *"No Matter What They Say"* (2000), from her *Notorious K.I.M.* sophomore album (and similar to Madonna's *"Music"*), illuminated the dissonance between women's use of male techniques and their lyrics—even as these same women dubbed those techniques problematic. The women's use of them suggests that male-implemented techniques are inherently viable. The second verse states:

> I'm just trying to be me doin what I gotta do.
> So why y'all keep hating on me and my crew?
> (Yo I'm saying QB look at them and look at you.)
> True.
> If I was you I'd hate me too.
> Louis Vuitton shoes and a whole lot of booze.
> Every other week a different dude, another cruise.
> I make offers nobody can refuse.
> You might even see me on the channel 9 news.
> I get paid just for laying in the shade,
> to take pictures with a glass of lemonade.
> My rock shine like it was dipped in cascade
> (uh uh Kim been fly since she was in the 5th grade).
> Wake up in the morning to breakfast from a maid.
> Wanted me so bad you went and copped a bootleg.
> Y'all niggas played like a high top fade.
> Some of the shit I hear don't know how it got played.
> Y'all rock Versace and y'all went out and bought it.
> I rock Versace and y'all know I ain't paid for it.
> My fam deep with security in the jeep.
> When the queen come in town, everything shut down.

In the video Lil' Kim talks directly to spectators about her accomplishments and material gain with hip-hop successes Missy Elliott's and Mary J. Blige's presence to support her claims. Dressed in lingerie and platinum jewelry, Kim claims mastery of the rap stage with money, cars, and selling CDs to prove it. She surrounds herself with similarly clad women, who serve as a visual and vocal fan base for her. The mise-en-scène attests to this as the camera centers Kim and focuses on her whole person more often than not. The camera empowers her also by giving her consistent low-angle shots.

FIGURE 21

Lil' Kim and P. Diddy
(a.k.a. Puff Daddy) in
"No Time."

From the beginning of the video Black women's bodies receive validation. Although most of the dancers are slender, the larger Missy Elliott shakes and parades with all of them comfortably. Even as Kim twirls on the runway, in the dressing room, and with male fans, she seems to have a wonderful time centering the narrative. Throughout her wardrobe changes and dance maneuvers, Lil' Kim promotes the idea that empowerment comes in many forms—regardless of "what they say."

Yet similar Lil' Kim imagery exists in many 2 Live Crew, Jay-Z, and Mystical videos. Indeed, imitation remains the highest form of compliment. And as Audre Lorde emphatically claims, "the master's tools will never dismantle the master's house."[107] Although women rappers like Lil' Kim, Foxy Brown, and Da Brat have found success in their mostly male-written but women-performed lyrics, they advance a complex womanist discourse visually and theoretically. Lil' Kim believes that she is helping to build the feminine side of hip-hop culture while still bringing the hard-core stuff (fig. 21).[108] Other examples from popular culture involved even more complicated emancipatory video practices. These contributions came mainly from voices and visions outside the mainstream.

ALTERNATIVE VOICES

Beyond rap women, artists outside generic music culture subverted Black women's objectification through their lyrics and videos. For the purposes of this work I define *alternative* as musical styles that defy neat generic categorization. Artists such as Tracy Chapman, Me'Shell NdegéOcello, Erykah Badu, Lauryn Hill, Jill Scott, and Indie Arie entered unexplored territory with their artistry, visual presence, lyrics, and marketing. Despite Black alternative-music legends such as Eartha Kitt, Jimi Hendrix, Nina Simone, Living Color, and Dianne Reeves, artists have enjoyed only limited popular acceptance. However, newer artists like the aforementioned have received greater acceptance, a result not only of their musical styles, as heard on the radio, but of their presence in music videos.

In 1988 Tracy Chapman became visible to the American music purview while studying at Tufts University. She performed both in coffeehouses and on the street corners of Cambridge. Quoting James Baldwin, Chapman believed that "[a]rtists are supposed to be disturbers of the peace. I feel like I'm challenging people." [109]

Widely lauded by music critics, Chapman wrote lyrics that called for a feminist revolt and a revolution of poor, marginalized people—a revolution, she claimed, already in progress. Nelson George donned her today's Black woman, "optimistic about social change and personal liberation." [110] However, her music defied the precise categorization that the industry requires—labeling her everything from an "urban folk singer" to "the queen of protest pop."

Her debut album, *Tracy Chapman*, ranked number one in the nation and sold over ten million copies worldwide. In 1989 her follow-up effort, *Crossroads,* was certified platinum. Over the ensuing decade Chapman produced five albums that reached international audiences. She says, "People have to dream and they also have to have all sorts of pragmatic things, they have to speak up and voice their opinions." [111]

Fox's *In Living Color* satirized Chapman's style and ambiguity in one of their episodes. Kim Wayans, in Chapmanesque black garb, portrayed the singer in a hippie-like apartment with beads, sparseness, and mix-matched furniture. The skit emphasized the simplicity, realism, and perceived eclecticism of Chapman's lyrics and persona, which were quite antithetical to the "real" blackness of the 1990s. Wayans sits by the window with guitar in hand and describes what she sees. This response was perhaps reflective of the larger Black community's disconnect with Chapman. Despite this estrangement, her videos carried an important impact for Black women as these same videos ushered her into mainstream prominence.

For example, in Chapman's 1996 release *"Give Me One Reason"* her raspy, authoritative voice and simple musical accompaniment defy the hyperactive music, movement, and editing of the 1990s videoscape. Filmmaker Julie Dash directs Chapman to play the guitar and sing in a would-be juke joint. Covered with locks, a long dress, and boots, Chapman delivers lyrics that center a woman asking her love interest why she should stay (fig. 22).

Dianne Reeves serves as the mute narrative protagonist in this video. Her

FIGURE 22

Tracy Chapman in
"Give Me One Reason."

presence brings depth and a cultural specificity to a mise-en-scène replete with lush and rich colors, straight-on camera angles, and beautifully toned and alternately coiffured Black women and men. Although not a staple of BET's programming rotation, the video received considerable coverage on MTV and abroad. Chapman's early alternative genre style and visual approach afforded much opportunity for edgier artists to follow.

Me'Shell NdegéOcello, for example, was one of Chapman's benefactors. In her performance she offered layered and multifaceted examples of word and image recuperation for Black women artists (and spectators) concerned with consistency. A hip-hop philosopher of sorts, her first release *Plantation Lullabies* (1993) blended rap, hip-hop, jazz, and funk. Signed onto Madonna's Maverick label, NdegéOcello received critical acclaim but limited radio airtime. The same excuses and labels that haunted Chapman faced NdegéOcello. Tired of hearing music that "didn't speak to me," NdegéOcello created a sound that blended "the gap between Southeast D.C. and the more middle-class bourgeois parts of town, between go-go and quiet storm, between hard-core funk and romantic music." [112]

In her lyrics/video *"If That's Your Boyfriend"* from this CD she aimed to transform. [113] *"If That's Your Boyfriend"* begins with a Black woman in braids tooling with her hair and saying, "I feel like such an ass." While various other women exchange monologues of bad feelings, NdegéOcello sings. Close-ups and additional text underneath direct NdegéOcello's continuous dialogue, rescuing these women from anonymity. Disembodied parts are not allowed. Full head-shots or NdegéOcello's mouth are the only close-ups featured. This technique personalizes and empowers by according the women a recognized and visible voice.

The lyrics narrativize a woman, NdegéOcello, who has unashamedly slept with another woman's boyfriend. She tells the girl, "If that's your boyfriend, he wasn't last night." Visually, she inverts this bad-girl image by dressing as a

FIGURE 23

Me'Shell NdegéOcello
in *"If That's Your
Boyfriend"*

bad boy (bald head and suspenders) while maintaining a "feminine" edge with shiny, dark (presumably red [the video is shot in black and white]) lipstick. Different from the CD, the video features various women (talking heads of various ages, ethnicities, and presumably sexual desires), who speak the mind of NdegéOcello. They relate their/her problems with men and relationships.

NdegéOcello opens a site for multiple interpretations of self-definition. All of her sites (these women) form a part of herself—her situated identity. She claims African-American, woman, musician, mother, and bisexual as all parts of her identity. With this stance she recuperates male space in her dress and often in her lyrical positioning. For example in the video she plays the bass (fig. 23), using it as a faux penis while stating:

> Ooh ooh baby baby, Look to the 'lastic at the bottom of the bag it.
> Ooh, baby baby, Make you wanna do things that you never have.
> Ooh, baby baby, Mad sex and when we're through,
> I really have no problem actin' like I don't know you.

She turns her back, walks away, and begins to play her bass—leaving the spectator wondering whether it is the Black woman of NdegéOcello's biological construction saying this or the sexualized Other claiming her space.

NdegéOcello's attempt at androgyny may be the most daring statement an artist can make, particularly in a cultural climate that still demands definition. Pat Aufderheide suggests that when one takes this stance, "Gender is no longer fixed; male and female are fractured into a kaleidoscope of images."[114] Indeed, as NdegéOcello asserts, Black women may need to negotiate their multiple selves differently and defiantly to survive virtual, visual, and actual erasure and continual disfiguration.

REPROGRAMMING THE CHANNEL

John Caldwell contends that "coexistent with American mall culture, stylistic designations foreground television's obsession with merchandising and consumerism."[115] The style, the beat, and the pitch of music videos make them a medium of unparalleled precedence. As an extremely successful marketing tool, music videos not only introduce artists but provide opportunities for them to reinvent themselves repeatedly in the visual realm.

Different types of music air via music videos, largely positioned within musical genres. From punk to gospel, most successful artists forward their lyrical sound from the domains of visual commercial centers known as music video. They offer literally hundreds of visual and aural pieces of information in a snapshot. With their proliferation and sensory depth, they often overwhelm spectators "by combining visual, spatial, gestural, and iconic signals."[116]

Music videos have become sellable commodities in and of themselves. This marriage of the visual realm of television to music has meant a "commercial success for people who lack even basic technical skills of musical performance."[117] Music videos give context and meaning to lyrics. Sometimes, as in T.L.C.'s *"No Scrubs"* (1999), they even reinterpret lyrics, pushing them in a direction that the song alone does not substantiate. Yet as many have argued, visual images are polysemic. Meanings change and refuse fixity in time. They are not the same for everyone, nor do they remain the same for anyone.[118] Music video illustrates televisual excess better than any other video form. As such, they offer a privileged site for public negotiation of gender, race, sex, and power. Their very excess opens up a space for resistance by Black women performers bent on shaking up racial and sexual politics.

Across musical genres, representations of Colored women vary little. Overwhelmingly, Black women decorate the cars, the parties, and the poolsides of Black (and White) men's music videos. Black women, particularly young ones, often comply with the negative way they are portrayed. Some offer their bodies as a form of belief in the power conferred to them (like the woman who touched Jesus for healing). Others (known as chickenheads) sweat young rap men for the paltry monies made (after recoupables) only because of their funds. A small study conducted on students watching music video found that "exposure to rap laden with sexual imagery fostered distinctly unfavorable evaluations of Black women. Following exposure to sexual rap, as compared with exposure to popular romantic music or to no music exposure, the assessment of these women's personality resulted in a general downgrading of positive traits and a general upgrading of negative ones."[119]

Videos that display women sexing it up by the pool, in the car, on the street corner would not be possible without women's participation. And, more tangibly, women participate by buying CDs, concert tickets, and other paraphernalia of artists that debase them. So yes, Black women need to recognize and take responsibility for their complicity in their own oppression and objectification. Yet I still maintain that music video retains emancipatory potential.

Tricia Rose suggests that through listening to women rappers we gain an understanding of young urban Black women's mechanisms for coping with familial and structural oppression.[120] The homegirls not shown in music videos are young sistahs who attend school regularly, set goals, contribute to their communities, and refuse to make drug use or sex their only choice. In fact, these particular Colored women appear infrequently across all television (and filmic) genres. Many believe (even the young girls themselves) that "acknowledging their existence wouldn't sell. Violence and sex sells."[121]

Yet although Black women artists are not immune to or outside of the video or recording structure, some manage to write and perform empowering lyrics that have accorded them subjecthood heretofore unimaginable in the realm of mainstream musical acceptance. Revolutionary material will not (cannot) come within industrialized norms of television. The challenge, then, is to create a balance between defining and choosing without confining. Music video maintains the potential to alter the visual and cultural ground for Afro-American women artists whose future can be glimpsed with these artists' ability to flourish in emerging (and proliferating) technologies such as on-line streaming video. Possibilities come with business ownership, management, continued lyric writing, directing, and producing while participating in the sociopolitical world beyond the music and the image.

4

PUBIC HAIR ON MY COKE AND OTHER FREAKY TALES

Black Women as Television News Events

Some man did a woman wrong. Now she wants to rip us off.
Her hate is exposed like an itch. She's sick, she's sad, what
  a bitch.
Maybe one day she will meet
A real fine man who'll treat her sweet
She will not be a bitch no more. . . . She will not be a witch
  no more.
She will not make a bitches brew.

             —Christopher N. Hall

Christopher Hall's "Bitches Brew" characterizes African-American women this way. Ironically, the words, coarsely amplifying notions of the late 1960s, prefigure contemporary descriptions of Black women. This foreshadowing gave way to the posts. As defined in *Webster's New International Dictionary*, the prefix *post-* (after: later, behind: posterior to) foregrounds late-twentieth-century dialogue on differences and opposition.[1] Academia presently celebrates the liberation of the posts—movements and cultures. It creates a supposed place for the margins to speak without being marginal, and it recognizes an equality of perspectives. It suggests access to these discourses as solicited and necessary. In other words, in this post- era that academics claim and foster, everyone, every thought, and every action has moved beyond tangentiality and parenthetical mention to central space-subjectivity. But from the perspective of many told that they now occupy the spotlight, postideologies have simply created a perpetual life of endings—endings still attached to their beginnings. Thus, despite the alleged destruction of modernism, colonialism, and structuralism, the nouns before *post-* still prevail.

As shown in previous chapters, among this cultural-intellectual debris, many of the -isms—sexism, racism, and classism—continue to prosper as well. This rubble cements certain ways of thinking and forces spectators to live among only "invisible ruins of cultural memory."[2] It provides a nomadic space of ruin where Teshome Gabriel's "multifarious identities, memories, nostalgias, stories and experiences reside."[3] In other words, mainstream visual culture preserves certain images, and the imagined must differentiate themselves from being ruined and the ruin itself. In no more evident and systematic way is the solidified rubble of people's lives articulated than in television news, where critical issues impact Black women's lives daily. Where vast amounts of complex and dense information require dissemination in three minutes or less, shorthands for race, gender, and class converge within narrative and visual structures. African-Americans endure a unique and rigid type of construction through this forum. Their lives air primarily in ruin on television news, making that rubble—that space between post- and -ism—a viable ground for interrogation. By examining television news spectacles in which objectification escalated to new authoritative and legitimized heights, this chapter shows how, when, where, and why the Negra figure turned newsworthy.

TELEVISION NEWS STUDY

Scholars have devoted abundant critical attention to the study of television news. Variant academic disciplines take up this field—extending its depth and reach. Whether examining the economic viability of local newscasts, representations therein, or ideological systems, news pervades academic discourse. In communication studies, concerns revolve around quantity: interrogating the numbers of Black anchors and reporters, the number of stories on a particular topic, or the number of Black newspapers.[4] In both versions of the *Window Dressing* study these areas appear.

In two seminal essays, "The Determinations of Newsphotographs" and "The Whites of Their Eyes," Stuart Hall sets a foundation for textual examination of news content.[5] By implicating both racialized and gendered constructions as implicit elements of reporters' and media producers' understanding, he draws detailed analyses of how ideology directs the viewer's interpretation of news content. Often segments dealing with Blacks maintain an "unstated and unrecognized assumption that the blacks are the source of the problem."[6] Others examine television's nonfiction world by focusing on the development of local news. Elayne Rapping, for example, suggests, "Local television . . . tends to deal with those issues that affect us personally: our communities, schools, personal disasters and achievements. . . . National programming [on the other hand] . . . is more educational in the sense of explaining and highlighting major national and global happenings and issues. It is the voice of our national leadership telling us what's going on, what it means and where it is leading."[7] In other words, national news defines the world for us. This chapter addresses this national "voice." Trapped between the voice-of-God narration that narrates stories and visuals with implicit codes, Black women's representations appear to be under attack.

Addressing constructions of race and gender in television news has a place in academic discourse. During the 1995 O. J. Simpson trial, for example, Black women were physically absent, yet their figures endured damnation. Postverdict, the Black female jurists; O. J.'s first wife, Marguerite Simpson; his mother; and his daughter Arnell moved front and center. They were assailed, found lacking, and condemned as simpleminded and stupid, exemplifying what Michele Wallace has described as "present absence."[8] Depicted as possessors of perpetual character flaws, even African-American women's absent figures accorded them degradation. Along with the examination of this case's implications, another major television news story, the Senate confirmation hearings of Clarence Thomas, helps determine whether he or Anita Hill was more truthful.[9] Others, such as John Fiske, probe the Los Angeles riots. This chapter foregrounds these specific critical engagements of television news.

BLACK WOMEN IN REALITY

Work got lighter as the children grew up and moved away to college, but it never did stop. Forty years of washing clothes, cooking, making love, grocery shopping, cleaning, ironing, making love, sewing, mending, making love, looking at TV, making sex and reading books.

—J. California Cooper, *A Piece of Mine*, 1984

As I suggested in chapter 2, working Black women in the 1980s and 1990s appeared more politically visible, more corporately viable, and more economically virile than their predecessors. However, their actual economic numbers demonstrated a different reality. In 1988 Black female-headed households constituted approximately 44.1 percent of the nation's Black families. These same Black female-headed households earned a median income of $7,349, whereas Black males garnered $12,044, White females $9,103, and White males $19,959.[10] Further, Black women more often than not served triple duty. They worked full-time jobs, headed their households 54 percent of the time, and committed extensive amounts of time and financial resources for community affairs.[11] And still men, regardless of their occupation, generally earned more than women. Only female fashion models and prostitutes earned more than their male counterparts—an indication of gender inequity and patriarchal control.[12] By the end of the century the income numbers reflected increases across the board but found Black women still at the bottom.[13]

These figures contributed to the condition of African-American women who gained economic empowerment from their work but sustained higher levels of fatigue. Chronic health problems like high blood pressure, cancer, obesity, and myomas ravaged African-American women's bodies. Black women evidenced 50 percent more diabetes than White women, especially if they were obese.[14] In addition, Black women carried higher risks associated with marked obesity.[15] Both incidence and mortality rates for cervical cancer were approximately 2.5 times higher among Black females than among nonminority women.[16] By 2000, with the lowest life expectancy of all women, they died increasingly from heart disease and were 2.5 times as likely to have AIDS.[17] At least a portion of these poor health conditions can be connected to Black women's explicit undervaluation and devaluation in the most prized area of America's capitalistic psyche, work—reflecting a form of oppression analogous to the trappings of colonialism.

Anne McClintock suggests that an "internal colonialization" exists when the dominant aspect of a society treats a group or region as poorly as a foreign colony.[18] African-Americans in general and Black women in particular fall into a colonized group category based on their continued lower standards of living, education, housing, and employment. Both groups endure this form of colonization. Furthermore, government and media attacks have been directed at Coloreds, women, and the poor, all of whom possess little power to exercise opposition.

Simultaneously, these disenfranchised groups have endured condemnation for perceived hierarchy manipulation. For example, Caryl Rivers attests that, "Since the Bakke decision (1978) the American media have exhibited what can only be called a tidal wave of disapproval for affirmative action. . . . A NEXIS search reveals no fewer than 5,732 stories on 'reverse discrimination' and nearly three hundred on 'affirmative discrimination' from 1985–1995."[19] Ain't nothing *post-* about Colored colonization, yet media representations of Black women as newly arrived members of the bourgeoisie persist.

It seemed that, irrespective of class, the 1980s brought a news assault on the image of Black women as their personages experienced several defeats. African-American women were relegated to their assigned place, behind everyone else. Tangible evidence of this action surfaced in attacks on welfare, unemployment, and underemployment on the lower end of the Black woman's economic/social/educational scale to censure of women in human resources, the academic community, and cinema that continued through the end of the century.[20] Ironically, the strongest complaints about perceived hiring preferences for and elevation of Black women came often from Black men. In her study of the historic roles of Black women Jeanne Noble maintains, "It seems as if too many . . . [Black men] believe that black women should not be given a chance in the world of work if there is the slightest possibility that a black male might be threatened"—so much for racial solidarity.[21]

NEWS IN REALITY

Television news communicated these societal attacks with the help of the computer information explosion and the alteration in news presentation format. Similar to music videos' transformation of television's look, television news changed visually and fundamentally in response to the growth of cable, music television, and Fox Television. John Caldwell theorizes that the changes in televised presentation occurred along several axes. One of those axes was the formal evolution propelled by the launching of Ted Turner's Cable News Network (CNN) in 1980. Caldwell suggests that "without any apparent or overt aesthetic agenda—CNN created and celebrated a consciousness of the televisual apparatus: an appreciation for multiple electronic feeds, image-text combinations, video graphics, and studios with banks of monitors that evoked video installations." [22] In other words, reality became constructed by the visual, electronic, and graphic markers of the story at hand. Semiotic codes for the "real" and the "simultaneous" became the story. Plus, these electronic markers emphasized the notion that more is necessarily better.

Some media theorists, such as Fredric Jameson and Jean Baudrillard, have argued that what most people consider "real" has actually disappeared anyway. In spite of assertions for reality that Ella Shohat and Robert Stam detest, Jameson believes that in this postmodern era history's continued subjection to interpretation mandates visual imagery's integral focus. Reality has been funneled through a contemporary vision of the image. Their arguments are borne out within television news and reality-based programs. A poignant example of reality's erosion exists with the videotaped beating of Rodney King.

What appeared as objective, real evidence by virtue of the videotape became what Kimberlé Crenshaw and Gary Peller call disaggregated: "The videotape images were *physically* mediated by the illustration boards upon which the still pictures were mounted, and in the same moment of *disaggregation* they were *symbolically* mediated by the new narrative backdrops of institutional security's technical discourse and the reframing of King as a threat rather than as a victim." [23] This reframing, it seems, was predicated on race. In other words, the reality of any videotaped imagery stands as legal evidence depending on the technological framing, the politics at stake, and the ideology of the spectator involved. Another example of racist ideological tampering surfaced with the demonizing of O. J. Simpson on the June 27, 1994, cover of *Time* magazine. By drawing him darker, the artist brought forth a real psychological referent. Black men as dark, closeted, and well-dressed demons became embodied in Simpson.

Talk formats, magazine shows, reality-based adventures, courtroom cases, as well as "catch the crook" shows such as *COPS,* offer other fascinating points for discussion of the real and race. Most of these programs are admittedly hybrids of reality and fiction. In *COPS*, for instance, the scenario is real, the cops are real, and the people they investigate are real. However, the projected criminals must agree to participate, thus making them quasi actors. The best scenes are ones selected from numerous others. With the lights, cameraperson, and producer all in full production mode, the police/perpetrator relationship becomes dramatized—drama that often grounds itself in a White American fear of the Other and the idea of lack. Fiske suggests that these shows offer viewers assurances that "the system can protect its vulnerable."[24]

With its pervasiveness, immediacy, and claims to reality, television affects how and what spectators view as news. It offers portrayals that the viewer processes as information. It teaches things about behavior, expectations, self, and others. Often, as Ernie Sotomayor suggests, the "lessons may be confused, contradictory, and distorted. Nevertheless, they cannot be ignored."[25] Since the 1980s Black men and women have appeared in physical custody of police officers more often than other persons, suggesting, as Robert Entman states, that "even when accused of similar crimes, blacks are more dangerous than whites."[26] Sound bites featured loud, argumentative, and demanding Black spokespersons who seemed only to list grievances and demand compensation for past wrongs. Many Black women emerged as victims (or alleged provocateurs) of sexual violence (for example, Tawana Brawley, Desiree Washington, and Robin Givens).

Although the major oracle of this misinformation, the mainstream press did not function alone in the sustained denigration of people of color. Black women themselves contributed to these very same television news perspectives as reporters, producers, and anchors. However, their finite presence came quite late to the news-gathering process—too late to persuasively challenge embedded ideology easily or substantially. They held limited power.

Not until the 1960s did Black reporters actually even appear in newsrooms. As cameras rolled on fires raging in Watts, Chicago, and Philadelphia, editors felt (and saw) the void of these "problem people" in their newsrooms. African-Americans and women like Charlayne Hunter-Gault, Max Robinson, Bernard Shaw, and Carole Simpson cut their reporting teeth as beacons into this previously ignored culture. Their continued work serves as one of the ways in which agency is recuperated for Black women, as addressed later. Yet nothing they and others accomplished in the newsroom prepared American television for the decades following their entrance.

By 1992 *Nightline* producers felt comfortable enough with and knowledgeable enough of the Other to run regular in-depth stories on the race problem (translated as the problem with Black folks) a week after the Los Angeles riots.[27] Preceding a discussion featuring Barbara Walters, Jesse Jackson, and

Bill Bradley, reporter Jeff Greenfield presented a background piece on the Black situation. In voice-over he stated that "words, numbers, cold facts . . . paint the most vivid pictures" as videotape showed mostly Black and Latino men robbing stores, burning buildings, and attacking truck driver Reginald Denny.[28] Yet what followed was a litany of statistics and images that indicted African-American *women* as instigators of this lawlessness by virtue of their procreative ability, illegitimate children, welfare dependency, and, of course, heading of households.

Submerged within and contributing to this media blaming of Black women came three poignant stories that positioned Colored women as "objects of scorn" via television news. The stories were media events—events that are, according to Fiske, "not a mere representation of what happened, but [something with] its own reality, which gathers up into itself the reality of the event that may or may not have preceded it."[29] Narratives, technologies, and visuals combined in evening newscasts to damn Black women, with redemption following only as they rose from the ashes, like the fabled phoenix. The crowning and subsequent dethroning of Vanessa Williams as Miss America, the testimony of Anita Hill at the Senate Confirmation Hearings of Clarence Thomas, and the welding of welfare across the bodies of Black women all provided unique yet representative examples of ideological imperatives within television presentation. The presumption of guilt, the television apparatus, the sociocultural preconceptions, and the circulating racist, sexist, and classist narratives, collectively vilified these women, reduced them to harlots, and subsequently lauded them only as vanquished (yet reclaimed) victims. Only through their respective falls have these women been able to find redemption, acceptance, voice, and, sometimes, success.

VANESSA WILLIAMS
(BLACK WOMAN AS OBJECT OF THE NATION)

On September 17, 1983, Vanessa Williams represented New York State in the *Sixty-third Miss America Pageant* in Atlantic City, New Jersey. Williams's victory secured for her a unique place in history as the first Black woman to wear America's crown. As the news of her achievement traveled, many Americans expressed pride and faith that race relations between Whites and Afro-Americans were advancing. African-Americans were particularly encouraged.

Black newspapers such as the *Chicago Defender* ran extensive front-page articles about Williams. A picture of her being escorted by two police officers along the Atlantic City beach was captioned, "Victory Stroll."[30] The article focused on her self-proclaimed disagreement with the stereotype associated with the term *beauty queen*—which deemphasized her other abilities. The *Los Angeles Sentinel* featured two medium close-ups of her on its cover. The paper reported not only Williams's win but also other Black firsts for 1983.[31]

Yet despite general enthusiasm over her win, Black communities also expressed some negative reactions to the choice of Williams as the "first Black" Miss America. With her light skin, green eyes, and hair texture normally associated with Europeans, the Congress of Racial Equality (CORE) issued a statement claiming that Williams was not "in essence, Black."[32] This unusual contention between an example of Black American progress and the people's response to it suggests pervasive latent sociocultural currents surrounding Williams's win.

With her subsequent fall, however, a totally different dimension erupted. Williams's descent became a major news event. Several ideological themes circulated around this news story, themes such as the articulation of beauty within contemporary visual culture, the notions of Blackness in the 1980s, the Miss America mythology; and the confluence of woman with America—aka the Nation. These threads of discourse merged with racist, sexist, and classist ideologies to behead the queen.

THE BEAUTY MYTH

As discussed in chapters 2 and 3, beauty in the United States has been defined as youth, European features, light skin, and slenderness. Based on this standard, many Black women internalized White assessments of their unattractiveness founded on their Blackness and their bodies. With their hair texture (bad), their bodies (diseased and overweight), and their skin color (just wrong), Black women consumed, or at least negotiated, racist and sexist articulations about their capacity for beauty as they diligently tried to fix it.[33] Yet Naomi Wolf submits that beyond physicality itself, "[t]he beauty myth is always actually prescribing behavior and not appearance."[34] Positioned as hypersexual, matriarchal, or athletic, African-American women are rarely accorded the adjective *beautiful,* either in reference to their physical appearance or their behavior. They seem to consistently fall short of the "ideal." Vanessa Williams initially proved an exception to this rule.

"Black was beautiful last night in Atlantic City," Sam Donaldson proclaimed on *World News Tonight (WNT)* the day following Vanessa Williams's win, harkening to a 1960s civil rights mantra.[35] Although CBS and the *MacNeil/Lehrer NewsHour* failed to cover the news of her win, in almost every other national television news forum Williams was described as beautiful, intelligent, talented, and the "First." Yet reminiscent of Wolf's observation, Natasha Barnes contends that "beauty is not 'natural' but ideological: it has a certain kind of face, certain features, hair texture, eye color, shape of nose and lips. . . . [B]lackness becomes identified as it usually is in the United States, simply through the presence of a black progenitor, and hence the proof of . . . 'Negro' identity."[36] Some insisted that Williams's win occurred at the expense of blackness—that her looks approximated Whites as closely as possible without actual achievement. Williams even sought to distance herself from the race factor. Her sound bite in Bob Berkowitz's report explained, "I hope to prove that I can do just as good, being a person, being Miss America *by the chance* that I am Black, and prove that I am *worthy* of the position *despite* my color."[37] With antagonistic notions of race circulating, the terms of blackness and beauty seemed predestined to collide and rupture.

As the tickling bone in situation comedy and as an urgent African beat in music video, defining blackness was imperative during the 1980s. While discussions of whiteness became popular, African diasporic scholars struggled to find a definition for Black in and for contemporary usage. Herman Gray offers one such definition of blackness. Gray's is a blackness that produces a "constellation of productions, histories, images, representations, and meanings associated with black presence in the United States."[38] He argues that the "demonization of blackness" through the "welfare queen" and "the aggressive black female" (along with the menacing Black male criminal) enabled the "mobilization of a counterimage of blackness—the figure of individuality, competence, exceptionalism—as difference (as opposed to 'other')."[39] Stuart Hall suggests that *Black* (as in Black popular culture) has come to signify all these things, "the black community," "the black experience," "the black aesthetic," and the "black counternarrative."[40] Carole Boyce Davies insists that " 'Blackness' is a color-coded, politically-based term of marking and definition which only has meaning when questions of racial difference and, in particular, white supremacy are deployed"—as mentioned elsewhere, blackness is provoked by whiteness.[41] Assuming their presence in public discourse, I suggest that these fluid and overlapping cultural exchanges of the term existed to produce a Miss America who served simultaneously as a credit to her country and her blackness and as an achiever despite it, particularly in a bastion of whiteness called the Miss America Pageant.

HERE SHE IS . . .

The mythology of the Miss America Pageant stems not only from a fairly lengthy history of the pageant itself but also from a nation and world enamored by pomp and profit. Whether for gain or glory, worldwide pageantry has prevailed and kept women as objectively central. No fewer than twenty-five pageants existed in the United States alone, yet the Miss America ceremony stood as the grande dame of them all.[42] Beyond generating revenue, beauty pageants allow spectators a type of escapism. White Americans, pre-Williams, could flee from the Colored reality of a continually different nation to a world of grandeur, femininity, and colorful clothing (or lack thereof) on White bodies.

In their work on global beauty contests, Colleen Ballerino Cohen, Richard Wilk, and Beverly Stoeltje describe pageants as events that surpass the constructs of femininity, beauty, and even competition. These contests "evoke passionate interest and engagement with political issues central to the lives of beauty contestants, sponsors, organizers, and audiences—issues that frequently have nothing obvious to do with the competition itself. By choosing an individual whose deportment, appearance, and style embodies the values and goals of a nation, locality, or group, beauty contests expose these same values and goals to interpretation and challenge."[43] Or in the case of Williams, the challenge presented itself on her racialized body.

The Miss America Pageant originated to bolster Atlantic City tourism in 1920. Early contestants' selection was based on their pedigree (much like animals), and inclusion was denied or celebrated because of it. The first Colored woman actually appeared in the program as a slave in "His Oceanic Majesty's Court" in 1922.[44] Robin Morgan queries, "Where else could one find such a perfect combination of American values? Racism, militarism, and capitalism— all packaged in one 'ideal' symbol: a woman."[45] Despite the slave debut, however, the contest held to one specific rule concerning non-Whites.

Organizer Lenora Slaughter described rule number seven as "the one that specified that 'only members of the white race' could enter Miss America." She remembered that "it was sometime in the middle 1950s when it went out."[46] Beside the Negra slave figure, then, no other person of color appeared in the pageant until 1970.[47] And although still predominately about sex, nation, and the Great White way, by the 1980s the pageant (and the nation) needed a facelift because of declining participation and, more important, declining viewership. The pageant found the necessary boost in the form of Vanessa Williams and the promise of what she could mean to the nation.

Williams's win uniquely illustrated the historic bonding of women's bodies to their countries. Nationhood's inscription across women's bodies has grounded common patriarchal ideology and fed information dissemination. In other words, men's nations have been characterized by the feminine state, always. "Mother Russia," "Miss America," and "Mother India" are a few narrative examples of the synergy of woman and nation. Nevertheless, although women serve symbolically as nation and "function as primary workers for a number of nationalist struggles . . . [they end] up not being empowered political figures or equal partners."[48]

In describing this relationship between women and nation, Nira Yuval-Davis suggests that women "symbolize the national collectively, its roots, its spirit, its national project. Moreover, women often symbolize national and collective honour."[49] The 1996 NBC telecast of the centennial Olympic games illustrated U.S. nation/woman synergy excellently.[50] With a heightened mode of nationalism elevating the feminine, NBC produced sustained coverage of the gymnastics events (similar to the coverage of ice skating during the winter games). They illuminated these events with young, petite girls/women, performing graceful, feminine (soft), amazing tumbles and leaps with accompanying narration from John Tesh.

In its traditional and continued context this competition sustained a preponderance of White women who realized and supported the feminine ideal. These women emblematized their homelands. Symbolically and actually, gymnastics remained the only sport that broadcasters focused on sans the U.S. team throughout the seventeen-day games. Even when the heavily favored U.S. (dark) women's basketball team played, the televised competition often remained on gymnastics.[51]

In their racialized bodies Black women threaten the nation/woman fusion. bell hooks suggests that "[i]n a white supremacist sexist society all women's bodies are devalued, but white women's bodies are more valued than those of women of color."[52] Racial discourses seem to disrupt the traditional structure of gender and nation. For example in Natasha Barnes's examination of beauty pageants' relationship to Jamaica's national identity, she finds that " 'Miss Jamaica' is not a trivial matter nor is it removed from the everyday manifestation of power and privilege on the island. . . . Wrapped in a mantle of respectability and civility that was denied to black people in general and black women in particular, beauty contests became the place for the making of feminine subjectivity in a racial landscape where femininity was the jealously guarded domain of white womanhood."[53]

Similar to Nick Browne's supertext theory of television scheduling, David Goldberg argues that race often cuts across national boundaries or defines the characteristics of a set of people, depending on the historical moment.[54] Yet I suggest that a very specific definition of race manifests itself when we discuss people of color. Race becomes biological, ahistoric, and incompatible with the nation, even in a sexualized (aka woman's) body. In America the sacredness of the nation's fusion with White women's bodies as represented by the Miss America Pageant remained unspoiled until 1983.

The 1983 Miss America Pageant appeared late on that Saturday night on NBC, forcing the news of her selection to air on the subsequent day's newscasts. Comparing Williams to Jackie Robinson, NBC's *Nightly News (NN)* placed the story in the third-quarter of the program—looking at the pageant and its history of racial exclusion. Reporter Norma Quarles voiced-over Williams's singing performance and her wave as she walked the runway as the new queen of the nation. The New York City multiethnic community expressed their delight in her win through quick sound bites. On ABC's *World News Tonight* Williams appeared also in the third quarter and was introduced by Sam Donaldson as "the first Black Miss America" (fig. 24).[55]

The *WNT* segment announced the win of Williams and the Black first runner-up, Suzette Charles, Miss New Jersey. It featured Williams's participation in the contest, her celebration with her parents, and reactions from her community of Millwood, New York. In both *WNT* and *NN*'s follow-ups the next day, representatives of Black communities described what they considered a momentous and glorious event for the elevation of "black beauty." *NN* consistently stressed her blackness in spite of Williams's distancing. Reporter Bob Berkowitz suggested that to Miss America purists, winning the swimsuit and talent competitions virtually secured the title. But his vocal intonation framed the remark as a quandary, which eventually led to commentary by Southern Christian Leadership Conference (SCLC) leader Joseph Lowery.[56] Yet, perhaps more covertly, Berkowitz's quizzical tone implied skepticism about whether this precedent holds when a Black woman wins those competitions. The report stated that even President Reagan called Williams to say "what a wonderful thing her win was for our nation," inviting her to the White House (this invitation coming as he struggled to improve his popularity rating among Blacks).

Unlike other contestants' encounters with the press after their wins, Williams received inordinate amounts of initial national news coverage. Yet after the first few days limited amounts of video aired nationally on Williams for the remaining ten months of her reign. She did, however, continue to receive substantial coverage in the Black press, which widely regarded her win as a triumph for Black America.[57] BET failed to carry news programming at that time. Nevertheless, throughout her reign her status as the first of her race merited Williams excessive amounts of local press attention as a Miss America winner. This same mass of coverage fed and led to her objectified status.

On July 20, 1984, when it became public that pictures of Williams posing nude would appear in *Penthouse*'s September issue, press coverage of Miss America exploded. From San Francisco Peter Jennings announced that Miss America had seventy-two hours to resign her crown because of an indiscretion.[58] Sandwiched between reports on the Democratic National Convention and apprehension of a Black rapist, *WNT* reporter Steve Taylor exposed the scandal.[59] He reported that the pageant requested the return of the nation's

FIGURE 24

Miss America 1984, Vanessa Williams
(Courtesy of Jerry Ohlinger's Movie Material Store)

crown. The segment showed Williams singing then cut to a nude photo of her standing above a White woman, presumably in an unseen sexual act. Taylor reported that Williams was not only the first Black Miss America but also the most visible and popular, according to local accounts. He presented footage of appearances procured from different localities throughout her reign. In an interview *Penthouse* publisher Bob Guccione stated that the pageant had "promulgated this tooth fairy image of the vestal virgin . . . that simply doesn't exist anymore," particularly, it would seem, in regard to a Black woman.[60] This *WNT* story covered the press conference with Albert Marks, pageant director, who stated that Williams violated a morals clause in her contract by not upholding the dignity of the pageant. It extended to her home in Millwood, where a morally outraged citizen defaced property with a demeaning epithet. This report mostly showed, however, Williams's community expressing sympathy.

The *NN* segment took this opportunity to reflect, perhaps, its misgivings about Williams as Miss America, particularly as the sponsoring network. Like a vaudevillian vendor selling tickets to a peep show, Tom Brokaw decried that "Miss America Took Off Her Clothes!" Like all the other programs, *NN* exhibited portions of the pictures. But instead of the straight cuts normally used in hard news stories, *NN* chose to dissolve and zoom-in slightly—their presentation resembling a quasi-pornographic montage. Independents, like INN, appeared more tabloidesque. In its report INN described Williams's "lesbian sex poses" and concluded by reporting that Williams had received a job offer from Guccione. No less than five times did they display as much as permissible of the photographs.[61]

Beyond the aforementioned programs that carried Williams's initial win, her nude body merited her reign newsworthy on CBS and the *MacNeil/Lehrer NewsHour*. On CBS's *Evening News (EN)* Dan Rather began with the words "prurience and the symbol of purity" and paused, seemingly in an effort to verbally distance the actual and the ideal.[62] The *EN* had Guccione appear, too, stating, "What she did was newsworthy. And as a journalist, it is my immediate feeling to see that it be brought to the attention of the public."[63] This report focused on the scandal in relation to Williams's pageant prize money and entertainment aspirations. This particular angle positioned Williams as a sex worker, either by pageant or posing. In a way it justified Guccione's earlier remarks.

Over the weekend CBS aired another report, which hinted that Williams might fight for the crown.[64] The curious portion of this segment came during its setup. The graphic positioned behind anchor Morton Dean fed into historical and prevailing myths about African-American women's sexuality (fig. 25). A color medium close-up of Williams in full queen regalia has been superimposed onto a black-and-white profile shot in soft focus. In the "pornographic"

FIGURE 25

The beheading of
Queen Vanessa

profile Williams is wearing (apparently only) a facial expression of . . . ecstasy? This graphic implies that the real side of all Black women, salacious and sexually ravenous, lies underneath their clothes.

As a consequence of this "media hype," by July 23, the end of the three-day deadline, both NBC and ABC led their newscasts with the Williams story.[65] At a press conference of regal importance Williams abdicated her title. Harkening to early-nineteenth-century yellow journalism, each newscast gave nearly three minutes to the story, repeatedly exhibiting portions of the photographs of Williams and stressing her presumed lesbian positioning with another woman. NBC's John Palmer stated, "During her reign she wanted to be a role model; buffeted by commerce and controversy she may have just succeeded. Not as a model but as a martyr."[66] Four of the pictures continued to be interspersed through the piece. By this time Guccione antagonized that Williams "did bring it upon herself."[67] CNN aired large portions of her press conference. They alone covered Black models who protested outside the press conference, chanting, "Long live the queen."[68] One model even claimed a "pimp mentality" for Guccione because of his offering Williams a job with *Penthouse* magazine after her abdication. *Penthouse* profited tremendously, with sales of approximately $5.5 million, compared to a $3.4 million average.[69] Sales so far exceeded production that Guccione canceled the magazine's anniversary party because of lack of copies to distribute.

In a newspaper editorial Bebe Moore Campbell addressed Williams's downfall as a first. Lauded in African-American communities, firsts always symbolize success, acceptance, assimilation. She reasoned, "Everyone is entitled to make a mistake. Black Americans, perhaps more than any other people, have earned that right."[70] Campbell encouraged the larger Black community to discard the self-inflicted feelings of collective failure and to continue to celebrate achievement. Failure, she maintained, allows for humanity. This suggestion, however, came as a learning lesson post-Williams's reign.

After Williams's resignation the remaining stories of the Miss America scandal focused on the following pageant. Dan Rather said that others predicted that Williams's "sex acts" might "contaminate the contest's down-home blend of cheesecake and apple pie."[71] Three days before the 1984 contest, Guccione announced that he possessed pictures of another contestant to be published upon her winning.[72] Despite deploring the publicity and being "royally damned" if the pageant would be disturbed again, Marks confessed that the controversy would probably bring twenty million more viewers to the pageant.[73] Hotel room bookings rose, more tickets sold, and the "loss of innocence" seemed all to result from the "naughty girl" who left.[74] Commented Bob Simon, "With Vanessa Williams, the sex crept out of the closet and into the *Penthouse*."[75]

The Vanessa effect produced a deep backlash in the U.S. pageant circuit that forced a retreat to an almost Aryan ideal. The new Miss America for 1985 was Sharlene Wells, a twenty-year-old from Utah who expressed pride in her Mormon heritage, her conservative values, and her virginity. Wells played the harp "as of course, do angels." Tall, blond, and blue-eyed, she nearly glowed (perhaps it was the lighting) with her belief in "God and my country." According to reporter Stephen Geer, "the dream was reborn" as the country returned to the vestal (White) virgin.[76]

Over nineteen stories appeared through the major national television venues from July 20 through September 16, 1984, on the dethroning of Miss America and the Miss America Pageant. This count fails to account for the additional stories that aired on independent news outlets, national entertainment television magazine programs, local newscasts, printed press, and, of course, the *Penthouse* photos themselves. In other words, during this period a viewer could learn about, ponder, and reiterate (through the VCR) on a daily basis the pornographic act of a Colored woman who wore the nation's crown. Currently, Vanessa Williams continues to receive substantial press but in glowing reviews of her highly successful singing career, her run on Broadway, her film and television appearances (figs. 26, 27), and her marriage to L.A. Laker Rick Fox.[77] The pageant even asked her to come perform. She declined.

hooks attributes Williams's new national notoriety to her public disgrace. She argues that "by appropriating the image of sexualized vamp and playing sexy roles in films . . . she assumed . . . the rightful erotic place set aside for black women in the public imagination. The American public that had so brutally critiqued Williams and rejected her had no difficulty accepting and applauding her when she accepted the image of fallen woman."[78] Without

FIGURE 26

Vanessa Williams *(left)*, Nia Long *(center)* and Vivica A. Fox in the film *Soul Food* (1997).
(Courtesy of Jerry Ohlinger's Movie Material Store)

denigrating her vocal or acting abilities, Williams herself concedes that she probably would not have achieved her current successes without the scandal. Some have theorized that a conspiracy existed from the beginning to dethrone Williams for a profit.[79] Regardless, it seemed odd that other Miss America contestants that possessed less than pristine backgrounds did not sustain the denigrative and totalizing coverage of the first Black Miss America.

For example, Miss Iowa 1968 held a position as a go-go dancer prior to the pageant but was able to participate because of her family's status. Miss America 1976 used her reign to speak out on the legalization of abortion *and* marijuana. Miss Florida 1982 held an arrest record for drunk driving but remained in the pageant after the charges were reduced. Miss Ohio 1994 pleaded "no contest" to shoplifting. Guccione's claim about nude photos of another contestant after Williams's fall indicated that she probably was not the first and clearly not the last.[80]

Although Williams's actions denied her the potential for agency in that forum, her win not only propelled her into stardom but opened the possibilities

FIGURE 27

Vanessa Williams and Chayanne in the film *Dance with Me* (Haines, 1998). *(Courtesy of Jerry Ohlinger's Movie Material Store)*

for other African-American women. The agency that comes through acquiring voice in an information age gives Black women a chance to speak on their heretofore silenced concerns. Did she pose? Yes. Was it news? Yes. But the motivation behind the extensive coverage was not that she posed nude. Underlying this media offensive were embedded stereotypical preconceptions about Negras that erupted and seemed to confirm previously held notions.

Through phrases commandeered by reporters and anchors—"lesbian sex poses," "despoiler of American womanhood," "prurience"—and through abbreviations for bad Black women (and Black women in general) a savagery and depraved sexuality was suggested that tied Black women to their national role of property. The confluence of beauty, pageantry, blackness, and nation along with racism and sexism helped dethrone Williams and relegate her to her rightful place. The quantity of coverage, importance accorded it, circulating narratives about Black women's sexuality, and, of course, sex worked through and with television techniques to condemn Vanessa Williams for her beauty (like theirs) and her blackness. It placed a sort of collective check on a "BABW—a Bad Ass Black Woman" who dared to vie for and win a position reserved both in actuality and in ideology for White women.

ANITA HILL
(BLACK WOMAN AS OBJECT OF LAW/JUSTICE)

Seven years later in another news story, the same intersections of gender, race, and the televisual joined the law to silence and marginalize yet another African-American woman through historical, ideological, and technical means. The opening of the "Anita Hill/Clarence Thomas Show" minimized Hill's accomplishments and presented the ideal subject for a Freudian revenge of projected male desire/hatred of the Other. In other words, the hearing provided an opportunity for Negroes to perform on television—for real, though. Hill posed a critical threat to political and media power structures because of her perceived class status, her credibility, and the confluence of blackness and womanhood.

As articulated by television news reports, Clarence Thomas embodied the American dream. Promoted as a beneficiary of the bootstrap theory, Thomas attended private Catholic primary schools and Holy Cross College. He proceeded to Yale Law School. Politically conservative, Thomas worked in both Reagan's and George Bush Sr.'s administrations. When working with Hill, he served as her supervisor both at the Department of Education and at the Equal Employment Opportunity Commission (EEOC).

Anita Hill, a middle-class, educated, conservative Black law professor, also professed the bootstrap method as the youngest of thirteen children from an Oklahoma farming family. She attended Oklahoma State University and Yale Law School. From there she worked briefly at a Washington law firm and subsequently moved to the Department of Education as Thomas's assistant. Hill began teaching at the University of Oklahoma Law School in 1986. Although the two were similar, Hill, as a Black *woman,* negotiated additional demands on her success.

Historically, the presumption of uppityness or snobbishness was assigned to women like Hill. This labeling resulted from the legacy of inequity in Black achievement across gender. Despite the label, however, these same women have been held accountable by the community for the uplift of the race through their education, professional status, and behavior. They often "wear the masks" that Paul Laurence Dunbar's poetry speaks of to cope with their contentious status. Wearing these constructed masks has availed them opportunities, more often than Black men, to obtain white-collar positions.[81]

Black women's roles have been defined and confined often to moving within the right circles, which translated to White alliances or affiliations with Blacks just like them. Some believe their actions fostered identity crises because of alienation from the masses of Black people and other Negras. With their professional status, methods of raising children, associating only with certain types (à la *Sugar Cane Alley*), and always obvious presence, Black middle-class women bore the brunt of criticism in "all visible matters" of Franklin Frazier's bourgeois Black.[82] Anita Hill's background reflected this tradition. As such, she became a trained and formidable wrench in the Senate Judiciary Committee's wheels of progress.

The Senate Judiciary Committee determines a Supreme Court candidate's fitness for the position. The Senate has traditionally defined its role as "trying to satisfy itself that a nominee has the intellectual capacity, competence, and temperament, the good moral character, and the commitment to upholding the Constitution that are required for the Supreme Court. In the post-Bork era, however, the confirmation process has also become a means of members of the Senate . . . to try to influence constitutional interpretation."[83] Despite or possibly because of that questionably new propensity toward constitutional interpretation, when sex hit the Senate floor, all other concerns became moot. The committee's job to evaluate each candidate as objectively as possible seemed more complex with Clarence Thomas. Not only was his "good moral character" on trial; his race and the nation's history were under examination as well. Frantz Fanon's belief that "for the native, objectivity is always against him" became a crucial idea in this case.[84] With layers of existing covert issues and concepts, Anita Hill's charges easily became less about sexual harassment and more about sex per se. Hill, a major component of this sexual equation, converged on a system that was prefigured on her gender although denied to that same racialized body.

As Williams's gendered body stood for the nation, the figure of woman also emblematizes justice and the law. The U.S. symbol of justice, the Goddess of Justice (Justicia or Themis), is a statue of a blindfolded woman holding a scale in one hand and an unsheathed sword in the other. The law recognizes her as the goddess of social order and the collective conscious of a society. According to the *Law Library Journal,* Themis sets an example "for those who do judge disputes so that they will remain dignified, holy, austere, incorruptible, and unsusceptible to flattery and inexorable towards the wicked and guilty, vigorous, lofty, and powerful, terrible by reason of the force and majesty of equity and truth."[85] In other words, she ensures that "what ought to be, is."[86]

Yet as Themis blindly holds the scales of justice, actual women serve merely as the prize for which men fight, as protectors of those same men, and as the producers of children. Some women have been encouraged to excel—up to a point. Invariably though the request (and demand) still comes for them to walk a few steps behind the menfolks. Such embedded ideologies shape women's success trajectory. Although absent from American law books, laws similar to those in countries such as Pakistan, which explicitly designate a woman's testimony as half of a man's, implicitly constitute a part of America's legal system.[87]

The departure of Supreme Court Justice Thurgood Marshall launched the battle between two African-American conservatives during the final trickle-down days. Apparently, President George Bush felt pressured to appoint another Black to the bench. Choosing the conservative Thomas filled the void. Not only had Thomas served Bush's and Reagan's administrations effectively, but his judicial acumen had neither been questioned, tested, nor widely circulated. The first round of hearings, September 10–16, 1991, aired only on National Public Radio and the Public Broadcasting Service, with highlights on the networks. Despite some debate among conservatives and liberals about his qualifications and his political views in regard to race, his confirmation seemed assured—that is, until October 6. On that day National Public Radio correspondent Nina Totenberg, in an interview, broke the story that a woman, Anita Faye Hill, had alleged charges of sexual harassment.[88]

Substantial political posturing occurred subsequent to that broadcast—broadcasters, politicians, and the American public demanded an explanation from the Senate as to why it had failed to act on these allegations when clearly it knew of them much earlier. As the tension escalated and the vote disintegrated, Thomas himself called for a delay in the vote in order to "clear his name." His supporter and friend Senator John Danforth (R-Missouri) sorrowfully read Thomas's statement before the Senate. "They have taken from me what I have worked forty-three years to create."[89] With Hill agreeing to cooperate fully with the committee, the players and stage were fixed for the show, masquerading as *hard* news.

LIGHTS, CAMERA, ACTION!

The second round of the Senate confirmation hearings of 1991 opened on a peculiar case in American history, which pitted an African-American woman and man against each other in a quasi-legal battle within the television frame. The case proved unusual because of (1) the nature of the subject, (2) the race of the principals, and (3) the inordinate attention accorded both. Beyond this, the second round aired entirely live!—an honor usually accorded only to critical news stories. Every network led with the story from October 6 through October 15, with additional coverage supplementing the lead story. The subject of sexual harassment rarely, if ever, appeared before the Senate Judiciary Committee, especially involving a Supreme Court nominee. It became doubly unusual for the major players in this drama, or any drama of national import, because they were Black. The attention given to this confirmation hearing via television and, more important, to a noncrime, nonsports subject involving African-Americans was (and still is) virtually unprecedented.

Within three days the public witnessed testimony from two intelligent and articulate human beings. Augmenting them, testimonies of five panels of other articulate and intelligent human beings aired. Most of the participants were African-American. Besides entertaining the populace through situation comedies, sports, music videos, and television crime news, this event probably hosted the largest number of Black faces appearing on television at one time.

Similar to Vanessa Williams's victory walk, the Senate hearings exuded a feeling of pageantry. Lights, cameras, reporters, spectators all filled the Senate hearing room, yielding to a kind of carnivalesque—a dreamlike music video. Says Mikhail Bakhtin, carnival "celebrated temporary liberation from the prevailing truth and from the established order: it marked the suspension of all hierarchical rank, privileges, norms, and prohibitions."[90] Carnival functioned to "liberate from the prevailing point of view of the world, from conventions and established truths, from cliches, from all that is humdrum and universally accepted."[91] Despite John Fiske's advocacy for this type of high/low collision, which, he suggests, provides a healthy ground for the low to vision itself, the reverse seemed to occur when the visual space held previously by the high was determined to prevail.[92]

Fiske argues that performances normally associated with low economic or cultural status subvert "high culture's" claim on superiority. Blacks, by virtue of their color and their type of entertainment, seem to always occupy this lower spectrum. Their mere presence allows for predetermined racial hierarchies to manifest themselves. Yet their presence in the Senate hearing room assimilated them into White culture despite their color.

Allegorical references abounded in this theater—this made-for-TV drama. Lynching, hypermedia, and the spirituality of Thomas, Hill, and the moral minority all came forth to participate. To counteract Hill's testimony, Thomas pandered to race. He seethed that the whole ordeal functioned as "a high-tech lynching for uppity blacks who in any way deign to think for themselves," indicting both the committee and the media.[93]

This reference to lynching and race galvanized the Republican supporters, silenced the Democratic detractors, and reflected Thomas's recognition of how this spectacle appeared in the visual frame. Thomas's past as a Catholic intellectual and purveyor of justice paralleled Hill's construction as an intelligent law professor whose commitment to improvement via bootstraps was equally evident. Their puritanical backgrounds were not lost on the committee or the television narrative to be told.

These Senate hearings began October 11 and lasted approximately thirty-three hours. They ended twenty-two witnesses later on October 13 at 2:00 A.M. Similar to the McCarthy hearings, African-Americans who participated in this process seemed like "pigeons in a confidence game of a White man's squabble."[94] The Committee leveled probing questions, especially at Hill. They sat as judge and jury, and the visual framing reflected that. As the colonialist masters in the film *Burn!* (Pontecorvo, 1970) literally sat above, so too did the senators. Yet their table, equal in height to the one where Hill and Thomas sat, only appeared elevated. This formulaic television device of Othering a subject framed these hearings.

Hill's eloquence and her silence conferred her credibility. Her cool, encapsulated within her speech, infused the hearings with a feeling of the surreal. But because silence is so often positioned against speech, even within the visually centered arena of television, it indicated trouble. Says Sally Steenland, "Women's everyday experiences were being examined by powerful men under glaring lights, and the men jumped with surprise to hear us talk."[95] Nevertheless, mainstream notions of Colored women's progress derailed with the camera's positioning of Hill. Black women resumed their place once again.

Hill defined her space by her physical presence, direct gaze, and quiet pose. Because of that, the audience developed sympathy for her. This sympathy realized itself despite the aesthetic formulated to castigate her. During her testimony, Hill was consistently framed in extreme close-ups (fig. 28). This technique severed her visually from any supporters, familial structures, or ties to humanity. She became a fanatical, one-woman crusade. Scorned and angry, she tempered her rage, but it remained nonetheless. The framing implied that a Negra's anger could not be legitimate.

Thomas's figure, on the other hand, was framed with his wife and supportive senator John Danforth visible behind him (fig. 29). He was surrounded by whiteness, perhaps most powerfully represented by his conspicuous prize—his wife. In *Black Skin, White Masks* Fanon insists that Black men believe, "By loving me [a White woman] proves that I am worthy of white love. I am loved like a white man. I am a white man. . . . I marry white culture, white beauty, white whiteness."[96] This inference was not lost on people operating the video equipment.

Crenshaw and Peller believe that videotape and videotaping are seductive because they seem "to transcend the partialities of objectivity and impersonality, like the allied distinctions between fact and opinion, between color-blindness and discrimination—and between law and politics . . . in our social context, the terms of a particular discourse of power."[97] Television news, like the videotape format it uses, asserts a hierarchy of evidence and meaning.

FIGURE 28

Anita Hill, all alone.

FIGURE 29

Clarence Thomas,
surrounded by support.

It presents a vantage point of an ephemeral objectivity that purports to distinguish between fact and opinion. As it professes to center issues, it perpetually adds bias. This (de)centering of Hill along with the senators' questions led viewers to conclude that she was untruthful.

Many senators held that Hill's following Thomas to the EEOC as a career move lacked rationality for "moral" or "reasonable" women, that is, if her allegations were true. Yet, as Noble insists, "morality is more than the sum of kisses and sex [for the Black woman]. There is the morality of justice, freedom, and fair play."[98] From many people's perspective, moral and reasonable women rationalize that food, shelter, and stable income are important. As a twenty-five-year-old with no job prospects, Hill's decision to follow Thomas represents a certain rationality.

Alongside this, the American material ethic of keeping up with the Joneses, or just keeping a job, still functioned. Sometimes for African-Americans "culture and refinement [stem] not from a careful sorting of ideas of values and experiences, but a slavish dedication to a white lifestyle which they [view] from afar." [99] In that light, and in light of her particular situation, Hill's actions squared with her goals. Negotiating preconceived notions about heightened sexuality and other attributes associated with African culture (and specifically Black women) often demanded trade-offs for social and professional status. Indeed, Thomas had made similar trade-offs, as illustrated by his mate, his ideological/judicial positions, and the camera's portrayal of them.

Under a colonialist paradigm the Anita Hill/Clarence Thomas spectacle re-affirmed a perpetual relegation of African-Americans in general to performers and of Black women to Jezebels and liars. All of these roles coalesced in one villain, Anita Hill. Clarence Thomas was confirmed to the U.S. Supreme Court on October 15, 1991, with a Senate vote of fifty-two to forty-eight, the narrowest margin ever.[100] Women's absence from the judiciary committee (and the news-gathering realms) certainly played key roles in the way these intersections came together and the outcome. Yet something more occurred.

The visual spectrum and constructed institutions of race, gender, and the law colluded to find Anita Hill guilty of ambition, treason, and sexual appeal. By her presence all attendant men (the committee, camera crew, and audience) assessed (begrudgingly) their own conduct within the workplace. Sexual harassment now had a face—one of a woman aligned with a group of women who have traditionally been abused, raped, and ignored. However, the answers to the questions Hill raised still render silence. Men and the television structure refuse to face fully their own indiscretions and transgressions.

Some concluded that the event appeared unmediated because these hearings, first, aired at all, and, then, without interruption. Says Steenland, "TV functioned as it rarely does—as clear glass, a window. It neither created the events, nor cast them, nor scripted them. Only minimally did it offer comment. There were no tidy lessons at the end. Only unsettling ambiguity." [101] In actuality, no ambiguity remained but for a different reason than what Steenland suggests. Clearly, Anita Hill committed perjury as pronounced by the visual framing. Every televisual impulse confirmed that. The evidence of her guilt produced by the visual apparatus condemned her almost as strongly as the videotape of Rodney King's police assailants condemned them.

Beyond the live hearing coverage for those three days, each television network carried independent stories and highlights of what transpired pre- and posttestimony. Reports fleshed out the drama, with each network displaying graphics that dichotomized Hill and Thomas. Stories queried, "Who is Anita Hill?" Reporters went to her home, and they interviewed people who knew her. They conducted polls asking the nation which person seemed more truthful and whether Thomas should be confirmed. Producers assigned reporters to various "hot spots" of the case: his house, her house, the White House, and the Senate.

However, the issue of sexual harassment dominated the network's coverage of the hearings. Reporters used White female pundits to frame the issue and the debate. Consistently, representatives of the National Organization for Women (NOW), various attorneys, and civic activists described what sexual harassment meant to America's women in the workforce. With the volume and choices of voices favored, the feminist and television impulse once again elided the reality of race and how it factors into Black women's work environments. In network presentations race stood as a separate issue, apart from harassment. Hill was a woman, whereas Thomas was Black.

Herman Gray concludes that for all the Hill/Thomas show included, it failed to address the power relations and politics of gender, class, and sexuality at large and within African-American communities in particular. He notes that both Thomas's and Hill's historical narratives were inadequately addressed: "In this television spectacle, blackness operated as an empty signifier. . . . Television audiences who watched were treated to the spectacle of black male-female hostility, judgments about black intellectual competence, displays of white male patronage, and titillating talk about black bodies and sex." [102] Anita Hill gained some control of her body by reclaiming her memory, using her voice, and negating national (and racialized) interest as inscribed on her female being. Mona Fayad suggests that with this retrieval of memory the body becomes transformed from object of male desire to a "desiring force"—rejecting "subjugation to a narrative of erasure. The grounding of identity not in the passive earth, which is the focus of the national allegory, [or with the law] but in a body that insists on its presence forms a notion of identity that resists being subsumed under sameness." [103]

THE RETURN TO NORMALCY

I believe that they both thought they were telling the truth.

—Bill Clinton

Interestingly, continued probing into Hill's allegations further corroborated her story. ABC's *Turning Point* featured African-American reporter Michel McQueen Martin discussing the case with many seen and unseen players in the drama.[104] Despite the insightful and detailed analysis provided and interviews Martin conducted, a White presence, Forrest Sawyer in this case, still served as a quasi overseer. He introduced and concluded every segment—in what registered as a stamp of approval and a legitimization of the conclusions reached. One could argue, I suppose, that perhaps this action took place in an effort to help those who otherwise would refuse to see or hear a Black woman.

Since her testimony Hill has written a book about her experiences in prime time. She also lectures widely on sexual harassment, teaches at Brandeis University, and serves as a regular contributor on Court TV's *Crier Today*. Furthermore, Hill's testimony paved the way for Kathleen Willey, Gennifer Flowers, Paula Jones, and Monica Lewinsky to confront the highly sexual, it seems, Bill Clinton. Several military officers have faced court martial proceedings because of their inability to keep their hands to themselves. And educational institutions have constructed extensive posted policies on sexual harassment. Because of her stance, Hill now stands as an important icon in White feminist solidarity circles and as an illuminator on issues of sexual harassment—which still neglect to deal with the racial aspect of her harassment. She has profited personally and made the way better for many U.S. women to address this issue but perhaps at the expense of her ability to claim the whole truth of her tragedy.

WELFARE ROLLS
(BLACK WOMEN OBJECTIFIED BY MOTHER NATURE)

Seems to me that every time they have a money crisis problem or tax crisis, they always talk about people on welfare. And it seems as if we're being used as scapegoats.

—Ruth Robinson, *World News Tonight*, February 19, 1981

The War on Welfare Mothers: Reform May Put Them to Work, But Will It Discourage Illegitimacy?

—*Time*, June 20, 1994

Vice President Gore and I took office in 1993 with a pledge to end welfare as we know it. Thanks to comprehensive reform, a renewed sense of responsibility, and the strongest economy in a generation, millions of former welfare recipients now know the dignity of work.

—President Bill Clinton, December 16, 2000

A particularly insidious form of television objectification surfaces when Colored women's reproductive ability crosses with the economic viability of the nation. Television news links African-American women to welfare. This connection resembles music video's sex and commercialism fusion with Black women's bodies. This portrayal reflects also the criminalized description frequently reported for Black and Latina male suspects. I assert that because of this pervasive and normalizing tendency, the union of welfare, nation, and nurture may be the greatest denigrative aspect of Black women's television representations.

The U.S. government's policy toward welfare and its connection with Black women was articulated best in a 1992 fund-raising speech. When the Republican White House, particularly adept at both code words and code visuals, sent Vice President Dan Quayle to speak on family values, it reaffirmed its vision of and for the nation. Normally newsworthy only in a humorous vein, Quayle leveled an attack on a fictional television character, Murphy Brown, for having a baby out of wedlock. Scholars and media assailed him for this but failed to fully address his extended comments, which had larger implications. Quayle focused on the 1992 Los Angeles rebellion/riots as a segue to (or as grounded upon) the bodies of Black women. He surmised that

> the lawless social anarchy which we saw is directly related to the breakdown of the family structure, personal responsibility and social order in too many areas of our society. For the poor, the situations compounded by a welfare ethos that impedes individual efforts to move ahead in society, and hampers their ability to take advantage of the opportunities America offers . . . the underclass seems to be a new phenomenon. It is a group whose members are dependent on welfare for very long stretches, and whose men are often drawn into lives of crime. There is far too little upward mobility, because the underclass is disconnected from the rules of American society. And these problems have, unfortunately, been particularly acute for Black Americans. The intergenerational poverty that troubles us so much today is predominately a poverty of values. Our inner cities are filled with children having children; with people who have not been able to take advantage of educational opportunities; with people who are dependent on drugs or the narcotic of welfare. To be sure, many people in the ghettos struggle very hard against these tides—and sometimes win. But too many feel they have no hope and nothing to lose. This poverty is, again, fundamentally a poverty of values.[105]

By Quayle's using certain phrases such as "breakdown of the family structure," "inner cities," "narcotic of welfare," and "whose men," he specifically blamed African-American women. In other words, with Negras the noun *welfare* became their adjective. Unlike Anita Hill, who could reclaim her body through the ashes of memory (and subsequent voicing through books, talk shows, lectures, and the classroom), lower-class Black mothers as nation have been set in a dual role in which they must carry within their bodies both the narrative dismemberment and the re-membering. Says Mona Fayad, it has become a case in which "Woman is written into history as the necessary blood-sacrifice that precedes the birth of the nation."[106]

Beyond gender, this sacrifice has evidenced itself through race. Stuart Hall describes this racial aspect as "inferential"—visually capturing the welfare focus. Embedded ideologies naturalize "representations of events and situations relating to race whether 'factual' or 'fictional,' which have racist premises and presuppositions inscribed in their set of unquestioned assumptions."[107] Statements emerged without ever bringing into awareness the racist presumptions on which they were grounded.[108] Even in simple shots of hands receiving food stamps, color stigmatization occurred.

Hall's theory highlights problems endemic to the news reporting process and its necessity to generate advertising revenue. Yet the codes used for marginalized groups move beyond class systems. The early study *Window Dressing* found that 1970s television news coverage of both minorities and women tended to be brief and to occur later in the program.[109] Contemporary analysis sustains these findings in general. But seemingly, like Anita Hill and Vanessa Williams before her, Black women achieve lead-story status when their sexuality, perceived promiscuity, and character frame the story.

Hayden White has suggested that facts and discourses work in tandem to validate each other, claiming that placement of facts in a narrative discourse "sanction[s] the interpretation to which it is meant to contribute. And the interpretation derives its force of plausibility from the order and manner in which the facts are presented in the discourse."[110] In other words, narratives forward ideas not only through content but also through organization, placement, quantity, and historical context. According to contemporary television news articulations, the welfare program and the women it helped functioned in a substantially different manner from what was envisioned at its inception. This perceived change directly impacted Black women and the nation's embracing of the program.

THE EMERGENCE OF U.S. HELP POLICIES

As one of several social programs instituted by the federal government in the early 1930s, welfare served as a cure-all for the Great Depression. In conjunction with programs such as Social Security and Medicaid, which were intended to help Americans at large, Aid to Families with Dependent Children (AFDC) was designed to help widowed, divorced, and abandoned women and their children. Welfare's implementation reflected cultural attitudes of the period that demanded women stay at home to care for their families. Richard Cloward and Frances Fox Piven argue that historically, poor relief was used as an instrument of social control of the workforce, mainly to prevent disorder.[111] Although the program was deemed as simple assistance and a little-noticed allocation for years, it began garnering substantial economic, political, and media attention in the 1980s.

One reason, according to Jill Duerr Berrick, is not that our attitudes toward the poor changed; rather, our perceptions of *who* was poor changed.[112] For example, by 1993 ABC questioned whether the country had reached the end of welfare as then known. The news segment opened with Rebecca Chase saying, "This is the reason some Americans hate the welfare system."[113] The image accompanying that text and for two natural sound seconds later shows a Black woman with her son. Despite Chase's later commentary, the viewer was already directed to hate Black women, their children, and their perceived profiting as welfare recipients. For all purposes the image completed the text.

Berrick believes that "the slight shift from widowhood to single parenthood may have been responsible for the change in public attitudes toward welfare . . . [so that] welfare became synonymous with morally questionable behavior," behavior that is connected to the color of those who became eligible.[114] It seemed that once African-Americans started to participate, the program required particular monitoring. With Black women's hypersexual reputation, a certain fear emerged that these women would cause a "race suicide" for Anglo-Saxons who claimed America exclusively for themselves.[115]

As more women of color were enabled to access these programs, press coverage increased correspondingly. One significant part of Ronald Reagan's election platform, which ushered in a new era of social conservatism just as America was emerging from an economic downward spiral, was to denounce and blame welfare and its recipients for the economic crisis. "Welfare reform" became the rallying cry of the Right. Cutting the program 15 percent in his first term, Reagan leveled an attack that political, social, and media workers all appropriated.

Running for office in 1992, presidential hopeful Bill Clinton usurped Reagan-Bush rhetoric as part of the Democratic platform. He promised to reform welfare as it had never been reformed before. After several years of modifications and based on his inaugural promise, he signed the Personal Responsibility and Work Opportunity Act of 1996 (HR 3734) (fig. 30). The act eliminated AFDC, giving states the fundamental role in assisting needy families. It delimited the food stamps program, the SSI Disability program, and benefits to noncitizens, substantially. Families who had received assistance for

FIGURE 30

President Bill Clinton reforming welfare, surrounded by those he believed needed reforming.

five cumulative years were made ineligible for cash aid, and after two years of assistance adult members had to find work, regardless of whether this work provided sufficient income for the family.

In 1999 *CNN* showed the policy's "success" based on one Black woman's employment at the White House. News stories disclosed that little had changed in the status of the poor, except that they were now poorer and more destitute, but the federal government announced that the welfare rolls had been reduced by one-half. All of the rhetoric rarely reflected the fact that these programs constitute about 1 percent of the federal budget.

With the pendulum swinging in one direction from both parties, two main strands of thought (implicitly grounded in racialized and gendered constructions) framed the welfare debate, particularly in visual culture: "nature"— which manifests itself in biological reproduction, out-of-wedlock children, and Negras' sexuality and perceived promiscuity—and "nurture"—which correlates Black women's presumed lack of work ethic and malfeasance with economic and political imperatives. Each served to confine Black women. Although these debates bore distinction and maintained their own discourses and controversies, their commonalities rested within women's vaginas and racialized notions that inhabited those spaces.

Nature

The most poignant visual images of welfare came via Afro-American women, their numerous children, and their solitude. The story that harbored the beginning quote by Ruth Robinson features Robinson, a large Black woman, with one child on her lap, one sitting beside her, a teenager walking through the frame and, suggested by her girth, potentially another baby on the way (fig. 31).

FIGURE 31

Ruth Robinson in her procreative abundance.

Linked with drug addicts, delinquent youth, and criminals, the voluminous display of Black woman's sexuality was used to connote an out-of-control status and a need for reform.[116]

In her work on women's biological reproduction and their confluence with the idea of nation, Nira Yuval-Davis asserts that often in countries like the United States, "people as power" outcries initiate a striving for "demographic balance." Historically, one of the main conduits for this balance came through the eugenics discourse—a pseudoscience covertly forwarded in the United States by Planned Parenthood founder Margaret Sanger. This movement did not concern itself with better nurturing but "attempted to predetermine the quality of the nation via 'nature,' by way of selective breeding."[117] Sanger maintained that uncontrolled fertility and large families were inextricably linked to poverty. She acted on that belief by placing clinics in poor, usually urban areas.[118] Yet a *Hastings Center Report* concluded that a tension remains between the notion of empowering poor women to control their fertility for their own best interest and limiting fertility among the poor and the underclass (usually Black and Latina).[119] This tension receives virtually no analysis in television news, even in light of twenty-first-century debates on genetic engineering.

What appears frequently is typified by a 1985 example. *NN*'s Lisa Myers delivered a report on the Massachusetts welfare program. The piece opens on a Black welfare mother who raised her three children for fourteen years with no education, no skills, and no confidence. In the piece she participates in a voluntary program aimed at getting women off the system. As one of the better and unusual segments for its variety of illustrations, the piece shows Black and White women welfare recipients training for jobs. Yet despite its equality of coverage, the lead-in to the story preframed the initial shot and the real problem. The story preceding it found Connie Chung announcing U.S. approval of contraceptive implants for American women.[120] More than a story tie-in, it served as an admonishment for and, perhaps, a more effective corrective to Colored women's unchecked procreative tendencies—the real baby makers. News failed to examine the issue beyond the Black body, deferring instead to clichés. These stories are not aberrations of the past. A 1998 CBS report looking at Wisconsin workfare centered White families as exemplars of achievement under welfare reform, whereas Jennifer Cameron, a Black woman, exemplifies the homeless-shelter occupant. A White social worker creates the context by citing an example of a woman with eleven children and no high school diploma as typical.[121]

Faye Wattleton served as the Planned Parenthood national spokeswoman for fourteen years. Touted as the face of abortion, this African-American woman embodied both the perceived animalistic sexuality of Black women and their depraved indifference to life. She often sat, as Hill did, in similar Senate hearings turned courtroom where the committee's actions reflected ideological predispositions.[122] Wattleton recalls one such meeting where the White male legislators paraded around the hearing room as judges in a courtroom. Describing it, she says that "the senators stepped down to the floor and slowly walked around a table laden with family planning and sex ed materials. They stopped for several minutes to peruse the covers and flip through some of the booklets, shaking their heads in disbelief."[123] Just what they did not believe is unclear. The historic connection of enslaved Black women's bodies with the national agenda should have illustrated the great unbelief—a memory, however, that continues to be erased. It has been replaced with official versions of media history that in this case cement Negras' sexuality to welfare and all of its implications.[124]

Again, the underlying and unpronounced discourses that circulate within Planned Parenthood and its vision for poor, Colored women are that these women possess no control of their sexual desires, have no rights to that desire, and need sterilization, of some sort. Beyond Wattleton, who is no longer with the organization, most Planned Parenthood proponents are White. Yet the organization's services largely impact Black and Latina women. It follows, as Rivers maintains, that "what enrages many people is the idea that tax dollars are subsidizing black sexuality."[125]

In a socially segregated country Americans harbor scant knowledge of the Other beyond visual representation. For example, new U.C.L.A. students are often told not to venture beyond certain points on the freeway—areas predominated by Black and Chicano residents. But logic dictates that this warning must have its basis in television news reports of the areas' inhabitants. How else would students know not to go to a place if they, and their friends, had never been there? Nationwide, I always can assess where Colored people live in mass just by where reports—news and social—tell me to avoid. These simple examples illustrate the impact television news has had on Americans' concept of its populace. The continued split image of Black women suggests that, indeed, "our moralistic attitude about sexuality on the one hand—combined with relentless promotion of sexuality on the other—combine to make the United States the Western world's leader in children having children."[126]

In segment after segment proposals from White, male legislators clamored for the sanctioning of African-American women's reproduction. Many proposed making a direct tie of benefits to the number of children born. For example, a 1992 New Jersey welfare reform proposal sought to deny benefits to all women who had more children while already within the system. The corresponding NBC news segment opened with a Black woman and her newborn.[127] Despite images of unbridled sexuality as a cause, research consistently has shown that economic hardship, racial discrimination, and disintegrated neighborhoods stand as the major reasons for increased and sustained high levels of pregnancy among Black teens—rates that actually have declined.[128] These cultural occurrences, however, are conspicuously absent from the discourses and visualization of the problem. This absence factors well into the implementation of nurture.

Nurture

Unlike earlier periods when welfare recipients (Anglo-Saxon women) were encouraged to find husbands in order to leave the system, public officials began proposing disincentives to women. Benefits were lowered, eligibility criteria tightened, and the application process made more complicated. Many women were required to register for work and/or a training program and to seek employment.[129] These actions (or reactions) were to remove what had been touted as a substantial burden to American taxpayers.

Yet only perpetuating mythologies fueled these measures. Contrary to common news wisdom, in no state did welfare lift a family above the poverty line. On average, women on AFDC had two children. Of the recipients, 42 percent had only one child, 30 percent had two children, and 16 percent had three children.[130] Most AFDC recipients were not African-American women. Although women of color constitute the majority, White women occupied 39 percent of the welfare rolls. Although reporters had access to the actual numbers, it appeared in some respects as if public opinion drove the AFDC program. The alignment of work and women's bodies translated into news items on welfare fraud as a form of prostitution and connected the program to chattel slavery.

For example, in one story CBS followed the Florida police on a welfare sting operation. The piece begins by trailing a Black woman on her way to turn herself into the police. Her crime—she held two jobs and did not report it. Thereby, she cheated the welfare administration out of $200.00. Throughout the segment White men gathered these criminals, loosely visualized as Colored women cheating the system. Surprisingly, no faces are shown in this segment (unusual for news coverage of Colored people). Yet the color and number of bodies suffices. The facelessness of representation (like the hands) indicted all Black women succinctly.

Television addresses poverty implicitly by showing images of its symptoms. Robert Entman concedes that "[t]he concepts of 'black person' and 'poverty' are so thoroughly intertwined in television news that the white public's perceptions of poverty appear difficult to disentangle from their thinking about African Americans."[131] In hundreds of segments examined from 1980 to 2001, Black faces framed the poverty discourse. Even within news organizations noted for their thoughtful analysis, this bonding exists.

For example, in an essay on the *MacNeil/Lehrer NewsHour* that acknowledged the birthday and legacy of Malcolm X, the essayist addresses poverty and feelings of destitution that, he surmised, encompasses many Black Americans. Yet visualizing what impoverishment means is determined differently depending on whose imagination conceives it. The White woman producer I worked for continually expressed dissatisfaction with the tape provided to her of African-American communities in indigent conditions. She maintained that the video was "not quite right"—meaning, not destitute enough. Her mind's eye was guided by previous in-house news pieces and recirculated CNN video. The idea of inferential knowledge resurfaces here as a problematic melding of poverty to race, with a specific black or brown face attached.

In traditional Black communities poverty elicited compassion, not damnation. bell hooks suggests that Blacks often acknowledged the economic existence of basically four groups: "the poor, who were destitute; the working folks, who were poor because they made just enough to make ends meet; those who worked hard and had extra money; and the rich." [132] Yet being poor in Reagan-Bush's America virtually constituted a profane act, in Clinton's White House an unseen anomaly. Inner city, welfare, welfare queen, affirmative action, quotas, drugs, homelessness, poverty, as well as menace, danger, and burden, all connoted African-Americans and, increasingly, Latinos. Reagan-Bush-Clinton did not invent these code words or their accompanying visuals, but their administrations perpetually connected them in speeches and legislation.

During Reagan's reelection campaign he exhibited even more hostility toward Colored women. Comfortable in and lauded for his stance on welfare, he questioned White Americans, "Are you better off than you were four years ago?" While surveying the Bronx, he took questions from Black and Latina women, who, frustrated with their economic plight, did not feel particularly better off. When asked about his plans to help them, he responded, "I can't do a damn thing for you if I don't get elected." [133] He was. And during his second term this same hostility, disrespect, and ignorance only increased.

One fitting illustration of Reagan's early Alzheimer's onset came through his misinformation about welfare housing (hotels) in New York City—hotels occupied predominately by Colored homeless families. Focusing on the cost of the hotel as printed in the *New York Times,* he complained during a news conference, "Why doesn't somebody build them a home for $37K?" He took an obscure, inaccurate figure and shifted the responsibility for the families to New York City, solo.[134] John Fiske maintains that this type of strategy is employed to maintain hierarchical control—both racialized and gendered. Like Clarence Thomas's castigation and reinvention of his sister's welfare status, "Stereotypes, such as that of the 'Black welfare mother,' are neither reflections of social reality nor merely distortions of it: they are active in producing it. The power interests that control economic and welfare policies also control the discursive policies that produce stereotypes."[135] In the construction of these fallacies, media most certainly matters.

Reporters positioned themselves against this backdrop of poor, urban Black neighborhoods (with a plethora of representations in the background to illustrate their point). By doing this they contrasted the perceived successes of mostly White children against the depravity of Black ones. Also, they ignored the fact that three-quarters of Euro-American children have never lived in poor families, whereas only one-third of Black ones have escaped it altogether. Consequently, "temporary poverty [is] more common to Anglo-American children but that among African-American children living in poverty, nearly one half [are] poor for at least five out of six years of their childhood."[136] This disparity yields virtually no reportage. In contrast, by 1988 twenty states had workfare legislation on their legislative floors.[137]

Although centering Black women, media coverage does periodically extend to White and Latina women's participation in welfare. But the coverage airs quite differently. Consistently, White women frame segments describing workfare and success in getting out of the system. Besides this, White women appear more frequently cooking for the family, cleaning the house, and overseeing homework, whereas in Black and Latina visual households, limited time goes toward showing these activities. These news stories, however, center on the White counselor, program administrator, sociologist, or, in some cases, police officer accounting for Black women's antiwork behavior.

Caryl Rivers suggests that one victory of the right has been to shift the debate about welfare from social policy to personal morality. The idea that Black women are lazy whores presents another riff on the Calvinist idea that the poor are evil. "If you are female, being poor *and* sexual is a double stigma."[138] Negras illustrate the moral deterioration of American society. One NBC story featured an elderly Black man helping a young, Black mother and others in general by providing them with food and clothes, helping to locate shelter, and arranging child care.[139] The reporter, Bob Dotson, voices the woman's working two minimum-wage jobs to sustain her family. But despite her efforts the segment repeatedly focuses on her return to welfare. As he shows her conditions, he increasingly uses the bodies of surrounding Black women to illustrate a certain point about Black women and motherhood. Some of the women shown clearly were beyond childbearing years, but their Colored, poor bodies seemed sufficient. Their mere presence stood for all sistahs. Working poor Black women were juxtaposed against Quayle's impulse to identify the Other. The mythical power and normality of whiteness served as the standard. As Fiske maintains, in drawing these defining lines around the identities of others, whiteness became a powerful and normalized status of being, simply, not the other.[140]

TO BE OBJECTIVE OR NOT TO BE . . .

Perhaps the cultural logic of these news condemnations comes through theories of surveillance. Fiske defines surveillance as the "power to know without being known, to see without being seen, and as ideally suited to development from the undefined position of superiority from which whiteness operates." [141] What could be rationalized as Laura Mulvey's "to-be-looked-at-ness," Jacqueline Bobo's "essentialist Black woman," and Lisa Lewis's "gender address" fails to account for the representation of actual, live, nonpaid bodies. More than in any other, this chapter's examples show objectification of Black women as a constant within television news. Yet agency for Black women has not been completely eliminated.

Once a text is in motion, objectifying forces control the image. Yet African-American women anchors, reporters, and producers play crucial roles in claiming and fostering an active agency. With limited access to the means of production, Black women's greatest reclamation of selfhood has come largely through the rebuttal. Atlanta's local CBS anchor, Monica Kaufman, has on numerous occasions undercut visual objectification through critical, postimage commentary. For example, one summer in the early 1980s Atlanta suffered an oppressive and sustained heat wave. The accompanying videotaped piece aired by WSB-TV showed Atlantans' responses to it. The centerpiece was a prominently featured African-American family on their porch—eating watermelon. This vision—beyond its historical presence—propelled racist and classist imagery once again into current usage. Once on camera, Kaufman responded to the tape by commenting, "White people eat watermelon, too." Although not able to revisit the visual metaphor, Kaufman, in this one statement, helped to reclaim the visual voice of a silenced racialized presence.

Further, a proactive agency can come through African-American and/or cognizant Other reporters and producers imputing or framing debates surrounding Colored representation. For example, Charlayne Hunter-Gault covered world and national news stories as assigned but also kept issues of race and gender at the top of the *MacNeil/Lehrer NewsHour*'s agenda, at least through the mid-1990s. After Vanessa Williams's win and dethroning, many Miss Americas have been Black. In fact, since 1983 the nation has crowned four Black Miss Americas, with the first Asian-Pacific American woman winning the 2001 crown. As the sacrificial figure, Williams, through her highly publicized fall, helped them win. [142] Women's presence in local and national legislative, executive, and judicial branches of government helps derail subsequent spectacles such as the Hill/Thomas Show.

With all of this so-called progress Black women must contend with pictures of actor Hugh Grant's unnamed Black prostitute, which were sold for Web-site decoration; with the characterization, abandonment, and firing of "quota" and "condom" queens Lani Guinier and Surgeon General Joycelyn Elders; and with Kemba Smith, who, sentenced to twenty-four years for affiliation with a drug dealer, was finally pardoned by Clinton in 2000. Covering mad Black women, ones whose wrath equals Lorena Bobbitt's, may best force patriarchal and racist news organizations to address their positionings and to strive if not for objectivity at least for balance.

5

YOU'D BETTER
RECOGNIZE

Oprah the Iconic and Television Talk

[By faith] women received back their dead, raised to life
again.
—Hebrews 11:35

I believe I will run on . . . See what the end will be. I believe
I'll work on . . . Find out what waits for me . . . Ooh, ooh,
ooh, ooh, Oprah."
—*The Oprah Winfrey Show*, 1998–1999

Freedwoman and abolitionist Sojourner Truth ignited an early White
Women's Rights group in Akron, Ohio, with her ire: "dey talks 'bout dis ting
in de head—what dis dey call it? 'Intellect,' whispered some one near. . . .
What's dat got to do with women's right or niggers' rights? . . . [S]ay women
can't have as much rights as man, cause Christ want a woman. Whar did your
Christ come from? . . . From God and a woman. Man had nothing to do with
him."[1] A century and a half later another free Black woman, Oprah Winfrey,
descended on American consciousness to answer Truth's call for women's and
"niggers' rights." Over the history of visual culture Black women's imagery has
teetered between disgust and adulation, depravity and excess, objectification
and agency. This pendulum has significantly impacted the lives of sentient
African-American women, but then came Winfrey. Oprah Winfrey's figure has
been positioned as both American and model minority. On her body the binaries created via White American male dominance reconciled, and Americans' quest for spirituality found refuge.

No other name (except perhaps O. J.) commanded comparable national recognition in late-twentieth-century pop culture. *Time* magazine lamented the
"full Oprahization" of American politics; *Publishers Weekly* claimed an "Oprah
Effect" over book sales; the "Oprah Factor" may have impacted the merger between New World Communications and King World, as well as *Time*'s subsequent buying of the distributor; and Christopher Buckley satirized a fictional
conversation between Oprah and Pope John Paul II as "Poprah." Because the

name, actuality, and talk show of Oprah Winfrey resonate with people, the mere enunciation "Oprah" conjures the sublime example of self-help, authority, and release. Depending on the context, the name transforms from subject to verb to adjective. As a multifaceted millionaire and international icon, Oprah Winfrey epitomizes both the objectified and the agency-assuming Black woman as created by the medium of television and exemplified in the preceding chapters.

As I have demonstrated, the latter part of the twentieth century found dramatic and contradictory disturbances within American economic structures, political ideology, and culture. Black firsts continued despite twelve years of Reagan-Bush trickle-down policies. Deregulation forced long-term employee outages. Clinton implemented a progressive yet duplicitous leadership, making way for another George Bush Republican administration. The Internet dominated communication. And of course the beat played on for the fortunate few. The changes and stasis of the -isms (racism, sexism, classism) increased consumer and spectator feelings of alienation, loss, and anger among all groups. Although these cultural shifts were not revolutionary, they took on a heightened significance. Perhaps this significance came from the proximity of the approaching millennium. More likely, however, the aesthetic called postmodernism—that new approach to art, politics, business, education, and entertainment—fostered dread and scorn within and against those whom it pretended to benefit.[2]

Despite, or perhaps in response to, these changes, I argue that Oprah Winfrey's iconic status emerged so pervasively because of two very specific, ongoing, and intermingled phenomena in American society. First, I suggest that Winfrey's figure symbolized and embodied the binaries of American culture, of multiculturalism itself. The confluence of her race and gender always already suggested bipolarity. Yet the duality of her Negroness and Americanness that W.E.B. Du Bois wrote about implicated the identifying characteristics of age, class, and sexuality, bringing to bear the force of "us and Other" configurations.[3] In this multicultural debate the assumption of whiteness established the foundation by which dialogue occurred. Consequently, her presence caused further collisions of race, gender, sexuality, and class with whiteness.

Further, Americans' feelings of instability and angst established by inequity and blame were displaced onto the body of Winfrey. Along with the rhetoric of multiculturalism, historically entrenched binaries—Black/White, rich/poor, privileged/disadvantaged, old/young, us/them, homosexual/heterosexual— elevated the Oprah Winfrey icon as an exemplar of dialogue. In other words, the hypocrisy and complexity of the signifiers—salad bowl/no color lines/melting pot/mosaic—congealed into a configuration of Black womanhood that inevitably alienated the signified—Winfrey—from part of her own identity.

Evelyn Hinz connects multiculturalism to religion. In "What Is Multicul-turalism? A 'Cognitive' Introduction," Hinz maintains that although religious overtones pervade the multicultural discourse, they rarely receive acknowledg-ment or consideration. She likens self-consciousness and self-reflexiveness to Catholic conscience; authenticity, transgression, honesty, and guilt to the site of the confession; and she adds that one should not overlook the "religious resonance of terms like 'purity' and 'impurity' in discussions of ethnicity, and especially when they are accompanied by a moralistic ridicule."[4] Hinz implic-itly condemns this religious tone, but I maintain that it is precisely within this vein, this "moralistic ridicule," that Americans express their loss of, search for, and forwarding of the Oprah Winfrey figure.

This brings me to my second assertion. I contend that the decline and vir-tual absence of spirituality in the lives of Americans has, at least partially, con-structed Winfrey as icon. Churches' decline in relevance has caused people to embrace salvation outside the bounds of established religion. Through her race, gender, talk show, and outside projects, Winfrey maintained ties to spir-ituality in the visual and oral folklore of Black representation. Beyond this, she emerged as a spiritual figure against whom the promise of tomorrow could be recuperated today. Symbolizing "core beliefs" as articulated by Nicholas C. Cooper-Lewter and Henry H. Mitchell in *Soul Theology*, Winfrey's figure achieved and activated an ideal balance for human existence.

According to *Soul Theology*, core beliefs empower individuals to affirm their own racialized, gendered, and ethnic construction while maintaining an other-centeredness and a self-giving focus. Balanced people are dependable without being rigid and are capable of expressing and controlling emotion. This bal-ance results in a positive sense of relationship to God and God's creations, how-ever that relationship is stated or envisioned.[5] In her presence on national and world stages Winfrey served simultaneously as an object of "credible" (implied atheistic) voice while connoting and claiming a balanced, spiritualized subject-hood. Thus, multiculturalism and the binaries that it excavated, coupled with religious absence, conjoined to form and forward the Oprah Winfrey star text. Her iconic status has ignited a complete redefinition of television and its growth. Winfrey has aided this redefinition not as a Black woman per se but as both a highly racialized woman and a de-raced, wealthy, American.

This chapter uses *The Oprah Winfrey Show* as a referential text to examine the genre of the talk show alongside other narratives that circulate about her omniscient presence. I use this strategy to uncover how overlapping discourses impacted representations of African-American women on television in the late twentieth century. Essentially, Winfrey's influence on American society has been examined and expressed through three distinct critical fronts: the scholarly, the production/economic, and the popular. Although they overlap, each possesses unique aspects of the iconic that work in tandem to both exalt and derail her.[6]

THE SCHOLARLY TALK OF TALK

The television talk show exploded in the 1980s as a distinctively American phenomenon.[7] Prior to this, 1950s talk shows were hosted by entertainers such as Dinah Shore, Merv Griffin, David Frost, Joan Rivers, and Mike Douglas.[8] In 1967 the talk landscape changed when Phil Donahue began broadcasting a television talk program as a phone-in show, similar to talk radio. The innovation of this format was its interactivity with the audience and its mixture of information and service. Donahue, comfortable with hard news topics, conveyed a sympathy toward other, "soft" news. However, viewers found Donahue's empathetic ear wanting. His lack created a space for Oprah Winfrey. Yet it was Donahue's talk show that led academics to begin investigating this new genre.

Television talk, like most daytime television, was theorized as female centered. Advertisers still idealized viewers as female homemakers, and they targeted cleaning women with cleanser, cooking women with food made easy, and mothering women with baby formula. Daytime advertisements were aimed at White women, married, and eighteen to thirty-five years of age.[9] Beyond demographic statistics, the commercials' racial composition reflected this. *The Oprah Winfrey Show* appeared within this very gendered and White weekday.[10]

Gloria-Jean Masciarotte's "C'mon, Girl: Oprah Winfrey and the Discourse of Feminine Talk" situates the talk show as a particularly female and somewhat liberating space. Through the prism of psychoanalysis she examines the Oprah Winfrey talk phenomenon, the history of talk itself, and the often-condemned feminine subject. She believes that the derogatory critical attention paid to the television talk show occurs because of patriarchy's gall at women's unrestrained speech on topics deemed feminine, their "painful experiences, [and] ongoing and ill-defined struggles."[11]

Further, Masciarotte's argument suggests that in the constitution of the subject, a series of *I*s instead of an *I/You* dichotomy forwards its trajectory in talk shows. Therefore, "resolving the issue is not the function of the talk show, [but] displaying the space for stories is."[12] In other words, women's speech and women's concerns become central and validated within the space of television talk. Topics ranging from premenstrual syndrome and breast cancer to plastic surgery and the glass ceiling fill the talk hour. This phenomenon, particularly in the context of a Negra bestowing subjectivity, accorded a quasi empowerment not only to the people (normally women) who were given voice but also to the racialized granter of the speech (Winfrey). In the final analysis Masciarotte maintains that because Winfrey was threatening, seductive, big, and aggressive, she defied and denied objectification and isolation. Hers was an "insistence on resistance, resistance to the dominant, curative, normalizing narrative."[13] This subjugation that Masciarotte claims advances the idea of Winfrey standing as a harbinger and beacon of difference.

Studies such as Wayne Munson's *All Talk: The Talkshow in Media Culture* pose key questions to the talk show genre itself: questioning whether they are more talk or show, conversation or spectacle, both or neither?[14] The familiarity of the format, the host, the audience, the set, and the relatively unscripted dialogue provide a forum in which the exchange of ideas takes place. Talk shows offer lively, useful information along with entertaining tidbits, unusual social practices, painful memories, reflections, and/or discoveries. Whether it is Donahue dressed as a woman on the issue of transvestism or Jenny Jones overwhelmed by her mastectomy, Munson concedes that talk shows "juxtapose rather than integrate multiple, heterogeneous, discontinuous elements. Rather than reconcile, talkshows (barely) contain."[15] But reactivating Masciarotte's point, perhaps containment denies dialogue. Resolution at the end of one hour may be more of a man's thing, a masculine construct that fails to follow women's acculturation or goals. This advocacy of reconciliation and heterogeneity surfaces in other scholars' investigations of the talk show genre as well.

Laurie Haag examines talk show intimacy, whereas Patricia Joyner Priest investigates why people participate. Dana Cloud's "Hegemony or Concordance? The Rhetoric of Tokenism in 'Oprah' Winfrey's Rags-to-Riches Biography" looks at the popularity of the format as dictated by its commercial success, its imitators, and demographic numbers. All engage in a dialectical discourse. Munson suggests that the talk show combines the elements of sensation, advice, and politics into a "promiscuous, hall-of-mirrors inclusiveness."[16] Yet in "Oprah Winfrey: The Construction of Intimacy in the Talk Show Setting," Haag argues that viewers have a certain relationship with Winfrey, parasocial she calls it, which allows them to feel intimately acquainted with her. Winfrey's specific success is attributable to "the evolution of both her personal 'legend' and her accessible communication style."[17]

For example, from *The Oprah Winfrey Show*'s inception participants (audience and guests) have always called and referred to Oprah Winfrey by her first name. This gesture indicated a certain familiarity not accorded or taken up by participants of *Donahue*, at least initially. Winfrey takes her audiences shopping, invites them to her home in pajamas, and rewards them for being "good" people. Haag says, "Only a good friend could tell a friend when she is not as cute as she can be."[18] Understanding and explicating the talk show while also revaluing its place in American culture and within the lives of spectators themselves helps to establish the talk show as a link between the interpersonal and the mass-mediated spectacle.

Munson suggests that this link serves a pragmatic and recuperative function. It reconciles technology and commodification with community, mass culture with the individual and the local, and production with consumption. Seemingly, this assessment reveals similarities among television platforms such as infomercials that feature doctors, psychics, therapists, preachers, and health gurus, as well as among the many reality-based programs that aired in the late 1990s. The televangelist movement falls within this linkage also. Munson maintains that in the combination of industrial and social, "the mythic American past of the participatory town meeting and the interpersonal 'handshake' politics of speech and presence meet the imagined 'present' of technological simulation, reproduction, and commodification."[19] This combination explains why the rhetoric of multiculturalism flourishes when Oprah Winfrey is the subject. Theories of postmodernism, as articulated by Jean-François Lyotard and Fredric Jameson, meld with capitalism. Additionally, they make clear the degree to which talk shows permeate American consciousness through business, education, politics, and consumerism. Yet beyond these concerns, still other substantial issues have pervaded the talk show domain.

I demonstrated in the four previous chapters that race, gender, class, and sexuality resonate within the television framework. In talk shows they predominate and provide much of the subject matter. Scholars such as Herman Gray submit that only within the talk show domain have discussions of race really permeated, despite their lack of depth.[20] Janice Peck disagrees. In her "Talk about Racism: Framing a Popular Discourse of Race on *Oprah Winfrey*," she maintains that because the inevitable goal of discussing racism on talk shows is to change perceptions, real-life problems are "discursively contained."[21] Following Peck's logic, for example, Winfrey's coverage of the 1987 and 1988 disruptions on race in Forsyth County, Georgia, did not alter substantially the demographics and perceptions of its inhabitants toward Blacks wanting to live there.

Similarly, Cloud argues that Winfrey's "tokenist biography" blames the oppressed for their failures. This biography is used to uplift and uphold the meritocratic American dream while justifying the inequities of the actual system.[22] Still further, Debbie Epstein and Deborah Lynn Steinberg contend in "All Het-Up! Rescuing Heterosexuality on the Oprah Winfrey Show" that Winfrey both problematizes and normalizes the boundaries of heterosexuality. The "common sense," the normalized and institutionalized notions of heterosexual coupling, subverts the complexity of power and patterns of social inequality.[23] Half of the debates about *The Oprah Winfrey Show* address its response to, interpretation of, or inscription of race, gender, class, and sexual orientation. The other half focuses on Oprah Winfrey and the talk show genre through the therapeutic aspects of talk.

Many scholars maintain that the central goal of the talk show is to provide a forum for displaced, and what they deem nonbeneficial, therapy, sabotaging real issues for superfluous coverage and ratings. The catharsis and comfort of confrontation, therefore, often only lead to further problems after airtime. For example, in Mimi White's *Tele-Advising: Therapeutic Discourse in American Television*, White uses psychoanalysis to assess "confessional practices" across differing teletherapy, television formats. White conducts this type of analysis to uncover "an agency for producing new voices and new subjectivities that nonetheless remain in fee to consumer culture, voices that both constitute and evade the forces setting them in motion."[24] Her assessments of the television talk show, and particularly of *The Oprah Winfrey Show*, make valuable and valid assumptions.

Winfrey's program has been filled with experts and needy patients/participants who cling to each other for resolution of problems. The audience is not only induced by but also implicated in this process because most of the issues discussed invoke fundamental malfunctions, curiosities, or joys harbored within human consciousness and families. Besides, these emotive displays elevate the spectator, many of whom feel superior to the talk show participants. But beyond prevailing theories of therapy, commercialization, identity construction, and the genre itself, talk show discourses highlight the binaries of multiculturalism and religious lack as founded by and on Oprah Winfrey.

Validating this assertion, many of the aforementioned theorists mention therapy within religious contexts. For example, Masciarotte likens declarations on talk shows to the religious activity of testifying or witnessing before a group rather than to undergoing therapy. This allows for the constitution of social citizen beyond the private sphere. Winfrey's creation of a particularly woman-centered, spiritual, and industrial space helped her to become therapist and patient, host and audience member. In examining Winfrey's 1992 series on race, Peck suggests that religious and therapeutic discourses blurred when racism was defined as a lack of understanding, "a failure to recognize others as divine creations, a violation of the 'golden rule,' and a resulting spiritual (and hence social) disharmony."[25] According to this logic normally distinct ideological territories now grouped individuals before God, the marketplace, and science in the talk show.

The religious tone permeating the late twentieth century came through politics, a resurgence of religious fundamentalism, televangelism, and the multicultural impulse. Bandied about within educational institutions, this dialogue/debate revolved around storytelling, whose story and who would tell it. On the other hand, the multicultural impulse, according to Ward Churchill, actually amounted to "monolithic pedagogical reliance on a single cultural tradition [which] constitute[d] a rather transparent form of intellectual domination, achievable only within the context of parallel forms of domination."[26]

The figure of Oprah Winfrey was situated somewhere in-between those domains. She acknowledged and completely embraced society's opposition of her being alongside her own life stories, testimonies, and real-life actualities. Fissures, along with her ability to work an audience, positioned her centrality through change, as accessible although completely unreachable and as wholly understood but an unknown quantity. These scholarly debates about Winfrey's figure overlapped with the production texts of her success and her assumption of manly (White) power in product creation.

THE PRODUCTION CODES

The public economic/production narratives of the real-life, multimillionaire Oprah Winfrey focused on her ongoing monetary deals with King World Productions, her production company, and her new projects. According to *Forbes* magazine, *The Oprah Winfrey Show* earned $115 million in revenue during its first two seasons.[27] Winfrey credits the acquisition of a new agent in 1985 for propelling her from "employee" to mogul: "I had to get rid of that slave mentality. . . . He took the ceiling off my brain."[28] By 2000 Winfrey's name appeared on "The Forbes 400," a list of the four hundred richest Americans, which placed her at number 354, with a net worth of $800 million.[29] By her fifteenth season, Oprah Winfrey had won thirty-four Emmys and had twenty-two million viewers weekly. Shackles, be gone!

Economic narratives increased in proportion to Winfrey's soaring ratings as compared to other talk shows, the program's ability to draw advertisers, and money generated. For example, *Broadcasting* assessed the potential for high ratings at a low cost as a major factor for the rapid increase in talk shows. In 1992 *The Oprah Winfrey Show* led the ratings and earned $705 million in revenue. One analyst remarked that "[t]hese shows really are high profit centers. . . . And you don't have to be Oprah to make money."[30] Not until 1998, in her twelfth year of broadcasting, was *The Oprah Winfrey Show* resoundingly beaten, by *Jerry Springer*, and not permanently.

When Winfrey entered her thirteenth season, in September 1998, King World Productions agreed to pay her $150 million dollars per year to continue the show through the 2002 season.[31] By 1998 she accounted for 40 percent of King World's annual revenue or about $200 million dollars.[32] This same year

Winfrey entered into an equal partnership with Geraldine Laybourne, Marcy Carsey, Tom Werner, and Caryn Mandabach to create a new cable station for women called Oxygen.[33] One of the largest cablers, TCI, committed to adding Oxygen to its basic service of seven million subscriber homes. Oxygen's premier in early 2000, along with the launch of her Web site, www.oprah.com, and *O, the Oprah Magazine* (the most successful magazine launch ever) all added to Winfrey's media omniscience.

Since 1986 Winfrey has produced several television works under the proviso of her Harpo Productions (*Oprah* spelled backwards and, coincidentally, the name of her character's husband in *The Color Purple*). They include *Women of Brewster Place* (March 1989), *Brewster Place* (May–June 1990), *Scared Silent* (September 1992), and *There Are No Children Here* (November 1993). The first two programs showcased Black women in dramatic fiction. The next two examined traumas that Winfrey herself endured in hopes that the exhibition thereof would end similar traumas. Her first feature film in collaboration with Touchstone Pictures, *Beloved* (1998), was produced also under the Harpo banner.

For "Oprah Winfrey Presents" Winfrey has delivered *Before Women Had Wings* (1997), *The Wedding* (February 1998), *David and Lisa* (November 1998), *Tuesdays with Morrie* (December 1999), and *Amy and Isabelle* (March 2001). *The Wedding* dramatized the 1996 book of the same title by Dorothy West. *David and Lisa* remade a 1962 classic of the same name. *Tuesdays with Morrie* won three Emmy awards, including one for Outstanding Made-for-Television Movie. All except *Beloved* and those projects under the "Oprah Winfrey Presents" logo appeared with the endorsement of nonprofit organizations. I will look more closely at the production and critical narratives surrounding the making of Toni Morrison's *Beloved* later in this chapter.

In September 1996 Winfrey launched the monthly "Oprah's Book Club" feature on her talk show. Its success gave an "atomic-powered boost" to sales of books selected and the authors themselves.[34] For example, the first book featured, Jacquelyn Mitchard's *The Deep End of the Ocean,* soared from an initial printing of one hundred thousand to eight hundred thousand after its announcement as a book club selection.[35] This ability to translate profits—to just speak it and have it be—gave Winfrey the status of a higher being. In fact, Vicki Abt called her a god, saying, "She has probably the highest Q [popular identification] rating of anyone on television. There may be better interviewers and smarter people elsewhere on TV, but no one markets charisma like Oprah does."[36]

While couched within the context of media moguls or media changes, *Variety, Broadcasting and Cable, Forbes,* and *Fortune* closely monitored the finances of this woman and of Harpo Productions. Similar to the coverage of professional Black athletes, Harpo Productions and Winfrey were discussed in terms of net worth and contracts. The racialized chutzpah of money and blackness propelled media propaganda about her. In other words, Winfrey's propensity to draw large sums of money both fascinated and appalled. Disgust came not so much in the amount of money per se (although that had a significant part) but more through ongoing arguments for racial reparations sought by some Black American citizens and a Caucasian sense that equality has been achieved. These types of production/economic narratives fed and merged with the scholarly to forward popular discourses.

THE POPULAR

Popular texts surrounding the Oprah Winfrey phenomenon have covered the star-generated projects, gossip, and fandom not addressed in the previous two arenas. From the beginning, articles appeared in magazines ranging from *Good Housekeeping, People,* and *Ebony* to *Ms., Nation, Time,* and *Essence.* Over twelve books have been written about Winfrey, specifically, and the talk show more generally. Many, quite tabloid-like, narrativize her life, increasing her fame. Several of these texts provide limited or no documentation and assume validation through pictures from *The Oprah Winfrey Show,* her character Sophia in *The Color Purple* (Spielberg, 1985), or Winfrey accepting one of several Emmy awards.

Her "rags to riches" story aired on the talk show through discussions of weight; her longtime suitor/fiancé, Stedman Graham; health; and wealth. Home, hairstylists, and favorite dishes were also popular narrative fodder. The personal and intimate details of her life came to existence through the realm of the popular. Even on the Internet she has received cultural and Web space in the form of tributes by fans, star biographies, promotions by stations airing the talk show, and through the *TV Guide* international schedule.[37] Her own site, www.oprah.com, promoted her talk show format, viewer participation, and new projects. John Fiske suggests that many of the sites related to fandom are cultural forums denigrated by the dominant value system. Thus through these fan formations the talk show became further associated with the cultural taste of disempowered people, the people Christians assert will be saved.[38]

For her role as Sophia in *The Color Purple* Winfrey received Oscar and Golden Globe nominations, as well as being named Woman of Achievement by the National Organization for Women in June 1986. Her role of Bigger Thomas's mother in *Native Son* (Jerrold Freeman, 1986) failed to receive the same accolades but kept her in the forefront of American cinematic consciousness. These acutely racialized, gendered, and age-specific roles did not tarnish her star status. In fact, a 1988 survey asked college students to give descriptors most frequently associated with television talk show hosts. For Oprah Winfrey they characterized her by her appearance and her concern.[39]

Although Winfrey distinctly personifies the accoutrements of success, her name and figure escape many of the stereotypical constructions of others who look like her, the damning relations of those as wealthy as her, and the pigeonholing of those as famous. This may be because of the sense of crisis that accompanies the construction of what Richard Dyer calls star texts. How stars speak to, embody, or condense crisis may reaffirm the "reality of people as individuals or subjects over against ideology and history, or else in terms of exposing precisely the uncertainty and anxiety concerning the definition of what a person is."[40] This need for crisis (and dialogue thereof) forwarded Winfrey's narratives.

In multiple unauthorized biographies Winfrey's rise from abject poverty to the *Forbes* fortune list predominated. Also popular was her own self-distancing from "blackness." She was quoted amply as not being into "that stuff" (dashiki-wearing, "power to the people" mantras) when in college, preferring to foster "excellence" as the key to combating racism, framed as if the two sit in opposition. Nods toward bootstrapping (à la Clarence Thomas and Anita Hill) loomed just below the surface. Yet Dana Cloud's analysis of these popular discourses found that tokenism promoted by Winfrey's stories elided the real-life barriers to success and wealth confronted by the majority of African-Americans.

Cloud suggests that this tokenism participates in the "hegemony of liberal capitalism in so far as it acknowledges black voices, but redefines oppression as personal suffering and success as individual accomplishment."[41] This idea harkens to Coco Fusco's expression of difference (see chapter 1) and to bell hooks's assessment of poverty and Black communities' historic response (see chapter 4). Similar to many now successful marginalized members, Winfrey's figure helped to lessen the significance of economic, racial, and cultural disparities. Moreover, within and through *The Oprah Winfrey Show* and her image, the dual selves of Oprah Winfrey confronted America's ability to just get along.

THE OPRAH WINFREY SHOW AND THE WOMAN BEHIND IT

Americans' love affair with this Black woman began with her talk show and her role in *The Color Purple*. Winfrey began her rise to iconic status when *The Oprah Winfrey Show* initially aired as *AM Chicago* in 1983. In the first six months the ratings for her show beat then reigning Phil Donahue in the same time slot. The King World Distribution Company saw the program and her appearance in *The Color Purple*. They approached the twenty-six-year-old Winfrey about syndicating her program nationally. In Winfrey, King World saw someone to compete against the virtually solo *Donahue*. Taking up the gauntlet, *The Oprah Winfrey Show* began broadcasting nationally in September 1986.[42] On initial syndication *The Oprah Winfrey Show* carried 120 stations. By the end of its first season the talk show held the number one rating position for daytime talk.

As *Donahue* provided the format for the daytime talk show's interactive style, Winfrey's program served as the progenitor to talk content as currently articulated. Winfrey supplied a warm, loving, and inviting space for viewers (women) and the in-studio audience to come and discuss their problems, concerns, secrets, and successes before millions. Aimed at a specific demographic, the show addressed and captured that audience in an unprecedented fashion. Coming to national attention on civil rights/affirmative action gains and battling (albeit subtly) Reagan/Bush attempts to reverse them, the show became the narrativization of one Black woman's life. This point proved to be imperative to her rise.

In succinct Americanesque storytelling Winfrey, the woman, grew up poor, struggled, overcame, and succeeded. Not trying to minimize or make light of her circumstances and successes, this brief account sums up her story. For marginalized folks dreaming of America, success must follow this type of narrativized trajectory. If the pitfalls had not occurred, similar situations would have been created. Indeed, it is the mandatory condition of the American dream. Like music video artists, talk show hosts submit to careful construction. Perhaps this construction aligns more closely with the actual lives of the hosts, but they are fashioned in a way that will make the host similar to the consumer, leaving room for and endorsing achievement. Although access to the American dream remained restrictive, scenarios such as Winfrey's were not unheard of for Black women growing up in this country in the late 1950s. Winfrey's tribulations began with her own conception.

Born to unmarried, teenaged parents, she suffered the shame of illegitimacy but benefited from the embracing of family. Although the phenomenon of children conceived by unmarried parents was fairly common in the United States, the progeny of that coupling often sustained open condemnation. For Afro-Americans W.E.B. Du Bois claims that a "red stain of bastardy" meant not only the loss of ancient African chastity but also held racialized implications of "the hereditary weight of a mass of corruption from white adulterers, threatening almost the obliteration of the Negro home."[43] This imagery played itself out in the public persona of Winfrey and other Black women. It underlies Halle Berry's and Mariah Carey's biracial status, Salt-N-Pepa's out-of-wedlock children, and Tawana Brawley's and the now defunct *Emerge* writer Lori Robinson's rape. It surfaced also within the context of Winfrey's show and other similar details of her life's tale. The importance of discussing these personal narratives was that they, particularly, became a part of Winfrey's talk show and iconic persona.

Most critiques extended from these personal tragic accounts. Criticisms of her talk show ranged from personal infusion to openly soliciting confessions without professional knowledge to handle them. But the judgment most pertinent to my argument was one that charged Winfrey with denying her blackness to ensure commercial success. Many African-Americans believed that Winfrey hugged more Whites than Blacks and befriended them more readily. For example, in a 1989 segment her guests included parents whose children had been fatally shot accidentally. Accidental shootings and gun control (which in and of itself bore a racialized component) were the topics. Winfrey, in tears, sat between a colored (Latina) woman and a White couple mediating and negotiating the ideological position of gun control and the personal feelings of loss.[44] In her brown body Winfrey effectively stood in for nonrepresented Black women who have lost their children through gunfire. But within a White articulation/framework of the problem, she decolorized it to assume salvation status. In other words, by embodying both the notion of mother and motherless with multiracialness, she positioned herself as someone for all people.

Like her audience, most of Winfrey's staff were White women. Winfrey justified and likened this racial composition to the viewership of her program. The demarcation between Winfrey's colored body and her White audience proved her ability to cross racial lines not only thematically but also through the use of her own body.

The girth of this body, her weight, probably represented Winfrey's predominate discussion segment, promotion ploy, and personal challenge in the show's first ten years. When *The Oprah Winfrey Show* began, Winfrey, at five feet seven inches, weighed 190 pounds. She lamented in the popular press, "I'm overweight. People tell me not to lose weight, I might lose my personality. I tell them, 'Honey it ain't in my thighs.'"[45] Often using her battle with weight gain as a springboard, she claimed that the turning point in her approach to weight came under the looking glass of a public event, the acceptance of the 1992 Emmy for best daytime talk show. Upset and depressed at her winning because of the necessity to go onstage, she wondered if someone was looking at the enormity of her butt. At the time she wore a size 24.[46]

Winfrey's weight and epiphanic experiences surrounding it commanded screen time and space, even beyond the talk show. As I pointed out in chapter 2, television condemns and devalues fat. Its enormity denies productivity and seems to allow women to take up too much space. Jeremy Butler argues, however, that Delta Burke's Suzanne in *Designing Women* became feminist in direct response to her weight gain. He remarks that Suzanne "shed the masquerade of femininity that women must preserve if they wish to remain visible *and powerful* in patriarchal culture."[47] Roseanne Barr, in person and in performance, reveled in the girth of her body, and Kathleen Rowe noted a power in Barr's self-described feminine fat and unruly laughter. But these women, in their anomalous bodies, retained the normality, the "possessive investment," of whiteness.[48]

With no such defense or cover Winfrey allowed America's obsession with thinness and youth to define her approach to weight. Ironically, although her weight fluctuations incited laughter in comedy, they helped to retain her power and popularity with everyday women. With a personal trainer and chef, Winfrey stabilized her weight by 1995. Both the trainer and the cook produced best-selling books based on their work with Winfrey. Indeed, the topics on *The Oprah Winfrey Show* and her own discourses played an important role in the construction of Winfrey as icon but also in rethinking Black womanhood and multiculturalism.

OPRAH, THE MULTICULTURAL ICON

Labeling Oprah Winfrey an icon of American success and credible voice requires definition and grounding. According to C. S. Peirce and Peter Wollen, icons are formed through linguistic sign systems that imply that language and meaning do not necessarily have direct correlation.[49] To Wollen the iconic is, "a sign which represents its object mainly by its similarity to it; the relationship between signifier and signified is not arbitrary but is one of resemblance or likeness."[50] As I mentioned earlier, Dana Cloud maintains that Winfrey's iconic positioning arose only through the rhetoric of tokenism. Cloud asserts that "liberal individualism requires the 'rags-to-riches' story as 'proof' that the dream of the individual achievement against all odds is real. This dream, in turn, justifies continuing inattention to structural factors, like race, gender, and class, that pose barriers to the dream for some Americans."[51] Yet in her Colored, big/small gendered body, Winfrey took on all the binaries and contradictions of the American dream for racialized, gendered, lower-classed, and sexualized Others. She epitomized the "give me your tired, your poor, your huddled masses" mantra of America. She became the Dream incarnate.

Beyond this, the rhetoric of multiculturalism turned increasingly from understanding, teaching, and accommodating difference to appreciation. Food, music, clothes, and arts became the essence of multiculturalism with the same hierarchical and privileging structures firmly in place. The social conservative movement astutely made multiculturalism synonymous with quotas, reverse discrimination, language, and anti-Americanness. Winfrey, however, eluded these distinctions by embracing and denying stigmas.

Even in a topic as superfluous as the "MTV Dance Party" Winfrey both defined and contained the -isms.[52] In the segment she defied stereotypes of Blacks' natural rhythm. She has none, nor can she sing. She possessed knowledge of contemporary cultural product but struggled with nouveau lyrics and beats. Her clothes reflected current trends but were not always suited to her frame. These types of minor, maybe superficial, contradictions signified larger ones that Winfrey strategically internalized, manipulated, and then exemplified as uniquely her own.

Certainly other iconic figures have emerged in American culture. Almost always appearing through the arts (music, literature, film, television) they include such figures as Marilyn Monroe, Elvis Presley, and, more recently, Madonna and O. J. Simpson. Perhaps the ability to say the icon's first name and have instant recognition across race, gender, generation, and class gives rise to their iconic stature. Yet only Madonna rivaled the space Winfrey occupied in the late twentieth century and in the psyche of national culture. Both singer and actress, through her own self-promotion and transgressive actions, Madonna inverted (or at least challenged) America's notions of sex, gender, and power. Madonna publicized her appropriation of the unspoken and taboo areas of America's moralist rhetoric and capitalized on it through the scandalization and titillation of the consumer.

Some have argued, however, that Madonna's insistence on solidarity with marginal groups and on moving between worlds was duplicitous. Dan Rubey suggests that she "presents herself as a female icon of white power functioning without sign or against white men. In this context, the assertion, 'It makes no difference if you're black or white, if you're a boy or a girl' seems cynical rather than naive."[53] bell hooks believes that her "power to the pussy" credo worked only to solidify Madonna's positioning on the backs of the marginalized. But Madonna, as producer of cultural ambiguity and openness, which was her profit center, marketed Madonna the performer. The sexual icon she constructed may indeed, then, accord power to the pussy.[54]

Yet despite Madonna's influence, her iconic status markedly differed from Winfrey's and in some ways was eclipsed by Winfrey's presence in American culture. In the 1990s Madonna's popularity declined. Lamenting that decline, Andrew Ferguson suggested that her "real crime" had been longevity. He maintained that "[t]he revolution craves novelty; it is rooted in the short attention span. And because its craving never slackens, it must create new icons and dismantle old ones with amazing speed."[55] But I suggest that the difference between Madonna et al. and Winfrey surfaced through Winfrey's ability to attack and control variant consumer visual venues.

Although all of the iconic figures mentioned were performers, including Winfrey, most lacked the ability to transcend their initial contact with the American spectator. Only Winfrey far exceeded her initial impact with television talk. She possessed a different persona. She acts, owns a production company (and restaurant, magazine, cable channel, and Web site), donates substantial amounts of money and time to various causes, and holds a college degree. These spaces not only mark her difference but also her scope and ability to reach ever more diverse sectors of the United States and the world. Even within this book, deciding whether to reference her by last name or the "Oprah" moniker sparked debate and reflection, a testament to the pervasiveness of her figure. Like religion, Winfrey assumed an omniscient presence, to be everywhere at once and to be all things to many. This religious resonance pervaded all her media forums and helped shape America's response to her.

THE IMPACT OF CHRISTIANITY

Alongside the free-love movement, the rise in religious fundamentalism grew steadily from the 1970s. Codified in social conservatism, it attacked multiple fronts simultaneously—politics, education, and media. Much of its rhetoric, particularly of the far right, positioned race, sexuality, and changing gender roles at the center of what's wrong with America. Dan Quayle's bemoaning of the "poverty of values" was only part of a larger move to restore the country to its previous hierarchical, conservative, and Eurocentric order. Prayer in schools, abortion, and gay rights were some of its core issues. By 1994 a study found that 90 percent of Americans considered themselves religious with 93 percent of those claiming Christianity.

Religious media became one of the most prevalent means to further the Moral Majority's agenda, reach backsliders, and make new converts. The National Religious Broadcasters organization claimed over thirteen hundred radio stations and television channels by 2000. With historic ties to religion and spirituality already, African-Americans, and especially Black women, faced a unique dilemma to this growing tide.

Against this backdrop a debate of Christianity's viability for African diasporic people began to rage in academic communities. One film of the period, Haile Gerima's *Sankofa* (1992), challenged the role of Christianity in the United States and its relationship to Africans in America, particularly. In this fiction about a Black American successful model in Ghana for a photo shoot, Gerima transports this woman metaphorically to pre-emancipation, where she confronts her blackness, the past, and its relationship to her future—all through the bonds of slavery. Christian doctrine served as a fundamental theme of this film to justify and maintain slavery. One biracial character (his mother a slave, his father an overseer) kills his mother in the name of God. Ultimately, the film questioned whether Christianity should hold a place for African-Americans wanting to remove the figurative shackles from their minds and souls.

Yet many African-American scholars fought the perennial charge that Christianity, as a compensatory and otherworldly religion, distracted Negroes from their tenuous American predicaments, as it encouraged them to accept their lot as the will of God, to "take this world but give me Jesus." Albert Raboteau writes that the Black men and women he remembers growing up with spoke with righteous anger and prophetic certainty about the destruction awaiting this nation unless it repented from the evil of racism. In that same vein he urges that "[a]ny form of Christianity that condones slavery or racial discrimination is to that extent false and will be punished[—]Ain't everybody talking 'bout heaven, gonna go to heaven."[56] Regardless of one's position, the idea of Christianity's fundamental necessity to the nation and the lives of the people elevated figures like Oprah Winfrey.

American evangelists such as Oral Roberts, Robert Schuller, Jerry Falwell, Jimmy Swaggart, Pat Robertson, and Creflo Dollar took their pulpits to the altar of television. Organizations such as Concerned Women for America, the Family Resource Council, and the Christian Coalition formed and mobilized to impress the word of Jesus on a drifting world and to castigate those outside of their "divine" interpretation. All of these so-called prophets prepared the American audience for a figure such as Winfrey—not in a one-leads-the-other way but as phenomena that mutually fed and forwarded each other. Through her sense and use of familiar Christian practices—testimony, catharsis, touch, resurrection, and salvation (her own spiritual, televisual style)— Winfrey gave voice to the unspeakable for intellectuals and atheists and confirmation for believers.

CONFESSION AND TESTIMONY

A part of Winfrey's style emerged through the use of confession and testimony. Confession makes up part of the Catholic principles of sacrament and penance. As articulated, God's grace and forgiveness come through the confession of sin to an ordained priest, who then directs, blesses, and forgives on God's behalf.[57] The confession always begins, "Forgive me Father for I have sinned," followed by admission of the sins of action, thought, and heart. This type of confessional practice appeared often in the talk show, particularly in the early *Oprah Winfrey Show* programs, and has been taken up by copycat programs spawned hence.

In 1985, for example, one of the most discussed confessional episodes occurred when an incest guest confessed that she had been raped by her own father. With that admission Winfrey broke into tears and called for a commercial break. On the show's return Winfrey revealed that at nine years old, she too had been raped by an older cousin. This confession, this on-air disclosure, drew 878 telephone calls to the show.[58] People accosted Winfrey on the street to thank her for bringing to light a secret they shared and endured. Early talk show confessions like this fueled the deluge of programs that succeeded hers in the late 1980s and 1990s.

With the introduction of talk shows hosted by the likes of Geraldo Rivera, Jenny Jones, Sally Jesse Rafael, Ricki Lake, Montel Williams, Morton Downey Jr., and Jerry Springer assorted sexual, relationship, self-centered, and work practices poured from the mouths and screens of the American public. In these programs no small amount of African-American women and men aired as defrauders of the welfare system, cheaters on their spouses, carriers of alternative men's children, and exhibitionists, all targeted at White women's consumption. One climactic case came from a murder resulting from a confession on *Jenny Jones*.[59] By the end of 1994 Winfrey publicly announced her disgust of the talk forum and vowed to rid hers of the "sleaze" factor. This change was visualized largely through another religious practice, testimony.

Winfrey's subsequent guests subscribed to the Protestant/Black Christian practice of testifying rather than to the confessional practices of Catholicism. The corollary to confession, testimony receives validation and actualization within the preponderance of television talk shows through celebratory pieces of success, ordinary heroes, miraculous deflections of death, and celebrity transformations. Yet for Black women on *Ricki, Jenny Jones,* and *Jerry Springer* their testimonies remained in the framework of stories that objectified their sexual and bodily travails.

Winfrey accelerated her commitment to affirming stories when she introduced "Change Your Life TV," the theme for her 1998–1999 season. The host turned singer in the show's opening credits. In the music video–like scenario, Winfrey stands/dances at a microphone surrounded by an ethnically diverse, young, pop choir. She says, "What I believe is that we all are looking for something deeper, greater."[60] This new program thrust, as the words at the beginning of the chapter indicate, was on making audiences' lives better through the uniting of spirit, mind, and body. In some ways Winfrey offered a nod to "new age" religion, with weekly appearances by the author of *Men Are from Mars, Women Are from Venus*, John Gray; Dr. Philip McGraw; and author Iyanla

FIGURE 32

Winfrey on the set of
The Oprah Winfrey Show

Vanzant, a Yoruba priestess whose 1993 *Acts of Faith* had more than seven hundred thousand copies in print. Winfrey's official Web site confirmed that, indeed, Winfrey recognized and assumed a certain spiritual testament and responsibility. Between changing people's lives and Oprah's Angels, this icon looked to make a difference.[61] This new direction, this new Oprah, overtly positioned Winfrey as a religious figure (fig. 32).

FIRE IN THE BONES: CATHARSIS, HOLY SPIRIT, AND THE LAYING ON OF HANDS

I have mentioned that criticism of Winfrey in Colored communities sometimes suggested that she favored her White guests and audience members over her Negro ones. Beyond language and quantity of Colored guests, this charge had some grounding in the quantity of touch she bestowed on guests. The religious denotation of the laying of hands on a person involves the transference of the Holy Spirit or Holy Ghost from one person to another in order to heal, cure, liberate (from curse), or relieve.

The general secretary of the National Council of Churches, Joan Brown Campbell, explained that the laying on of hands is an ancient form of ministry filled with spiritual richness. It symbolizes the outpouring of God's spirit through those present to one who is facing a time of crisis.[62] One audience member remarked that Winfrey touches people and that everybody needs touch in their lives. Touching seems to provide a space and means for catharsis to occur. Winfrey's touches, literally and visually, connected her to both the specific audience member and the at-home spectator. For people who lacked touch in their day-to-day lives this televised figure achieved a certain tactility.

This assessment may exude a Hallmark feel, yet many have used the power of touch to both embrace and condemn African-American women. Negra touches were invited into the homes of White Americans whose babies needed nursing and whose children needed raising. In Black homes the same rules have applied. Touch has received validation to harvest food, cultivate the lives of children in segregated schools, and rock abandoned crack babies in hospitals. Conversely, however, tactility endured condemnation when these same women possessed too much melanin, were designated as whores (at least in public), or retained too much education, drive, or attitude. Winfrey's tactility harbors a perceived healing quality normally reserved for White religious persons, the visualized White Jesus himself, whereas the racial component of her being was relegated to the nurturing and historic comforts of mammy.

RESURRECTION

Winfrey's biblical associations did not confine themselves to her talk show persona. They pervaded all of the discourses and visual manifestations that created her figure. In *The Color Purple* (1985), for example, the potential volatility of its White director, Steven Spielberg, visioning a Black woman's story and the issues presented brought to the forefront many of America's foibles, even though the story is set in the past. According to media of the time, Winfrey enjoyed her television talk show because of her success at it. But with acting, she felt that "you lose your personality in favor of the character you're playing but you use it to provide energy for your character."[63]

Alice Walker's *The Color Purple* (1982) chronicles the lives of several women and their relationships to a family of men, male culture, and themselves. But unlike the book, the film revolves solely around issues of power, particularly men's power over women, home, and sexuality. For example, in the book Celie and Shug engage in an intimate, passionate, and long-lasting lesbian relationship that the film barely acknowledges. Further, Walker incorporates a strong, anti-Christian, pro-God sentiment within the text. The film, however, revises the anti-Christian plot. These religious and sexual subversions, particularly as they impact Shug's behavior and sexuality, illuminate the lack of sexual power simultaneously accorded and denied to African-American women. They show also the impact this constant denial has on Black women and men's relationships in visual culture.[64] The denial of sexual freedom along with moral condemnation was critical to the disempowerment of African-American women and the elevation of a Christian ethos.

With this revisionist tactic in mind Winfrey played a central character in the construction of the film and, within it, offered the possibility of resurrection (fig. 33). One poignant scene opens with a shot of a white dinner plate with Sophia's (Winfrey) face reflected in it. At first the reflection and plate are

FIGURE 33

Winfrey as Sophia in *The Color Purple*

indistinguishable. When the shot widens to frame her full figure, the spectator sees that Sophia appears either asleep or subdued, rocking gently in her chair without speaking. This scene is the family's Thanksgiving meal celebration. Squeak (Rae Dawn Chong) asks Sophia how she feels. She replies, "Confused." Harpo (Willard E. Pugh) questions, "Aren't you glad to be home?" She responds, "Maybe." While the scene's dramatic tension actually concerns Celie's (Whoopi Goldberg) breaking away from Mister (Danny Glover), Sophia's presence confers a Christian ethos.

Celie calls Mister "dead horse shit," causing Squeak to laugh. The camera cuts to Sophia as she begins to stare meekly at Celie. Harpo commands Squeak to shut up, saying, "You know it's bad luck for a woman to laugh at a man." This declaration brings forth laughter from Sophia, a slow, loud, continuous, and solitary chortle. Her laughter silences everyone. Mr.'s daddy (Adolph Caesar) turns slowly toward her and remarks, "My God. The dead has arisen." With that, Sophia recounts the misery of her jail time: "I know what it like Miss Celie. Wanna go somewhere and cain't. I know what it like wanna sing, have it beat out ya. I want to thank you Miss Celie, for everything you done for me. . . . When I see'd you, I know there is a God . . . and one day I'se goin get to come home."

The possibility of resurrection has been key to African-Americans' ability to survive in the United States. Resurrection became a central mantra during Reconstruction. Reminiscent of Scarlett's declaration before God in *Gone with the Wind* (1939), Sophia's resurrection and her laughter made profound and progressive statements about Black women and their ability to survive and insert themselves into patriarchy, despite Spielberg's reconceptualization of the text. Thereby, Winfrey as Sophia and as a spiritual icon symbolized the possibility of resurrection.

Jacqueline Bobo examined Black women's responses to this film and literary text in *Black Women as Cultural Readers*.[65] Following the scene in which Sophia packs up her children in order to leave Harpo, the women in Bobo's study came to an interesting verdict about fictionalized representation and real-life situations:

Phyllis: You folks be talking about she [Celie] should have gone with her [Sophia], but you have to remember, girlfriend's mouth got her in jail for a while.

Whitney: That's true. Well, you gotta do what you gotta do. It's all about integrity.

Phyllis: First, it's about survival. Then it's about integrity.[66]

Therein lies the dilemma: whether to suffer in silence either through racialized, gendered, generational, or sexualized tropes and to, at some level, be saved, or to speak your mind and endure the consequences, which may be fatal. Inevitably, Sophia was punished for speaking her mind in this narrative, and the other Black women endured some form of oppression. Yet it was Sophia's specific oppression that represents issues of sight and, more poignantly, sound.

In the role of Sophia Winfrey occupied that anonymous space of the inner eye that I discussed in chapter 2. Sophia became a literal servant, but, more significant, within this designated sphere she failed to receive recognition (as in the scene with Miss Millie in the store and car). Although new to the visual realm, Winfrey used the words written by Alice Walker and the art of performance to secure her own resurrection from dire circumstances connected to her own biography. As borne out in subsequent visual texts, Winfrey's personal tragedies paralleled and equaled Sophia's, forcing the tangential connection linking the character in the film, the host of the talk show, and the actual lived narrative of Oprah Winfrey. These connections suggested that if Oprah could rise after all her trials, certainly the members of her audience could too.

SALVATION

According to Cooper-Lewter and Mitchell, everyone possesses a belief system that enunciates certain value judgments. Whether expressed or kept within, "an assumption inescapably involving some sort of faith determines all conscious choices and influences all unthinking response."⁶⁷ In the biblical text of Mark the demon-possessed, the leper, the paralytic, the dying child, the hemorrhaging woman, and the blind man all, in the face of apparent hopelessness, received divine blessings and mercy through God's freeing them from their pains and problems.⁶⁸ In this century these same types of individuals, broken through the loss of children, abandoned by friends, and alienated from society's norms, found themselves on and spectators of the talk show. The producers strove for a certain salvation-like peace at the end of each installment of *The Oprah Winfrey Show*, at least visually. For example, on the 1992 coming out day segment for abusive parents, tears flowed, confessions and apologies were offered, and testimonials were given. In this milieu Winfrey represented a saving grace, a conciliator. She brought warring parties together, initiated and directed the touch of flesh, and asked appropriate questions to elicit salvific responses.⁶⁹

Outside the confines of the talk show Winfrey represented salvation through her philanthropy. In September 1994 she announced her "Families for a Better Life" program, which literally attempted to rescue people from the life of poverty inhabited by members and residents of Chicago's inner city (that is, the areas where poor Blacks and Latinos live). Although Winfrey gave a considerable amount of money to initiate the program, it ceased operations after helping only five families.⁷⁰ In 1997 she challenged viewers to volunteer to help build 202 houses with Habitat for Humanity, one house in every city where a station carried *The Oprah Winfrey Show*. Donating monies to educational institutions and nonprofit children's organizations, Winfrey sought to make a difference, in cash. Interestingly, even when her efforts failed, as they did with Families for a Better Life, the failure inconsequentially impacted the perception of Winfrey's salvation ability. Winfrey was seen as a giver, but beyond financial philanthropy. She appeared to give of herself. In essence, then, salvation came to those who believed and followed her example. *The Oprah Winfrey Show*'s shift in focus from "Get with the Program" to "Change Your Life TV" confirmed it.

Beyond her prominence as a spiritual icon Winfrey pursued her dreams of stardom. In 1989 Winfrey's Harpo Productions produced Gloria Naylor's *Women of Brewster Place*. This four-hour, two-part television special showcased Naylor's novel with Winfrey as coexecutive producer. Winfrey starred as the central character, Mattie Michael, in a cast of African-American actresses who found themselves in a poor tenement on a street blocked by a brick wall. The program opens and closes with Mattie framed in the middle of a hole created by the women finally fed up with the horror of their lives.

Despite the visual flaws in Winfrey's aging process,⁷¹ the project made a significant statement. The financial and popular wherewithal to bring a story

FIGURE 34

Kimberly Elise, Oprah Winfrey as Sethe, and Thandie Newton in *Beloved*.
(Courtesy of Touchstone Pictures. Photo by Ken Regan/Camera 5)

about Black women to television spoke to the political and economic American culture of the late 1980s and the commercialization of Black women's stories. By then Black women seemed bankable. The main proponent of that profit was Winfrey herself.

Her most ambitious film project, however, has been the production of Toni Morrison's *Beloved*. Published in 1987, the book traces an escaped slave woman's encounters with her past, her present, and her future. For eleven years Winfrey struggled to produce a film version. She ultimately succeeded in 1998, bankrolling a coveted director who would allow her to assume the lead role of Sethe (fig. 34).

The film sets forth powerful iconography and performances to try to capture this painful and dense historical moment. However, audiences failed to value its efforts. Despite an enormous marketing blitz by Disney Communications and Winfrey herself,[72] the film ran only eight weeks. It generated just over $22 million, but it had cost $80 million to make.[73]

Critics faulted the surrealist nature, the "irrelevant protracted sequences, which sidestep the tragedy and pathos which should be its core,"[74] and, in some circles, Winfrey. Frank Rich complained that "the audience feared more sermon than drama from the increasingly more preachy Oprah."[75] I agree with some of this criticism, but the reality of the reasons for the film's failure goes deeper.

Despite Winfrey's popularity, this project positioned her squarely in her blackness. Beyond its economic agenda, slavery in the United States dehumanized one group of people (Black) for the sole benefit of another (White). Being 150-plus years past slavery's abolishment has failed to lessen its impact and has further shaped its legacy. Who can humanely reconcile Black women's bloody, beaten, and raped bodies and perceived animalistic tendencies (particularly those who still have Black and brown women in their kitchens and nurseries)? It seemed not many. Winfrey's recuperation of blackness at the expense of the multicultural impulse helped tank the film from the start.

OPRAH AS FICTIONALIZED NARRATIVE REFERENT

Beyond the discourses that circulated in the everyday lives of Winfrey's talk show viewers and her own acting forays, Hollywood utilized her omniscient name recognition for profit. In the blending of fact and fiction television comedy featured Winfrey, the actress, within their texts as "Oprah, the talk show host." The layers produced by this intertexuality harkened to both the historic nature of television and the postmodern aesthetic. But as I have shown, Winfrey moved beyond intertext to intratext. Winfrey's status coupled with her credibility made her opinions, her roles, and her personal life pervasive and intimately open to the spectator. In sitcoms and feature films Winfrey grounded self-referentiality and reality. She performed herself, was played upon, and used as a real-life construct in the world of fiction.

For example, in an episode of *The Fresh Prince of Bel-Air* the Banks family appear on *The Oprah Winfrey Show* (fig. 35). Winfrey plays "Oprah," the talk show

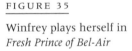

FIGURE 35

Winfrey plays herself in
Fresh Prince of Bel-Air

host, when the family comes as guests on a segment of political candidates. The episode, "A Night at the Oprah," illustrated once again why Winfrey became ingrained so firmly in the minds of the American public. She offers to buy Hilary a dress just like hers (in Hilary's size), features two families (one Black, one White), and draws out the secrets of her guests (Hilary living with Treavor, her fiancé). Even citizens who claimed not to watch television possessed an "Oprah" referential understanding.

An early *In Living Color* episode parodied Winfrey, *The Oprah Winfrey Show,* and her obsession with weight. The scene opens with Kim Wayans as Winfrey, dressed very elegantly in a blue silk dress, moving through the crowd. Announcing the day's subject, "men unable to commit," she comforts a young woman by pulling the girl onto her lap and rocking her. Returning to the audience, she opens a candy bar. She then begins to lament over her relationship with Stedman, to eat uncontrollably, and to rotisserie three whole chickens simultaneously, consoling herself by exclaiming, "Homeboy still throwing down in the bedroom."

Wayans as Winfrey gorges, cries, and rants about Stedman's spending her money and living in her condo. Visually, her body gradually expands, literally, as she yells, "Food is my lover; food is my friend." Presumably, the sheer weight of her enlarged body lifts her into the air outside of the frame until finally the body explodes, raining all types of food disgustingly to the ground. In this skit Wayans played the "Oprah legend" against the metanarratives that surrounded her. Food and fat, her relationship with Stedman Graham, her interaction with audiences, and her hybrid speech collided and exploded before the viewers' eyes.

These metanarratives not only formed a part of her star discourse but also, particularly in this case, lauded the Negro wit that helped frame and proclaim the Winfrey impact on the lives of African-Americans. In this instance Wayans's parody of Winfrey's performance confronted and extended the fiction in service to humor and grace. In mainstream television programming Winfrey was equally prevalent. For example, she served as Ellen's therapist in Degeneres's much-heralded coming-out episode, putting Winfrey on the cutting edge of cultural sexuality despite academic assessment otherwise.[76]

In cinema the beginning of *The Nutty Professor* (1996) played into the Winfrey mythos by dominating the fictional characters' dinner conversation. The Klump family (Eddie Murphy) are an obese, African-American, middle-class family, seemingly comfortable with their weight. The only concern comes from the eldest brilliant son, Sherman. When Sherman removes the skin from his chicken, the dinner conversation turns to America's obsession with weight. Father Klump exclaims, "You know where that come from? Watchin that damn TV. Every time you turn it on they got somebody on there talkin about lose weight. Get healthy. Get in shape. Got everybody lookin all anorexic talkin bout that's healthy. I know what healthy is."

As Father Klump rants, he piles his plate with greens, chicken, peas, and potatoes, followed by a dousing of gravy. Ironically, the fat content of this meal exemplifies one of the most pernicious causes of heart disease, obesity, and high blood pressure in Black communities. Nevertheless, the musing continues, and Winfrey becomes the subject of critical examination:

Father Klump:	And tell you somethin else. I don't know why everybody tryin to lose weight in the first place. Ain't everybody suppose to be the same size. We supposed to be all different. Big. Small. Medium. Midgets. You supposed to have all that . . . Like that Oprah Winfrey. She gone lose her weight. Whatn't nothin wrong wit her. She was fine. Oprah was a fox. She lost all that weight, her head look all big, skin hangin all off her . . . Oprah and Luther need to keep their ass one way cause I'm confused.
Mother Klump:	Yes, I hope nothing's wrong with Oprah. She doesn't look real.
Grandmother Klump:	Ain't nothin wrong with Oprah. I seen Oprah on *Hard Copy* last week. Was the picture of health. Got her a tall, young, strong gentleman named Stedman, so handsome . . .

These constant references to Winfrey's real and constructed selves fuse fiction and reality.

NEXT, ON OPRAH

The figure of Oprah Winfrey exemplified the psychosis of American society in the latter part of the twentieth century. For Black and White, dirt-poor and disgustingly rich, fat and thin, beautiful and unattractive, fiercely independent and completely dependent on male companionship, producer and consumer, this woman (and the man in her power) embodied and exploited accepted binaries. Although this ideological and polysemic displacement benefited the consumers of her texts (mostly White women in the case of the talk show), it virtually denied Winfrey's agency as a Black woman.

The surplus of her body, her presence, her talk, and her life marked out the territory of her iconic figure as individualistic, exemplary, and isolated. Winfrey personified a method for the coexistence of difference. She strove to present a moral and spiritual beacon for a country moving away from spiritual underpinnings as a sign of progress and intellectualism. The splitting of binaries across her body enabled her figure to move beyond the -isms. She achieved subjecthood while satisfying consumer demand. But the producer,

Winfrey herself, paid a price. She was absent in her presence. Standing on the ground of "excellence," her achievements were stripped from her colorized and gendered form and, in turn, were partially denied to women who look like her.

Winfrey bridged a gap that had been simply ignored for quite a long time. She encouraged victims of dubious circumstances to appear before a compassionate and similarly (but not identically) composed audience to hear them. The discussions on institutional problems (racism, sexism), relationship problems (marriage, adultery, dysfunction), and unspoken problems (rape, incest, molestation) touched nerves that ate at American consciousness. Although Phil Donahue's program covered similar categories, Donahue lacked the ability to move beyond the surface. Successful talk show hosts not only sympathize with but empathize with their audience and guests. Yeast production, for example, was not a topic of familiarity for Donahue.

Winfrey, like Jesus, placed herself in the framework of her guests and audience (often quite literally in the case of rape and weight issues), which endeared and promoted her as the voice for and the ear of the spiritual unseen and unspoken. However, as she continued to do this, to perpetually disclose information, her figure reinscribed sexist and racist constructions of Black womanhood. This propensity may eventually lead to her downfall. The beginning of this decline can be seen in spectators' responses to *Beloved* and in comments by Tom Shales, who says, "Of course Winfrey is wonderful and living-saintly and all things bright and beautiful. We all know that. But her evangelistic tendencies are beginning to spin out of control."[77]

Talk shows that emerged subsequent to *The Oprah Winfrey Show* featured Black women and lower-class Whites ad nauseam, often conflating the two. From young Negro girls impregnated by their sisters' husbands to those afraid of commitment (as in the *In Living Color* skit), African-American women represented the base and mythologized sexual vamps that permeated welfare debates, sexual harassment cases, and energized musical bodies. Talk show hosts Ricki Lake, Jenny Jones, and Jerry Springer exploited these women and their stories to get dramatic boosts in their ratings.[78] Lake would question incredulously, "You were pregnant, and he was only coming to sleep with you?" Her audience would respond, "Go Ricki! Go Ricki!" Even expressions such as these, extracted from Black talk, fed and fueled this kind of exploitation.

In these talk shows Black faces and bodies performed for predominately White audiences in a White, serialized context. Although most of the counselors, therapists, and audiences were White, the overwhelming proportion of guests on these shows were Black and Latina, poor, young, and unemployed. Jill Nelson describes these shows: "Young women of all colors are victims; or stupid, sex-addicted, dependent baby-makers, with an occasional castrating bitch thrown in. . . . It was initially interesting to see that a significant number of these couples are interracial, but the subtext quickly became clear: Penis-waving black men prey not only on black women who deserve/are used to it, but on White Women."[79] In her talk show and as her real star persona, Winfrey spoke in an inappropriate, private speech. Using terms of endearment, she comforted the broader American mainstream yet made them uncomfortable. Phrases such as "child," "girlfriend," "honey, please," beyond their tangential relationship to the South, erected notions of mythic internal relationships between African-Americans themselves that incorporated Whites.

The splitting of the American psyche played itself out across Winfrey's body. Few Americans remained unaware of Winfrey's success story. The discourses surrounding her personal, professional, and production life were documented on the television and through popular publishing. Her life story began in poverty, strife, abuse, and neglect then bloomed into Cinderella's night at the ball and an ongoing dance with the prince. Only in this case Winfrey served as both the Colored Cinderella and Prince Charming. She helped create the vision and guided its progress. After the ball Cinderella and the prince stormed visual fronts and conquered a good portion of them. Quintessentially American, the dream became accessible through Oprah Winfrey along with the contentious identity issues that buttressed that dream. Consequently, the dichotomies that divided her body never departed but dangled the potential to unite across difference.

EPILOGUE

African-American Women
in Twenty-first Century X

It is a waste of time hating a mirror or its reflection instead
of stopping the hand that makes the glass with distortions.

—Audre Lorde, "Good Mirrors Are Not Cheap"

. . . the voices of women and men from my old neighborhood
[remind] me never to forget from when and whom I came.
They don't say, "Feel guilty." They say only, "Remember."

—Gloria Wade-Gayles, "When Race Is
Memory and Blackness Is Choice"

I walk down the street and guys say, "Yo baby, yo baby, I'm
talking to you." . . . And when I don't speak, they say, "Yo,
fuck you 'cause you ain't fly anyway." I'm the type to turn
around and say, "Then why the fuck was you chasing me?"

—Roxanne Shanté, *Bulletproof Diva*

Let's keep it real here. I enjoy television. Whether it's the clever, parodic
commercial, the reality slash fiction slash reality show, the local news, or
Miss Cleo's infomercial, every aspect of the medium entices and provides entertainment.[1] It teaches something about the human condition, always. Call it
my guilty pleasure with scholarly backup. Thus, *Shaded Lives* is not meant to
solely bash commercial television for its failings. Rather, I think of this book as
an exploration, a quest to better understand the underaddressed and unex-
plained conflation of objectification and agency in television's portrayal of Black
women. It is also a beginning, a vehicle to encourage action in rectifying representations that do disservice to the world by providing limited vision.

The end of the twentieth century parodied Dickens's "best of times and worst
of times" with respect to living definitions of gender, race, class, and sexual orientation. During these decades of the postmodern push, cultural critics, legislators, and other invested citizens hoisted up diversity as a cure-all to the -isms
of daily living. Yet they often forgot that intellectual theories do little to ame-
liorate institutionalized health, economic, education, and legislative disparities.

As I examine images of African-American women, objectification emerges
as both a mandatory condition and a complex process. Sitcoms, music videos,

television news, and talk shows reflect the dialectic between objectification and agency, the negotiation between containment on the one hand and reappropriation and transgression on the other. By conforming to generic and economic television conventions, Black women in the twentieth century assumed roles that stabilized White normative standards. Against this dominant White patterning, blackness was defined. Further, objectification worked through ideology, particularly the myth and embodiment of the American dream. To find a national audience, some Negras mitigated racial specificity, negating racial and gender affiliation in order to gain prominence and success.

On the other hand, television exhibited Black women's ability to insert themselves into the larger cultural consciousness. This agency, in large measure, meant action. Black women talked and talked back, moved beyond appropriate speech, controlled or centered narratives, and redefined style-activated moments. Beyond these actions, Oprah Winfrey's and others' ability to visualize via ownership produced a subjectivity. Ironically, the findings show that in most instances objectification and agency are not true opposites. This in-between space, albeit slight, leaves room for advocating change.

WHAT HAPPENED?

Situation comedy provided ample examples of Negroes grinnin' and smilin', shuckin' and jivin' for Black folks and, by extension, Whites. The normality of whiteness framed Black-cast programs largely through stereotypes and reifications of minstrelsy. Negras found color-coded validation either through a hyper and overdetermined blackness (Sheneneh, Pam, Thea) or through nods to a certain White privilege (Gina, Hilary, Whitley). Herman Gray suggests that these programs excavated the menacing Black while lauding Otherness in lieu of difference. From appropriately effeminate dress and straight hair to "high yella" women and sanitized speech, Afro-American women could only tread in a world of comedic White ideals.

This book devotes a considerable amount of space to Black women's bodies with a focus on intragroup color conflicts, hair politics, and dress. Although some may argue against the relevance of narrative physicality, television is, after all, a visual medium. Preconceptions about women of color resided in mainstream psyches long before the articulation of words, making vision and viewing central in popular culture. Moreover, television portrayals offer perceptions and possibilities rather than what is (fig. 36). In *The Primacy of Perception* Maurice Merleau-Ponty suggested that the body serves as the site of outward human expression, "the visible form of our intentions." He maintains that "[e]ven our most secret affective movements, those most deeply tied to

Pam, Gina, and
Sheneneh engage in
one of their class- and
color-conflicted stances
in *Martin*.

humoral infrastructure, help to shape our perception of things."[2] Certainly, privileging bodily sites of humanity was crucial to interrogating the representational politics of Black women.

Although African-American women appeared within various television formats, they served predominately as narrative foil and cultural cliché—adding both colorized presence and irrelevancy to the pot. For example, Khandi Alexander as Catherine Duke in *NewsRadio* could only daydream about having Black coworkers in her lily-white sitcom work world.[3] Plus, this phenomenon was not confined to the sitcom. The sixth season of the award-winning drama *ER* found surgeon Peter Benton (Eriq LaSalle) being informed by his baby's mama (Lisa Nicole Carson) that their son may not, indeed, be his.[4] In the same season Jeanie Boulet (Gloria Reuben), a series regular, walks off unceremoniously into the Chicago night. No one noticed nor seemed to care about her departure.[5]

Cablers in the serial business, particularly Lifetime, HBO, and Showtime, have moved the bar slightly toward fuller representations. They recognize the economic benefit to making their programs reflect the look of the United States. At the turn of the century highly touted cable programs like *Any Day Now* and *Soul Food* emerged (fig. 37). The former program looks deeply into the lives of two women—one Black and one White—growing up in post–civil rights Alabama. The latter takes off from a film of the same name. It follows the lives of three African-American sisters and their families. Yet the prominence (and continuity) of these shows faces what may be the wave of the future. *Any Day Now* seemed positioned to directly compete with its Lifetime station mate, *Strong Medicine*. *Strong Medicine* featured the lives of two women doctors—one White, one Latina—in an urban environment.[6] Likewise, *Soul*

FIGURE 37

Soul Food on-line home page (2001)

Food was positioned constantly against its cable mate *Resurrection Boulevard,* the story of the boxing Santiago family from East Los Angeles. Entertainment seems disposed to replace rather than expand its Colored presentations.

From 1995 to 1997 *Living Single* was the most watched program by Negroes. It featured authorial Black feminine voices and furnished roles that centered the concerns of Black women. *Living Single* allowed for Black sexuality to transcend whorishness. It dislodged Colored women from the role of narrative prop and gave them subject status. But by 1998 it had been canceled because of low majority viewership ratings.

Further, although the end of 1999 found *The Parkers, Moesha, For Your Love,* and *Malcolm and Eddie* capturing top-ten spots in African-American households, these same programs failed to appear in the top one hundred of all others.[7] By fall 2001 only one program survived. Television comedy reflected the spaces where what is considered funny split along racial lines—maybe because it was also the only genre, beyond music video, where viewers could view more than one Colored at a time.

Already into the twenty-first century, music videos offer homegirls and hoochies as the predominate visual ideal. With virtually no lyrical voice, Colored women's bodies and their allusion to sex sell young consumers not only music product but also ideas of who Black women are or could be. The genre maintains a tremendous impact on the growth and success of African-American women artists. Plus, it resonates with young Black women (and men and Whites and others) who watch them. Joan Morgan argues in her book, *When Chickenheads Come Home to Roost,* that many of the choices made by Black women artists stem not only from the patriarchy of an evolving commercial environment but also from the struggles addressed (or unaddressed) in Black communities.

Across musical genres, the videos of Boyz II Men, 2 Live Crew, and Puff Daddy (P. Diddy) present scantily clad, light-skinned, long-haired, and silent Negras as living accoutrements of the entertainer's success. When these young women's mouths move, the masculine voice of the male artist (or writer) surfaces. Female artists themselves are not immune from these same television and recording structures, not even those few artists who hold the economic clout to make a claim for agency. And, indeed, some do. Progressive impulses came from artists like Da Brat, Foxy Brown, and Lil' Kim. However, their lyrics and videos reinscribe materialism and sex as commodity exchange. The bad bitch aesthetic carries out an industrial imperative that promotes Black female bodies as wholly and in parts sellable. Plus, as T.L.C. demonstrate on their release *Fanmail*, this newfound power fails to keep men from approaching them for a ménage à trois. Yes indeed, African-American women artists faced daunting challenges in the music industry when trying to assume a progressive stance. While still nodding toward capitalism, however, some managed to write lyrics and translate those words visually in ways that moved toward empowerment.

The idea of Black women as subjects advanced in the gender-bending music genius of Me'Shell NdegéOcello's lyrics, the bad girl dressed and acting like a bad boy; the reconstitution of looking relations in Salt-N-Pepa's *"Shoop"*; the demystifying and recuperation of women's sexual pleasure in Janet Jackson's *"Any Time, Any Place"*; and the blending of variant musical forms, bodies, and styles with the works of Lauryn Hill, Erykah Badu, Macy Gray, and Jill Scott. Further, African-American women's physical movements progressed beyond pure sexuality through their athleticism and hip-hop dance swerve, as in Mary J. Blige's *"You Remind Me–The Remix"* or many of Missy Elliott's cuts. Tracy Chapman, Whitney Houston, Janet Jackson, and Queen Latifah offered viable creative, intellectual, and business paths for establishing and maintaining agency, lyrical potency, marketing, and ownership.[8] Moreover, as Tricia Rose suggests, by listening and really hearing women rappers and other artists, an audience could learn much about the meaning and lives of Generation X.

These video times found White rocker Meredith Brooks, like many others, attempting to recuperate the female dog in presumably all of women's beings. In her song "Bitch" (1997) she sings, "I'm a bitch. I'm a lover. I'm a child. I'm a mother. I'm a sinner. I'm a saint. I do not feel ashamed. I'm your hell. I'm your dream. I'm nothing in between. You know you wouldn't want it any other way."[9] Okay. But instead of Brooks just being a bitch by herself, she punctuates her video with the bodies of Black women and men. An older Black woman in prayer and a Black familial couple represent Brooks being a bitch, perhaps explicitly visioning the space of real-life bitches.

I acknowledge that explicit lyrics that position Black women (and other women) as passive, inept, gold-digging hoes did not begin with Generation X. Johnny Taylor's "It's Cheaper to Keep Her" (1973), Prince's "Head" (not shampoo, 1980), and Marvin Sease's "Candy Licker" (1987) existed well before Jay-Z asked "can I get a fuck you to these bitches from all of my niggaz who don't love hoes? They get no dough."

Further, female entertainers have always kept up, in some measure, with gendered smack downs. Millie Jackson's "The Rap" (1974) and Gwen Guthries's "Ain't Nothing Going on but the Rent" (1982) made Amil's response to Jay-Z above, "Can I get a woop woop to these niggaz from all of my bitches who don't got love for niggaz without dubs," all the more understandable, disturbing, and predictable. But perhaps the difference in the latter part of the century was the visual component.

While artists of the past, both men and women, dished up the other in often raw fashion, it was all talk. As Noella Cain attests, in down-home nightclubs artists offered up many tantalizing ditties, but on record the lyrics were sanitized.[10] With music video the talk found backup in visual action. Remember the adage, children learn what they see, not what they hear? Further, the propensity and profit of publishing profanity found acceptance in this era. The major vehicle for this Black visioning, twenty-year-old Black Entertainment Television, was sold to Viacom at the end of 2000. With Viacom's incredible audience reach, now even more people can get a woop, woop to the detriment of African-American women!

Television news continued its perpetual castigation and elevation pendulum swing. Surgeon General Jocelyn Elders and Civil Rights Division nominee Lani Guinier entered the hall of shame for the championing of men's masturbation and suggesting that quotas may be necessary to balance an imbalanced world, respectively. Television news served as the genre in which objectification of Black women became the most totalizing. Once a news text began, objectifying forces seized and controlled the image trajectory. Both Vanessa L. Williams and Anita Hill were visually condemned for displaying a Colored sexuality—Williams for the allusion to it, Hill for the articulation of it. The coverage of welfare showed the persistent connection, degradation, and marginalization of Colored women's figures as a social identity. Societal anxiety with gender became displaced onto their Black bodies.

In January 1995 then–Speaker of the House Newt Gingrich cited welfare for turning young people into young animals, saying, "[T]here is a level of barbarism in this society that *we wouldn't have dreamed of as children.*"[11] ABC illustrated his point with what appeared to be Latino young men shooting at each other at a gas station. But these images were pre-Columbine, pre-Georgia, pre-Arizona, where the shooters, at least, were all White and affluent. Instead of welfare, these killings result from this particular society's foundation on constitutional gun rights, barbarism, and manifest destiny. From the genocide of American Indians to slavery of Africans to the actual and now virtual rape of Black women, Newt's American dreams have been nightmares to Colored folks. Since the shootings, not much has been said about the "welfare state."

Despite this inclination toward complete objectification, subjecthood was not impossible in television news. Black women claimed centrality through vigilance and rebuttal. African-American women producers and anchors interrupted the visual narratives not only with their own Colored and gendered presences but also through the selection of video illustrations and informed commentary. In these instances agency came both reactively and proactively.

Finally, in many ways the highly publicized construction of Oprah Winfrey encapsulated the contradictions of this book's subject. Her success came through an elision of race, gender, and class, while recuperating all of these identifying markers. Her iconic figure reflected the representations of Black women across genres. Through texts that defined her as "Oprah," as well as ones she created, the notion of a democratic, liberal, meritocratic ideal emerged. Her willingness to deny blackness made her particularly palatable and supremely consumable by mass audiences and to those who wrote about her.

Winfrey's popularity never waned. One fan told her, "I want to be a white Oprah." Winfrey responded, "You want to be a white Oprah? What does that even mean?" [12] Although Winfrey stood in the gap for the difficulties of living life as an African-American woman, her embodiment of said binaries left her only partially accessible to other Black women as a completely credible sign of empowerment.

On the other hand, Winfrey commanded recognition as subject. Through her economic leveraging of *The Oprah Winfrey Show*, Harpo Productions, and other media entities, she made her voice heard. She talked back through philanthropy and the courtroom while addressing issues that impacted Colored women directly. In her figure the theoretical ability to break binaries grounded itself.

TELEVISION'S FUTURE

If the personal TV and digital are the wave of television's future, then what representations will we see of Black women? Increasingly, television reflects and produces programs for White teenagers; middle-class, White businessmen; blue-collar, White midwesterners; and gay/lesbian White Generation Xers. Television executives also seem to have a target demographic called Black—programming for young, old, rich, poor, professional, unemployed, undereducated, or Ph.D.s indiscriminately.

The strategy for delivering Black consumers to advertisers is to view the needs, outlooks, and intelligences of thirty-five million people as homogenous. This thinking is evident with the newest network additions. Warner Brothers Television (WB) and United Paramount Network (UPN) entered the television landscape by once again appealing to Anglos but featuring African-Americans. The majority of their initial programming has featured Black-cast sitcoms with happy characters who possess readily solvable, sitcom concerns. I suspect increased majority viewership will find the networks moving in the way of Fox—whitewashing the screen while keeping black fringes in commercials, diegetic music, diegetic entertainment, and sports. Thus, the new television world centralizes whiteness and maleness, offering no substantial shift from the past—in these high-tech, TIVO times.

So what is African-American women's future in situation comedy (and other television fiction)? In a review of Donald Bogle's *Primetime Blues: African-Americans on Network Television,* John McWhorter considers the history of Blacks on television to be a clear sign that the "color line is ever dissolving in America." [13] In essence, Blacks who think like Bogle (and myself, I fear) will be remembered for "a time when black thought in America was unwittingly dominated by an appetite of self-defeat." [14] Perhaps it is defeatist to predict that television in the twenty-first century will not only look but also similarly reflect current motifs of African-American women and Coloreds in general. But given the history of this country, real change cannot come when narratives like the 1995 *Jefferson in Paris* transform Thomas Jefferson's and Sally Hemmings' master-slave coupling into a great romance. Maybe it's just me, but this revision of history seems to move our collective selves back in history rather than progressively toward an equitable and colorized future. [15]

For good or bad, the success of music video and music television makes palatable programs like HBO's *Pimps Up, Hoes Down* (1998). In this world of pimping, "Mr. Whitefolks" aside, Blacks dominate. In the program one pimp declares, "I gotta Ph.D.—a pimpin' hoes degree"; another comments, "You ain't servin no rotten mother fuckin product," in regard to women, their vaginas, and checkups. At the same time female pimp Big Lex was shown as a viable alternative. [16]

Within this nouveau documentary the same structures created to keep women in competition resurface. One prostitute defends her man against Big Lez, saying, "Ain't no hoe gettin my motherfuckin' money!" Presumably she feels this way because challenging a "motherfucking man" to get her earned money is without question.

Journalists and radio personalities such as Farai Chideya, Tavis Smiley, and Tom Joyner continue to take culture to task for distorted and limited portrayals by utilizing every communicative format available and accessible—including cable, radio, and the World Wide Web. Their mission, it seems, is to put news in service to the public. They also put their talk to work by raising money for historically Black colleges and universities, organizing critical conferences, and physically moving their messages around the country. Viacom was none too pleased to receive hundreds of calls related to Smiley's firing from BET.

In the manifestation of "The Age of Oprah," as a 2001 *Newsweek* cover suggested, her iconic figure tilts more and more toward exceptionalism rather than example. Then–presidential candidate George W. Bush appeared on *The Oprah Winfrey Show* to make himself more palatable to *White* women. One viewer gave insight as to why Winfrey may no longer ideologically "belong" to the group labeled Black women, at least not presently. When asked about the appeal of Iyanla Vanzant, who began her talk show in fall 2001, the Oprah fan spouted, "I don't think [Iyanla] could ever be as big because she's not universal."[17] Therein lies the key. Winfrey prefigures in the larger American consciousness *not* as an African-American woman (with certain histories, limitations, failings) but as a universal (that is, White) figure. That is what the fan meant earlier by envisioning herself as a White Oprah.

Contrary to the implications of Michael Jackson, the reality of race relations in the United States secures the idea that Winfrey cannot escape her blackness. Nor do I think she has ever wanted to. But the television structure, like other economic/political businesses, tries continuously to cut off and exceptionalize individuals from their cultural positioning in order to crown them in the mainstream. When they fail to conform properly, like Lil' Kim, Venus and Serena Williams, and Tiger Woods, censure looms.

Dancing in September (2001), an HBO film, tackles the irony of network television, race, and gender. As the character Tommie (Nicole Ari Parker) accepts an award for her minstrelized, then canceled, network sitcom, she asks rhetorically, "Why do we care how we're represented?" She answers herself, saying, "Because there is power in what we do, if we do it right."[18] Although my Black women students from Spelman and Clark Atlanta discussed women of color representations and began ideologically moving beyond restrictive binaries, they still needed to worry about their survival outside the classroom. In this new century certain inferences made about Colored women based on dress, gender, and their racialized bodies form part of a larger social life and daily threaten their safe return from the library. In those situations abstract and fictionalized discussions of the social construction of identity failed to substantially matter.

SNAPSHOTS OF THE FUTURE, TODAY

Picture 1. In 1999 Judy Goodwin, a Black female, filed a lawsuit against KLOS-FM radio station and its parents Disney and ABC for violating anti-

FIGURE 38

Cita, telling it like it is?

discrimination laws. On the nationally syndicated "Mark and Brian" show, dark, plastic gardening tools were given away as gag prizes to on-air listeners and advertisers in their "Black Hoes" contest. Goodwin contended that the station used this promotion with the "conscious aim and intent of providing offensive, sexually charged entertainment for its primarily White male listening audience and advertising clients."[19]

Picture 2. According to scholar Shannon Mcrac, "[t]he body is rapidly becoming redundant in an age of progressive denaturation."[20] This idea receives confirmation in twenty-first-century Black programming. In 1999 BET introduced a computer-generated show host named Cita (fig. 38). Cita virtually represented an urban, "round the way" young woman—one who is, according to BET music programming VP Stephen Hill, "a ghetto girl who is far too 'street' for television."[21] Like Barbie, she boasted an extremely curvaceous body, was prone to gossip, and exhibited a Southern/lower-socioeconomic status—as evidenced by her speech. Cita's main job was to introduce videos and dish dirt—the new Black woman figure?

Picture 3. Even the promise of the Internet continues to look only marginally encouraging for women of color. When in the late 1990s I attempted a simple Yahoo search for Black or African-American women, I was assaulted by pornographic images. Some sites' technical aggressiveness forced me to shut down the computer in order to exit. The new millennium finds an exponential improvement in Internet search results because of the increased numbers of African-American women creating Web sites. However, three or four pages in, a search will lead one right back to pornographic sites on Black women. Moreover, input "black and girls" concurrently and you will find yourself in the throes of Colored punnany.

WHERE NEXT?

The danger of analyzing representations within popular culture is in supposing finality. The possibilities of this work for both spectators and producers lie in its ability to persuade each to engage television more critically, with an open mind, and to foster substantive discussions with women whose lives are impacted by television scenarios. A media literacy workshop conducted with young Black girls illustrates my point.

I knew that these young women already held an incredible media savvy just by virtue of their having grown up with BET and reality TV. But what became clear to me was what level of complicity and understanding they form with television and the Internet. For them these media vehicles are both all meaningful and meaningless. Negotiating with them about why conferring "hoochie" status on a Black woman in a short skirt is problematic is doable (despite trying to get a definition of *hoochie* that does not elicit giggles). But to hear them tell it, television tells the truth of our lives just because. It is at this juncture of indeterminacy where intercession becomes crucial.

We can all act. Academics can teach media literacy beyond the walls of the academy—in K–12, community centers, religious houses, many venues. Students can share the tools learned in class with friends and family. All of us need to be much more proactive about our likes and dislikes. The Internet makes it easy to lodge a concern, complaint, or compliment. Further, and this goes especially with music and music video, we can refuse to purchase items that demean, degrade, or stifle. Television, music, and film are businesses that respond to consumer desires. The adage of putting your money where your mouth is has never been as important as it is with media literacy and advocacy.

Not only do broader representations serve marginalized populations, but they accord daily life greater meaning for all. What seems to get lost in the rhetoric about representation, access, and multiculturalism is that acknowledging one thing does not necessarily take away from the other. More specifically, calling for and embracing fuller representations of African-American women does not diminish anyone else's imagery. What it does do, ultimately, is deconstruct, or at least decenter, systems of power. Only through vigilance, control of vision, direction, and distribution will the representations of African-American women begin to consistently resist, reposition, or possibly even escape objectification and assume sustained and affirming agency. *Shaded Lives* welcomes the challenge.

APPENDIX

Black Situation Comedies, 1980–2001

SHOW	NETWORK	DATES AIRED
227	NBC	September 1985–July 1990
704 Hauser	CBS	April–May 1994
Amen	NBC	September 1986–July 1991
Arsenio	ABC	March–April 1997
Bernie Mac Show, The	Fox	November 2001–present
Between Brothers	Fox	September 1997–January 1998
Between Brothers	UPN	January–August 1999
Built to Last	NBC	September–October 1997
Charlie and Co.	CBS	September 1985–July 1986
Checking In	CBS	April 1981
Claude's Crib	USA	January 1997–March 1997
Cleghorne!	WB	September 1995–December 1995
Cosby	CBS	September 1996–April 2000
Cosby Show, The	NBC	September 1984–September 1992
Damon	Fox	March–July 1998
Different World, A	NBC	September 1987–July 1993
Family Matters	ABC	September 1989–August 1997
Family Matters	CBS	September 1997–July 1998
For Your Love	NBC	March 1998–May 1998
For Your Love	WB	September 1998–August 1999
Frank's Place	CBS	September 1987–October 1988
Fresh Prince of Bel-Air	NBC	September 1990–September 1996
George	ABC	November 1993–January 1994
Getting Personal	Fox	April–October 1998
Gimme a Break	NBC	October 1981–May 1987
Girlfriends	UPN	September 2000–present
Gregory Hines Show, The	CBS	September 1997–March 1998
Hangin' with Mr. Cooper	ABC	September 1992–August 1997
Here and Now	NBC	September 1992–January 1993
Homeboys in Outer Space	UPN	August 1996–June 1997
Hughleys, The	ABC	September 1998–April 2000
Hughleys, The	UPN	September 2000–present
In the House	NBC	April 1995–May 1996
In the House	UPN	August 1996–September 1998
Jamie Foxx Show, The	WB	August 1996–January 2001
Jeffersons, The	CBS	January 1975–July 1985
Just Our Luck	ABC	September–December 1983

Kenan and Kel	Nickelodeon	October 1996–September 1999
Linc's	Showtime	August 1998–February 2000
Living Single	Fox	August 1993–January 1998
Malcolm and Eddie	UPN	August 1996–May 2000
Martin	Fox	August 1992–August 1997
Me and the Boys	ABC	September 1994–August 1995
Minor Adjustments	NBC	September–November 1995
Minor Adjustments	UPN	January–August 1996
Moesha	UPN	January 1996–May 2001
My Wife and Kids	ABC	March 2001–present
On Our Own	ABC	September 1994–April 1995
One on One	UPN	September 2001–present
Out All Night	NBC	September 1992–July 1993
Pacific Station	NBC	September 1991–January 1992
Parent 'Hood, The	WB	January 1995–July 1999
Parkers, The	UPN	August 1999–present
PJs, The	Fox	January 1999–September 2000
PJs, The	WB	October 2000–May 2001
Redd Foxx Show, The	ABC	January–April 1986
Rhythm and Blues	NBC	September–October 1992
Robert Guillaume Show, The	ABC	April–August 1989
Roc	Fox	August 1991–August 1994
Royal Family, The	CBS	September 1991–May 1992
Sanford	NBC	March 1980–July 1981
Show, The	Fox	March–June 1996
Sinbad Show, The	Fox	September 1993–July 1994
Singer and Sons	NBC	June 1990
Sister, Sister	ABC	April 1994–June 1995
Sister, Sister	WB	August 1995–May 1998
Smart Guy	WB	April 1997–May 1999
South Central	Fox	April–August 1994
Sparks	UPN	August 1996–August 1998
Steve Harvey Show, The	WB	August 1996–present
Tall Hopes	CBS	August–September 1993
True Colors	Fox	September 1990–August 1992
Wayans Brothers, The	WB	January 1995–present
Webster	ABC	September 1983–September 1987
Where I Live	ABC	March–November 1993

NOTES

INTRODUCTION

1. K. Sue Jewell, *From Mammy to Miss America and Beyond: Cultural Images and the Shaping of U.S. Social Policy* (New York: Routledge, 1993), 12.

2. J. Fred MacDonald, *Blacks and White TV: African Americans in Television since 1948* (Chicago: Nelson-Hall, 1992), 250.

3. bell hooks, *Yearning: Race, Gender, and Cultural Politics* (Boston: South End Press, 1990), 147.

4. Carole Boyce Davies, *Black Women, Writing, and Identity: Migrations of the Subject* (New York: Routledge, 1994), 5.

5. Trinh T. Minh-ha, *When the Moon Waxes Red* (New York: Routledge, 1991), 157.

6. All of these defunct series air continuously in syndication.

CHAPTER 1 ▪ THE MADDENING BUSINESS OF SHOW

1. See "NAACP Blasts TV Networks' Fall Season Whitewash," in *NAACP Convention News*, July 12, 1999 <http://151.200.0.60/president/releases/naacp_blasts_tv_networks.htm> (accessed September 28, 2001).

2. Jannette L. Dates and William Barlow, eds., *Split Image: African Americans in the Mass Media* (Washington, D.C.: Howard University Press, 1990), 265.

3. Miriam Hansen, *Babel and Babylon: Spectatorship in American Silent Film* (Cambridge: Harvard University Press, 1991), 39.

4. Ella Shohat and Robert Stam, Donald Bogle, and James C. Scott all argue for "liberatory possibilities" or "hidden transcripts" in marginalized people's performance. Although I agree with these nuanced ideas and their potential, they fail to apply in this instance.

5. For more on early Black cinema and its participants see Charlene Regester, "Lynched, Assaulted, and Intimidated: Oscar Micheaux's Most Controversial Films," *Popular Culture Review* 5, no. 2 (February 1994); Thomas Cripps, *Slow Fade to Black: The Negro in American Film, 1900–1942* (New York: Oxford University Press, 1993); and Daniel Bernardi, ed., *The Birth of Whiteness: Race and the Emergence of U.S. Cinema* (New Brunswick, N.J.: Rutgers University Press, 1996). For a good filmography see Larry Richards, *African American Films through 1959: A Comprehensive, Illustrated Filmography* (Jefferson, N.C.: McFarland, 1998).

6. Donald Bogle, *Toms, Coons, Mulattoes, Mammies, and Bucks: An Interpretive History of Blacks in American Films* (New York: Continuum, 1991), 31–33.

7. Ibid., 36.

8. I have found no Hollywood film that centers Black women or their lives before *Imitation of Life*. During this period, however, Josephine Baker stars in *La Sirene des Tropiques* (1927), *Zou Zou* (1934), and *Princess Tam Tam* (1935). Yet these films were made in France and were shown most successfully there. Although films by Oscar Micheaux—e.g., *Within Our Gates* (1919), *Body and Soul* (1925), and *The Scar of Shame* (1927)—all centered Colored women, these films were created and shown exclusively for African-American audiences outside of Hollywood.

9. For an in-depth analysis of the war and Hollywood see Thomas Cripps's *Making Movies Black: The Hollywood Message Movie from World War II to the Civil Rights Era* (New York: Oxford University Press, 1993). Cripps constructs a historical and cultural look at how Hollywood aided the war effort.

10. Ella Shohat and Robert Stam, *Unthinking Eurocentrism: Multiculturalism and the Media* (New York: Routledge, 1994), 225.

11. See Dates and Barlow, *Split Image,* 254.

12. Melvin Patrick Ely, *The Adventures of "Amos 'n' Andy": A Social History of an American Phenomenon* (New York: Free Press, 1991), 98.

13. Ibid., 208.

14. MacDonald, *Blacks and White TV,* 32.

15. Dates and Barlow, *Split Image,* 262.

16. Ibid., 264.

17. MacDonald, *Blacks and White TV,* 29.

18. I will examine *The Nat King Cole Show* in chapter 3.

19. MacDonald, *Blacks and White TV,* 4.

20. Daniel R. Fusfeld and Timothy Bates, "Black Economic Well-Being since the 1950s," in *A Turbulent Voyage: Readings in African American Studies,* ed. Floyd W. Hayes III (San Diego, Calif.: Collegiate Press, 1997), 491–516.

21. For one particular reporter's story see Charlayne Hunter-Gault's *In My Place* (New York: Farrar, Straus, Giroux, 1992).

22. Television diminished an already declining film audience, and Hollywood searched for solutions to improve movie attendance.

23. The Department of Labor and Daniel Patrick Moynihan released a report in 1965 called *The Negro Family: The Case for National Action* (Washington, D.C.: GPO, 1965). The report suggested that matriarch-led families lay at the foundation of Black communities' weakness and that "[a]t the heart of the deterioration of the fabric of Negro society is the deterioration of the Negro family" (5). This factor, according to the department's criteria, fostered the racial unrest in urban America.

24. Bogle, *Toms,* 251. For how this phenomenon of Black women's anger was translated in 1990s cinema see my "Rock-a-Block, Baby! Black Women Disrupting Gangs and Constructing Hip-Hop Gangsta Film," *Cinema Journal* (Forthcoming, 2002).

25. Donald Bogle, *Blacks in American Films and Television: An Illustrated Encyclopedia* (New York: Simon and Schuster, 1988), 284–285.

26. For a look at 1970s White flight see Nathan Glazer, "The Hard Questions: Life in the City," *New Republic,* August 19, 1996, 37; George C. Galster, "White Flight from Racially Integrated Neighbourhoods in the 1970s: The Cleveland Experience," *Urban Studies* 27, no. 3 (June 1990): 385–399; and Heather Ann Thompson, "Rethinking the Politics of White Flight in the Postwar City: Detroit, 1945–1980," *Journal of Urban History* 25, no. 2 (January 1999): 163–198.

27. In the short-lived *Harris and Company* (March–April 1979), the show's creators strove to project "new images of African Americans in order to introduce a different perspective, a framework for thinking about black people based on their own African-American inspired vision of black reality" (Dates and Barlow, *Split Image,* 258). Although it received good reviews, NBC dropped it from the schedule after only four episodes. Dates forecasted that the "death of relevancy helped to ensure the stifling of television programs or stories treating serious issues affecting African-Americans" (ibid., 266). A pattern of devaluing Black stories in visually unfamiliar contexts continues, as seen by the short runs of the series *Under One Roof, Frank's Place,* and *City of Angels.* These series ran in the latter part of the century. Dates believes that their early demise not only reflects a changing network commitment to programming in general but, more insidiously, to its method of justifying not carrying this type of programming because "people just don't want to see that." *Under One Roof* ran from March to April 1995, *Frank's Place* from September 1987 to October 1988. *City of Angels* ran from January 2000 to December 2000. For an analysis of *Frank's Place's* unique ability to show Black life see Herman Gray's *Watching Race: Television and the Struggle for "Blackness"* (Minneapolis: University of Minnesota Press, 1995), chap. 7.

28. Interestingly, too, *Julia* left the air just as *The Mary Tyler Moore Show* arrived. Moore's show came without the baggage and racial yoke of *Julia*. It aired for seven years and spawned three series. I thank Deborah Jaramillo for bringing this irony to my attention.

29. Bogle, *Illustrated Encyclopedia*, 272.

30. MacDonald, *Blacks and White TV*, 206.

31. *Good Times* creator Norman Lear initially envisioned the program with a single-mother household, but veteran actress Esther Rolle refused the role unless a husband/father, John Amos, was added. Lear accepted these terms. The young, wisecracking son, J. J. (Jimmie Walker), however, began to dominate the program. Based on this reconfigured family balance, Amos left the show. Shortly thereafter Rolle left too. A similar reconstitution of the Black family existed in the long-running *Family Matters* (1989–1998).

32. Mother Jefferson (Zara Cully) and Florence (Marla Gibbs) appeared on *The Jeffersons*, Dee (Danielle Spencer) on *What's Happening!!* and *What's Happening Now!!*, and Florida (Esther Rolle) on *Good Times*.

33. United States Commission on Civil Rights, *Window Dressing on the Set: An Update* (Washington: GPO, 1979), 6.

34. W.E.B. Du Bois, *The Souls of Black Folk* (1903; reprint, New York: Norton, 1999), 5.

35. Gerald David Jaynes and Robin M. Williams Jr., eds., *A Common Destiny: Blacks and American Society* (Washington, D.C.: National Academy, 1989), 35–36.

36. In 1980 the United States population stood at approximately 228 million, with 180 million Whites, 26 million Blacks, and more than 14 million Latinos. Census 2000 results showed a nation of over 281 million inhabitants, with 198 million Whites, almost 35 million Blacks, and more than 33 million Latinos. Of that total, Black women constitute more than 18 million. Figures are taken from James E. Person Jr., ed., *Statistical Forecasts of the United States* (Detroit: Gale Research, 1993); the *Statistical Abstract of the United States, 1994*, by the U.S. Department of Commerce (Washington, D.C.: GPO, 1994); and *Census 2000*, available from <http://factfinder.census.gov/servlet/BasicFactsServlet>.

37. See Steven V. Roberts, "Washington in Transition: Reagan's Final Rating Is Best of Any President since '40s," *New York Times*, January 18, 1989, A1.

38. Coco Fusco, "About Locating Ourselves and Our Representations," *Framework* 36 (1989): 9.

39. E. Franklin Frazier, *Black Bourgeoisie* (London: Collier, 1969), 192–193.

40. Jaynes and Williams, *Common Destiny*, 274–275.

41. In *Common Destiny* Jaynes and Williams insist that the new Black bourgeoisie possess a predilection toward alignment with a Black lower class. They suggest that this may be the result of "structural liberalism," which stems from a shared interest, thus reinforcing considerations of ideology or race solidarity in seeing the public sector expand (169). Yet statistics in Black flight from Negro communities, the widening chasm of income, and the "look" of television force me to disagree with their assessment.

42. Wade W. Nobles, "African Philosophy: Foundations for Black Psychology," in *A Turbulent Voyage: Readings in African American Studies*, ed. Floyd W. Hayes III (San Diego, Calif.: Collegiate Press, 1997), 303.

43. Cornel West, *Race Matters* (Boston: Beacon Press, 1993), 15.

44. Conceived and carried out by President Johnson's civil rights legislation of 1968, affirmative action was to correct centuries of discriminatory employment, housing, and education practices. In 1980s cultural currency affirmative action was used as a code for Whites to scapegoat African-Americans, particularly for the nation's economic downfall, unemployment, and the increase in perceived unqualified Colored faces in corporate spaces.

45. On affirmative action see Darien A. McWhirter, *The End of Affirmative Action: Where Do We Go from Here?* (New York: Birch Lane Press, 1996); Hugh A. Wilson, "Does Affirmative Action for Blacks Harm Whites?" *Western Journal of Black Studies* 22, no. 4 (winter 1998):

218–225; and Clay J. Smith, "Open Letter to the President on Race and Affirmative Action," *Howard Law Journal* 42, no. 1 (fall 1998): 27–58.

46. The first wave had been in the 1920s, called the Harlem Renaissance. The second wave occurred in the 1960s and 1970s with the Black Nationalist Movement and the civil rights movement.

47. Sam Fulwood III, "An Identity," *Los Angeles Times Magazine,* April 9, 1995, 12.

48. This number includes Delegate Donna Christian-Christensen of the U.S. Virgin Islands.

49. These companies include conglomerates like Time Warner (owner of HBO; America Online; Time, Inc.; Warner Bros.; Warner Music Group; New Line Cinema; E! Television; Turner Broadcasting; CNN; and the Cartoon Network), Disney (owner of ABC Television, ABC Radio, ESPN, ESPN2, ESPN Classics, ESPNews, and Disney Enterprises), and Viacom (owner of CBS, TVLand, Blockbuster Video, Showtime, VH1, MTV, Nickelodeon, Comedy Central, KingWorld, Simon and Schuster, TNN, Paramount, CMT, Infinity, CBS Internet Group, UPN, and Black Entertainment Television).

50. David Atkin, "The Evolution of Television Series Addressing Single Women, 1966–1990," *Journal of Broadcasting and Electronic Media* 35, no. 4 (fall 1991): 522.

51. Tim Brooks and Earle Marsh, *The Complete Directory to Prime Time Network and Cable TV Shows: 1946–Present* (New York: Ballantine, 1995), 1202. Although *Hill Street Blues* did not feature an all-Black cast, nor was it a comedy, it hosted a large number of Colored actors, extras, and themes.

52. With programming and counterprogramming among all the networks, either Thursday or Sunday night became the fixed space for Black comedy. All situation comedies with Black casts aired before ten o'clock P.M., after which dramatic programming, serious people with serious lives, appeared. This narrowcasting pattern has been subsequently followed by both Warner Bros. Television (WB) and United Paramount Network (UPN).

53. Quoted in Patricia Mellencamp, *High Anxiety: Catastrophe, Scandal, Age, and Comedy* (Bloomington: Indiana University Press, 1992), 39.

54. Julianne Malveaux, section introduction in *Slipping through the Cracks: The Status of Black Women,* ed. Margaret C. Simms and Julianne M. Malveaux (New Brunswick, N.J.: Transaction, 1987), 8.

55. John M. Jeffries, "Discussion," in *Slipping through the Cracks: The Status of Black Women,* ed. Margaret C. Simms and Julianne M. Malveaux (New Brunswick, N.J.: Transaction, 1987), 131–132.

56. Ibid., 139.

57. Ibid.

58. Very few African-American women appeared in prime time outside of situation comedy. Full cast members in some dramatic series included Regina Taylor in *I'll Fly Away* (1991–1993); Diahann Carroll (1984–1987) and Troy Beyer (1986–1987) in *Dynasty;* Anne-Marie Johnson, Denise Nicholas, and Dee Shaw in *In the Heat of the Night* (1988–1994); Lisa Gay Hamilton in *The Practice* (1997–present); Gloria Reuben (1996–1999) and Michael Michele (1999–present) in *ER;* Vivica A. Fox, Viola Davis, and Gabrielle Union in the short-lived *City of Angels* (2000); and Lisa Nicole Carson in *Ally McBeal* (1997–2001). Lorraine Toussaint served as a colead in Lifetime's *Any Day Now* (1998–2002). And Vanessa Williams, Nicole Ari Parker, Malinda Williams, and Irma P. Hall appear in Showtime's *Soul Food* (2000–present). A handful of Black female characters also worked in daytime soap operas.

59. bell hooks, *Yearning,* 91.

60. bell hooks, *Talking Back: Thinking Feminist, Thinking Black* (Boston: South End Press, 1989), 42.

61. This situation changed slightly in 2001 when President George W. Bush appointed Condoleezza Rice national security advisor and General Colin Powell secretary of state. These two alone receive validation in the foreign affairs arena.

CHAPTER 2 ▪ LAUGHING OUT LOUD

1. *The Cosby Show* premiered on NBC, Thursday, September 20, 1984.

2. Founded in 1869, Clark College (now Clark Atlanta University) is a historically Black, coeducational college in Atlanta, Georgia.

3. Gil Scott-Heron, "The Revolution Will Not Be Televised," in *The Norton Anthology of African American Literature*, ed. Henry Louis Gates Jr. and Nellie Y. McKay (New York: Norton, 1997), 62.

4. Mellencamp, *High Anxiety*, 61.

5. Most Black television representations (as well as representations in cinema) are found in comedy. Thus, because of the cultural specificity of comedy, these representations fail abroad in traditional markets. This same phenomenon emerges for Black programs in domestic syndication. Claims of weak Black viewership ratings' power continue to impede these programs' progress. Although sitcoms at large do not perform well within international markets, drama and action-adventure series do. Programs such as *Baywatch, Wheel of Fortune, Colombo, Dark Justice,* and *ER* air in European, Latin American, and Asian countries. Says Meredith Amdur: "Many qualities make the action hour ideally suited for export. Visual appeal, fast pacing, and glossy heroes, all help move the emphasis away from dialogue, which can lose its edge when dubbed" (Meredith Amdur, "Action-Hour Appeal Is Worldwide," *Broadcasting and Cable*, August 29, 1994, 39). Because few Coloreds appear in these series, a racialized exclusion defines visual exportation. See Mike Fenan, "Ratings Block Minority Syndicators," *Broadcasting and Cable*, September 27, 1993, 30; Betsy Sharkey, "Give Them What They Want," *Mediaweek*, May 27, 1996; and Michael Freeman, "It's the Hour of the Hour," *Mediaweek*, June 6, 1994.

6. David Marc, *Comic Visions: Television Comedy and American Culture* (Boston: Unwin Hyman, 1989), 13.

7. Joseph Boskin and Joseph Dorinson, "Ethnic Humor: Subversion and Survival," *American Quarterly* 37 (spring 1985): 81.

8. Newcomb quoted in Jane Feuer, "Genre Study and Television," in *Channels of Discourse, Reassembled: Television and Contemporary Criticism*, ed. Robert C. Allen, 2d ed. (Chapel Hill: University of North Carolina Press, 1992), 148.

9. Darrell Y. Hamamoto, *Nervous Laughter: Television Situation Comedy and Liberal Democratic Ideology* (New York: Praeger, 1989), 34.

10. Lynn Spigel, "Television in the Family Circle: The Popular Reception of a New Medium," in *Logics of Television*, ed. Patricia Mellencamp (Bloomington: Indiana University Press, 1990), 88.

11. Lynne Joyrich, "Critical and Textual Hypermasculinity," in *Logics of Television*, ed. Patricia Mellencamp (Bloomington: Indiana University Press, 1990), 161.

12. Ibid., 165.

13. Kathleen Rowe, *The Unruly Woman: Gender and the Genres of Laughter* (Austin: University of Texas Press, 1995), 31.

14. Robin R. Means Coleman, *African American Viewers and the Black Situation Comedy: Situating Racial History* (New York: Garland, 1998), 220.

15. Ibid.

16. Andrea Press, *Women Watching Television: Gender, Class, and Generation in the American Television Experience* (Philadelphia: University of Pennsylvania Press, 1991).

17. Introduced in 1987, Lifetime Television was the first cable network that targeted women specifically and that promoted women consistently in the forefront. But like other media output, it privileges a specific group of women. Lifetime targets White women, twenty-five to fifty-four years old. Oxygen, which launched in 2000, targets a much ethnically broader and younger woman but as of this writing has yet to find its voice and vision.

18. Feuer, "Genre Study and Television," 153.

19. Ironically, one of the more popular programs in the 1980s, *Gimme a Break* (1981–1987), featured Nellie Harper (Nell Carter) as maid and nanny to motherless White children and their father. Jannette Dates maintains that Carter "continued in the role because it was a hit with crossover markets and because roles for African American women, scarce in all forms of mass entertainment, were especially hard to find in network television in the early 1980s. The opening song focused on the show's theme. Its lyrics, sung by the star, included the lines 'Gimme a break. I sure could use it. I've finally found where I belong!!'" (Dates and Barlow, *Split Image*, 275). The statement struck a responsive chord with contemporary sitcom audiences and forwarded derogatory and limited representations of Black women.

20. "Baby, It's You," *Martin*, writ. Darice Rollins, Fox, September 1993. Lawrence engages in a similar scenario with *Martin* actress Tichina Arnold in the film *Big Momma's House* (2000).

21. Shohat and Stam, *Unthinking Eurocentrism*, 180.

22. Andy Medhurst, introduction to *The Colour Black: Black Images in British Television*, ed. Therese Daniels and Jane Gerson (London: British Film Institute, 1990), 16.

23. Jacqueline Bobo's *Black Women as Cultural Readers* (New York: Columbia University Press, 1995) looks at Black women spectators and their responses to representations in film and narrative texts. bell hooks addresses also Black audience response to Black life on screen in her introduction, "Making Movie Magic," in *Reel to Real: Race, Sex, and Class at the Movies* (New York: Routledge, 1996).

24. Medhurst, *The Colour Black*, 16.

25. Both programs were created and written by Norman Lear. He also introduced the Black sitcoms *Sanford and Son* (1972–1977), *Good Times* (1974–1979), and *The Jeffersons* (1975–1985). Lear, noted for his social consciousness, has talked about the much-contested departure of John Amos from *Good Times*, when Amos's character left Florida (Esther Rolle) to raise the children alone. Lear reminisced, "We knew that we would have entirely new areas to explore in terms of the family. J. J., the oldest son, would have to assume the strong male role, with circumstances forcing him to reach toward manhood. We felt that would be very good for the characters, very good for the young people watching the show, and was a very valuable area for dramatic expression" (Norman Lear, interview in Horace Newcomb and Robert S. Alley, eds., *The Producer's Medium: Conversations with Creators of American TV* [New York: Oxford University Press, 1983], 186). What this move actually did was perpetuate circulating tropes of disintegrating Black families based on female-headed households.

26. Further, although soap operas have hosted a few Black women in their narratives from the 1970s, one of the most popular from the 1980s onward, *The Young and the Restless*, directed its interaction with them in a typical fashion—as maid to one of the central families. They called this Colored character Mamie. The character Mamie Johnson (Marguerite Ray, Veronica Redd-Forest) appears on *The Young and the Restless* from the early 1990s. Her character spawned and is thus tangentially related to all the Black characters on the program. When Redd-Forest assumed the role, she wore a wig, her natural short-cropped hair perhaps a bit too ethnic, too radical for the *Y and R* aesthetic. This not-so-covert contemporary capitulation to an offshoot of mammy and its association with Black women reverberated throughout situation comedy.

27. Atkin, "Evolution," 522.

28. Ruth Frankenberg, *White Women, Race Matters* (Minneapolis: University of Minnesota Press, 1993), 236–237.

29. John Fiske, *Media Matters: Everyday Culture and Political Change* (Minneapolis: University of Minnesota Press, 1994), 142.

30. Toni Morrison, *Playing in the Dark: Whiteness and the Literary Imagination* (Cambridge: Harvard University Press, 1992), 46–47.

31. Davies, *Black Women*, 6–8.

32. Nick Browne, "The Political Economy of the Television (Super) Text," in *American Television: New Directions in History and Theory* (Langhorne, Pa.: Harwood Academic, 1994).

33. For example, many of the visual texts acquired for this book came via an Air Force friend, Warren Singleton, stationed in Germany. Consequently, the integral intertextual materials on my video dubs dealt primarily with military concerns—a far cry from regular, television intertextual fare.

34. The same type of African-American absence and presence occurs in *Something Wild* (Demme, 1986).

35. Trinh T. Minh-ha, "Not You/Like You: Post-Colonial Women and the Interlocking Questions of Identity and Difference," in *Making Face, Making Soul—Hacienda Cara: Creative and Critical Perspectives by Feminists of Color,* ed. Gloria Anzaldúa (San Francisco: Aunt Lute, 1990), 373.

36. Jeanne Noble, *Beautiful, Also, Are the Souls of My Black Sisters: A History of the Black Woman in America* (Englewood Cliffs, N.J.: Prentice-Hall, 1978), 75.

37. Between Dionne Warwick, as the conduit for Psychic Friends, and the newest Miss Cleo, the West Indian Tarot Card reader, Black women continue to ground the prophetic imaginations/ruminations of Caucasian audiences.

38. The term *inner eye* comes from Ralph Ellison's *Invisible Man* (New York: Quality Paperback Book Club, 1947) and refers to the way majority populations fail to see Coloreds:

> I am an invisible man. I am a man of substance, of flesh and bone, fiber and liquids—and I might even be said to possess a mind. I am invisible, understand, simply because people refuse to see me. That invisibility to which I refer occurs because of a peculiar disposition of the eyes of those with whom I come in contact. A matter of the construction of their *inner* eyes, those eyes with which they look through their physical eyes upon reality." (3)

39. "Subterranean Homeboy Blues," *Law and Order,* NBC, September 20, 1990.

40. Or, in the case of these characters, they become honorary Whites.

41. Marc, *Comic Visions,* 178.

42. Diahann Carroll was the first Black professional to appear on television in the series *Julia.* However, as described in chapter 1, nurse Julia Baker lived in a multicultural (White) California world to which Black Americans beyond herself and her son had limited access. Further, although George Jefferson is a businessman in *The Jeffersons,* his manner and type of business (he owns seven dry-cleaning stores) situate him as working class, despite his East Side apartment.

43. Marc, *Comic Visions,* 217.

44. Ella Taylor, *Prime-Time Families: Television Culture in Postwar America* (Berkeley: University of California Press, 1989), 159.

45. I thank Mike Budd for guiding me to these ideas in his review of my work.

46. Dates and Barlow, *Split Image,* 269.

47. Fredric Jameson, *Postmodernism, or, The Cultural Logic of Late Capitalism* (Durham, N.C.: Duke University Press, 1991), 70. The emphasis on nonexistence is mine. These types of families failed to exist in White communities too.

48. See Sut Jhally and Justin Lewis, *Enlightened Racism: The Cosby Show, Audiences, and the Myth of the American Dream* (Boulder, Colo.: Westview, 1992).

49. Gray, *Watching Race,* 84.

50. See my appendix for a list of Black situation comedies from 1980. Many post-*Cosby* programs harken back to that series.

51. Kristal Brent Zook, *Color by Fox: The Fox Network and the Revolution in Black Television* (New York: Oxford University Press, 1999), 5.

52. John Thornton Caldwell, *Televisuality: Style, Crisis, and Authority in American Television* (New Brunswick, N.J.: Rutgers University Press, 1995), 11.

53. Zook, *Color by Fox*, 4.

54. Caldwell, *Televisuality*, 11.

55. Ibid.

56. Reagan's trickle-down impact on culture and its parallel to structural adjustment will be explored further in chapter 3.

57. Zook, *Color by Fox*, 5.

58. Gray, *Watching Race*, 141.

59. For example, by its 1993 season *In Living Color*'s Wanda character was the lead supporting character. Another female-impersonated character, as drawn by Jamie Foxx, further rendered Black women unattractive, self-aggrandizing, sexually frustrated, and pathetic.

60. Zook, *Color by Fox*, 101.

61. *3rd Rock from the Sun* (1996–present) and *Homeboys in Outer Space* (1996–1997) are indicative of the postmodern celebration of difference. Perhaps, too, all of the comedies aired with a scant more cheekiness, as shown in *Married with Children, Roseanne, In Living Color, Grace under Fire*, and *Martin*. The term *difference* used here comes from the writings of Jean-François Lyotard.

62. Stuart Hall, "Cultural Identity and Cinematic Representation," *Framework* 36 (1989): 69.

63. Franklyn Ajaye, "Apartheid TV Affects Viewers' Lives," *Los Angeles Times*, November 16, 1992, F3.

64. Nina C. Leibman, *Living Room Lectures: The Fifties Family in Film and Television* (Austin: University of Texas Press, 1995), 171.

65. As *Family Matters* (1989–1998) continued, White grew up—making the character more grotesque and absurd. A tall, attractive, young Black man, he continued to occupy the identity of a sniveling child. Although education endured condemnation quite liberally in sitcom characterizations and in larger American culture, in predominant (White) sitcom discourses balance existed. For every nerdish but smart White character like Kevin in *Wonder Years*, Screech in *Saved by the Bell*, and Arvid in *Head of the Class*, there appeared attractive, well-adjusted, smart ones like Alex in *Family Ties*, Doogie in *Doogie Howser, M.D.*, or Ricky in *Silver Spoons*. No corresponding male character existed in Black comedy. In 2001 an episode of Showtime's drama *Soul Food* shows a White kid's comfort with calling the young Black male character Ahmad (Aaron Meeks) a "bitch" for trying to do his schoolwork (writ. Salim Akil, "Who Do You Know?" July 11, 2001).

66. The work cited comes from a study conducted by George Gerbner as noted on the *Fact Sheet of the National Rainbow Coalition Commission on Fairness in the Media* (September 16, 1994), 28. At the time, all people of color represented 19.8 percent to 23.1 percent of the U.S. population according to *American Demographics* 12, no. 8 (August 1990).

67. Katherine E. Heintz-Knowles et al., *Fall Colors: 2000–01 Prime Time Diversity Report* (Oakland, Calif.: Children Now, 2001), 2. This report addresses the six networks' program diversity.

68. This perception is apparently pervasive according to a national survey conducted by the *Washington Post*, the Henry J. Kaiser Family Foundation, and Harvard University. In the survey researchers found that 40 to 60 percent of Whites believe that Blacks are faring as well or better in the areas of income, jobs, education, and health care. The reality is vastly different. See Richard Monni, "Misperceptions Cloud Whites' View of Blacks," *Washington Post*, July 10, 2001 <http://www.washingtonpost.com/wp-dyn/articles/A42062-2001Jul10.html> (accessed November 14, 2001).

69. Several Black comedies have received critical coverage. For example, two full texts explore *The Cosby Show*: Jhally and Lewis, *Enlightened Racism;* and Linda K. Fuller, *The Cosby Show: Audiences, Impact, and Implications* (New York: Greenwood Press, 1992). *The Cosby Show* serves also as the subject of numerous journal and popular articles. The series *A Different*

World, Frank's Place, and *In Living Color* receive a thorough examination in Herman Gray's *Watching Race.* Additionally, Kristal Brent Zook examines several Fox series in *Color by Fox.*

70. Gray, *Watching Race,* 101.

71. Medina says that the idea for this story came from his life growing up poor and Black in East Los Angeles. He chronicles his opportunity to live in the home (garage) of a rich, White family friend. For *Fresh Prince* Medina simply made the characters Black. See Laura B. Randolph, "The Real-Life Fresh Prince of Bel Air: Television and Recording Tycoon Benny Medina Proves That Hollywood Life Can Be Stranger Than Hollywood Fiction," *Ebony,* April 1991, 30–38.

72. Always vigilant of perversity, frequently even television servants' titles confer racial hierarchies. In series that feature White servants a title is given like Mr. French of *Family Affair,* Mr. Belvedere of *Mr. Belvedere,* and even Uncle Charlie of *My Three Sons.* However, with Black servants (male or female) a solitary name usually suffices. Beulah *(Beulah),* Benson *(Benson),* Geoffrey *(Fresh Prince),* Florence *(The Jeffersons),* Nell *(Gimme a Break),* and, of course, Mamie.

73. *The Fresh Prince of Bel Air,* NBC, January 1, 1996.

74. Zora Neale Hurston, "The Pet Negro System," in *I Love Myself,* ed. Alice Walker (Old Westbury, N.Y.: Feminist Press, 1979), 156, my emphasis.

75. Christopher John Farley, "Blacks and Blue," *Time,* November 22, 1993, 80.

76. Bambi L. Haggins, "Banter, Banter, Banter, Kiss: Evolution and Intransigence in Romantic Comedy" (paper presented at the Society for Cinema Studies Conference, Dallas, Tex., March 1, 1996), 2.

77. Ibid., 4.

78. Malaika Brown, "Sisterhood Televised: Yvette Lee Bowser and the Voice She Listens To," *American Visions,* April–May 1995, 42.

79. For Bowser's thoughts on the program see ibid.

80. Fox relegated the series to midseason replacement before the 1997 fall season. A massive Internet write-in, fax, and call-in campaign ensued, mostly from Black American consumers. The program returned that fall and finally ended with the episode "Let's Stay Together" in January 1998. See Lyle V. Harris, "Living Single," *Atlanta Journal and Constitution,* January 1, 1998, 1C.

81. "No Color Lines" was one of the station identifications for the very popular 92.3 The Beat radio station in Los Angeles. Its format is hip-hop and r&b, aimed at the urban youth market. "Can't we all just get along" came from a Rodney King press conference after the 1992 response/riots/rebellion erupted on the streets of Los Angeles.

82. A woman, presumably Fresh Prince's mother, is shown shaking her finger at Will before sending him to California. This woman, however, never appears in the series. When the Fresh Prince's mother does appear, it is not the same woman as in the opening. Besides, in national syndication many stations shorten the opening to provide more commercial space. The viewer hears only the first few bars of Smith's rap and sees him spinning on a throne.

83. Rudolf Arnheim, *Film as Art* (Berkeley: University of California Press, 1957), 182.

84. Bambi L. Haggins, "The Sitcom-Work," March 15, 1997, 22, Los Angeles, California, photocopy of unpublished manuscript.

85. Betsy Sharkey, "Teen Angel: Singing Sensation Brandy Is Lifting," *Mediaweek,* February 19, 1996, 20–23. This was an interview with the creators.

86. Plus, some of these series function as a cross between comedy and drama, according them more space for realistic settings.

87. Kim Reese (Charnelle Brown) of *A Different World* aspires to be a doctor. Phylicia Rashad plays an attorney on *The Cosby Show,* and both Dee (Sheryl Lee Ralph), of *Moesha,* and Regina (Wendy Raquel Robinson), on *The Steve Harvey Show,* work in education. These occupations appear so infrequently that studies have shown that when they do appear,

spectators consider them unreal. See Sandra A. Dickerson, "Is Sapphire Still Alive? The Image of Black Women in Television Situation Comedies in the 1990s" (Ph.D. diss., Boston University School of Education, 1991).

88. Gloria Naylor, *The Women of Brewster Place* (New York: Viking, 1980), 4.

89. None of the women represent the Caribbean or African communities that populate New York, and especially Brooklyn, the setting for *Living Single*. Even Sheryl Lee Ralph, who hails from Jamaica and New York, loses her Caribbean ancestry until the sixth season. Her Jamaican heritage then becomes a part of the excuse for Ralph to leave the cast.

90. These four characters were the principals in Terry McMillan's best-selling book *Waiting to Exhale* (New York: Viking, 1992) and the successful film (dir. Forest Whitaker, 1995) of the same name.

91. See Means Coleman, *African American Viewers*.

92. "Bundle of Joy," *Fresh Prince of Bel Air*, writ. Myles Avery Mapp and K. Snyder, NBC, January 25, 1993.

93. Says Hubert-Whitten, "They [NBC officials] kept calling me asking me to say the parting was mutual, but I'm not like that. I fight back. They intended to slap me on the wrist if I would behave like a good little nigger woman" (*Jet*, August 9, 1993, 17).

94. According to the Nielsen Media Research *Report*, "African-American viewers show a clear preference for programs with predominantly African-American casts." In the 1999 top-fifteen prime-time programs in Black households, ten of the fifteen were Black situation comedies. None of those ten, however, factored into the "all other" top-fifteen choices. *The Parkers* ranked number one with Black audiences during the 1999–2000 season. See Nielsen Media Research, *2000 Report on Television: The First 50 Years* (New York: Nielsen Media Research, 2000), 42.

95. *Living Single*, Fox, January 2, 1996.

96. *Living Single*, writ. David Cohen and Roger S. H. Schulman, Fox, September 15, 1994.

97. In 1997 Ellen Degeneres "came out" on her show, *Ellen*. This was the first time a character admitted being homosexual in prime time. The show was canceled a year later. However, it did open the door for series such as *Will and Grace, Normal, OH, Queer as Folk*, and characters within *Spin City*. Nevertheless, lesbian women have not successfully reemerged in television comedy.

98. Black spectators found it hard enough to address homosexuality among men, without even considering women. However, *Living Single* did address, very poignantly, Black lesbianism in 1996. In the episode "Woman to Woman" Max finds out that her college roommate (Karen Malena White) was to marry a woman. Later that same year Queen Latifah plays a female gangster in F. Gary Gray's *Set It Off*. In the film she is a gangster-girl butch lesbian.

99. Even this baby was not conceived in a conventional way. Max received a sperm donation that came miraculously from Kyle.

100. Jeremy G. Butler, "Redesigning Discourse: Feminism, the Sitcom, and *Designing Women*," *Journal of Film and Video* 45, no. 1 (spring 1993): 17.

101. Quoted in Raquel Cepeda, "Money, Power, Elect: Where's the Hip-Hop Agenda?" *Essence*, August 2000, 163.

102. *Gone with the Wind* (Fleming, 1939).

103. Bogle, *Illustrated Encyclopedia*, 95.

104. Review of *Fresh Prince of Bel Air, Variety and Daily Variety Television Review 1989–1990*, September 10, 1990.

105. "Take My Cousin. Please," *Fresh Prince of Bel Air*, writ. David Zuckerman, NBC, November 22, 1993.

106. "Break Up, Part 1," *Martin*, writ. John Bowman, February 1, 1993.

107. Marlene G. Fine, Carolyn Anderson, and Gary Eckles, "Black English on Black Situation Comedies," *Journal of Communication* 29, no. 3 (summer 1979): 28.

108. Ibid., 27.

109. In 1996 the Oakland School District voted to infuse Ebonics or Black English into teacher training to help children learn standard English. A national controversy ensued.

110. Shohat and Stam, *Unthinking Eurocentrism*, 191.

111. Marc, *Comic Visions*, 14.

112. Davies, *Black Women*, 152.

113. "My Funny Valentine," *Living Single*, writ. David Steven Cohen, Fox, January 15, 1995.

114. April Sinclair, *Coffee Will Make You Black* (New York: Avon Books, 1994), 3–4.

115. Kathy Russell, Midge Wilson, and Ronald Hall, *The Color Complex: The Politics of Skin Color among African Americans* (New York: Anchor Books, 1993), 150.

116. Kathleen Rowe, "Roseanne: Unruly Woman as Domestic Goddess," in Newcomb, *Television*, 207.

117. Me'Shell NdegéOcello is an artist whose work I address in chapter 3.

118. Quote by Bethann Hardison in Russell, Wilson, and Hall, *Color Complex*, 155.

119. Kobena Mercer, "Black Hair/Style Politics," in *Welcome to the Jungle: New Positions in Black Cultural Studies* (New York: Routledge, 1994), 104.

120. See the *New York Times*, September 23, 1987, 21.

121. Ingrid Banks, *Hair Matters: Beauty, Power, and Black Women's Consciousness* (New York: New York University Press, 2000), 42.

122. According to the *Nielsen Media Research 2000 Report on Television: The First 50 Years*, Flip Wilson was the first Black entertainer to host a top-rated network program.

123. Dates and Barlow, *Split Image*, 266.

124. Quoted in Vern L. Bullough and Bonnie Bullough, *Cross Dressing, Sex, and Gender* (Philadelphia: University of Pennsylvania Press, 1993), 233.

125. *The Flip Wilson Show*, head writ. Herbert Baker, NBC, October 8, 1970.

126. Bill Richardson, *Guy to Goddess: An Intimate Look at Drag Queens* (Berkeley: Ten Speed Press, 1994), 68.

127. F. Michael Moore, *Drag! Male and Female Impersonators on Stage, Screen, and Television: An Illustrated World History* (Jefferson, N.C.: McFarland, 1994), 2.

128. *A Different World* explored women's relationships quite well, particularly as the program entered its latter years.

129. On Showtime the series *Linc's* offered the same type of subtle humor as *Frank's Place*. Nevertheless, the series was canceled after two years.

130. *Broadcasting and Cable*, June 12, 2000, 64.

CHAPTER 3 ▪ I GOT YOUR BITCH!

1. See Ruth Forman, "Green Boots n Lil Honeys," in *We Are the Young Magicians* (Boston: Beacon Press, 1993).

2. Helen Kolawole, "Booting Booti Off the Box: What's behind the Female Flesh Cavorting around Swimming Pools in the Endless Stream of Rap and R&B Videos?" *Voice*, June 18, 1996, 27.

3. Pat Aufderheide, "Music Videos: The Look of the Sound," *Journal of Communication* 36, no. 1 (winter 1986): 57.

4. Home, however, is only one of several places where the consumer meets with music video. Music videos dwell in department stores, university lounges, shopping malls, student unions, bars, clubs, airports, and other places of public interaction and consumption.

5. This assessment refers primarily to the major cable networks. It excludes, somewhat,

pay cable channels such as HBO, which take more risks than networks accessible to the wider U.S. audience.

6. During this period many articles were written about corporate mergers. For an overview see "A Chronology of Recent Major Mergers and Acquisitions That Have Shaped the Media Industry," A.P., *Fox Marketwire*, September 7, 1999 <http://www.foxmarketwire .com/0907991/cbssidesml> (accessed January 11, 2000). In September 1999 Viacom announced a deal to buy CBS, and in January 2001 the merger between America On Line and Time Warner was approved.

7. Assertion posed by political scientist Deirdre Condit, June 20, 2000, at the Barbados Summer Institute on Women's Studies Curriculum Transformation, Barbados, West Indies.

8. The highest-ranking Black executive at a studio, Dennis Hightower, was promoted ceremoniously to CEO of Disney in March 1995 and one year later took an early retirement. No one was surprised.

9. Mellencamp, *High Anxiety,* 50.

10. See Caroline Waxler, "Bob Johnson's Brainchild," *Forbes,* April 22, 1996, 98-100.

11. MTV, as a matter of policy and "target," refused to air Black artists' videos until c. 1983, amid much controversy. The executives rationalized that the service was designed to feature rock music videos and would lose its core audience by adding Black artists. For more on MTV's inception see E. Ann Kaplan, *Rocking around the Clock: Music Television, Postmodernism, and Consumer Culture* (New York: Methen, 1987), 15-17; and R. Serge Denisoff, *Inside MTV* (New Brunswick, N.J.: Transaction, 1989), chapter 5.

12. Waxler, "Johnson's Brainchild," 100.

13. Spanish stations Univision and Telemundo began in the 1980s. Both of these stations aired regularly on VHF or UHF stations as independents. Galavision, which began in 1991, currently reigns as the only other ethnic cable station in the market. In 2001 NBC bought Telemundo.

14. Promotional video, Black Entertainment Television, Telemation Productions, September 10, 1980, UCLA Film and Television Archives.

15. In 1998 Robert Johnson bought all the shares back and returned the company to a private entity owned by himself and Liberty Media Corporation. See John M. Higgins, "Johnson Taking BET Private," *Broadcasting and Cable,* March 23, 1998, 92.

16. According to the *Cable/TV Fact Book, 1994,* the number of cable systems grew from around 6,200 in 1984 to approximately 11,217 in 1993. The number of subscribers escalated from twenty-nine million in 1984 to approximately seventy-nine million in 2000. Nearly 70 percent of the nation's homes are wired, but a large percentage of the unwired are African-American neighborhoods. As figures indicate, cable access has not been uniformly available to all. In fact, certain neighborhoods in New York City, one of the first cities to implement cable (1970), remained unwired in the latter part of the 1990s. This example of how quickly cable had (or had not) reached penetration in certain areas indicates how the industry is liberating only for some.

17. Felecia G. Jones, "The Black Audience and the BET Channel," *Journal of Broadcasting and Electronic Media* 34 (fall 1990): 484.

18. Comment from Deborah Jaramillo in dialogue about Black Entertainment Television, Tucson, Arizona, January 2001.

19. Snigdha Prakash, "Viacom-BET," *All Things Considered,* National Public Radio, November 3, 2000.

20. Quoted in ibid.

21. Throughout this chapter music video titles are italicized with flanking quotation marks. The song to the video is in quotation marks alone, and the album/CD is italicized without the quotation marks.

22. Kaplan, *Rocking around the Clock,* 30.

23. Of MTV's flow, Dan Rubey writes that "individual videos always intersect with *macro-*

narratives existing above and beyond any particular video or its individual narrative—other videos, live performances by the band, promotional campaigns, media articles, etc." (Dan Rubey, "Voguing at the Carnival: Desire and Pleasure on MTV," *South Atlantic Quarterly* 90, no. 4 [fall 1991]: 878).

24. Kaplan, *Rocking around the Clock,* 12. Kaplan compares this mode of production to advertisement construction. She maintains that "the reliance on freelance crews, the omission of production credits and the financial tie-in to the record companies all duplicate the production situation of ads" (13). In the 1990s directors' names began to appear on videos. First and foremost, however, the video belonged to the artist.

25. See Rubey, "Voguing," 875.

26. Aufderheide, "Music Videos," 66.

27. See Lisa A. Lewis, "Form and Female Authorship in Music Video," in Newcomb, *Television,* 252. Lewis argues that in female rock video, entering into the male-dominated space allows women to reconstruct it as their own and to provide uplift to the female audience. Like rock artists, many early women rappers do not write their material solo. Usually it becomes a combined effort of the male producer and the artist. Yet rap lyrics seem much more closely tied to the artist's being than do lyrics in any other musical form. This tie becomes especially problematic when a woman's space is entered under the proviso of safety.

28. Lisa A. Lewis, *Gender Politics and MTV: Voicing the Difference* (Philadelphia: Temple University Press, 1990), 110.

29. Ibid., 50–51.

30. Andrew Goodwin, *Dancing in the Distraction Factory: Music Television and Popular Culture* (Minneapolis: University of Minnesota Press, 1992), 18.

31. Ibid., 3.

32. Caldwell, *Televisuality,* 363–364 n. 48.

33. Robin Roberts, *Ladies First: Women in Music Videos* (Jackson: University Press of Mississippi, 1996).

34. The cover of Roberts's book is a sketch of Queen Latifah. Amazingly, even the racialized, cultural specificity of this rapper's articulation and presence are neatly marshaled to center gender.

35. MacDonald, *Blacks and White TV,* 13–14.

36. *The Nat King Cole Show* appeared on NBC beginning November 5, 1956.

37. The lip-synching itself replicated artists performing their recordings and, as a cultural phenomenon, spawned imitators all the way to the Grammys. See Dave Laing, "Music Video: Industrial Product, Cultural Form," *Screen* 26, no. 2 (March–April 1985), 81. For Grammy impostors see Milli Vanilli.

38. In 1984 *Soul Train* began awarding the "Soul Train Music Awards," along with producing other types of music specials such as the *Soul Train Women of Soul Awards.*

39. J. R. Reynolds, "No Stoppin 'Soul Train' Vet Cornelius: Producer Adds 3 New TV Specials in '95," *Billboard,* March 18, 1995, 24.

40. *Yo, MTV Raps!* began as a rap weekend special. According to its producer, Jack Benson, it was launched as a series in 1989. Its inception came with the help and success of BET's video format.

41. John Miller Chernoff, *African Rhythm and African Sensibility: Aesthetics and Social Action in African Musical Idioms* (Chicago: University of Chicago Press, 1979), 73.

42. See Rubey, "Voguing," 877.

43. Ibid., 877–878.

44. Armond White, "In Living Color," *Rolling Stone,* October 14, 1993, 77.

45. Ibid.

46. The notion of "positive" images continues to pose a problematic binary, especially in terms of African-American signifiers. "Positiveness" can range from simply having Black

faces in view (on magazine covers, in film and in television) to notions of "correct" or "moralistic" interventions. The debate for and on progressive, positive, affirmative, and accurate representation continues. More tangible problems, such as funding, distribution, and access, are shifted summarily to tertiary corners.

47. Sonja Peterson-Lewis and Shirley A. Chennault, "Black Artists' Music Videos: Three Success Strategies," *Journal of Communication* 36, no. 1 (winter 1986): 108.

48. A good example of this lack of image control is shown in the reality-based show *Popstars*.

49. Bill Flanagan, VH-1 editorial director, interview by Terry Gross, *Fresh Air,* National Public Radio, June 29, 2000.

50. Todd Boyd talks about the need to focus on this "hyperreal" beyond the actual when analyzing visual culture and rap. See Todd Boyd, *Am I Black Enough for You? Popular Culture from the 'Hood and Beyond* (Bloomington: Indiana University Press, 1997), esp. 70–72.

51. Mim Udovitch, "The Girlie Show," *Rolling Stone,* October 14, 1993, 69.

52. Ibid., 70.

53. Janice Faye Hutchinson, "The Hip Hop Generation: African American Male-Female Relationships in a Night Club Setting," *Journal of Black Studies* 30, no. 1 (September 1999): 82.

54. Rubey, "Voguing," 895.

55. Me'Shell NdegéOcello, "Soul On Ice," *Plantation Lullabies,* compact disc, Maverick Recording Company, 1993.

56. K. C. Arceneaux, "The Remix as Cultural Critique: The Urban Contemporary Music Video," *Popular Music and Society* 16, no. 3 (fall 1992): 117.

57. Queen Latifah, *"I Can't Understand,"* dir. Michael Lucero, video, 1993.

58. For a fuller exploration of the shackles of superwomanhood see Michele Wallace's pioneering text, *Black Macho and the Myth of the Superwoman* (New York: Dial, 1978); and Joan Morgan's *When Chickenheads Come Home to Roost: A Hip-Hop Feminist Breaks It Down* (New York: Simon and Schuster, 1999).

59. With the proliferation of videos every year and the doubling of women rappers, this chapter examines only a small sampling.

60. Arnheim, *Film as Art,* 181–182.

61. Rubey, "Voguing," 885.

62. Andrew Ross, "Back on the Box," *Artforum* (May 1995) <http://www.artforum.com/> (accessed February 6, 1997).

63. Caldwell, *Televisuality,* 93.

64. We know, however, that artists such as Elvis, the Beatles, and others appropriated soul music long before with little or no acknowledgment, credit, or financial compensation.

65. Marvin J. Gladney, "The Black Arts Movement and Hip-Hop," *African American Review* 29, no. 2 (1995): 294.

66. Rubey, "Voguing," 893. Rubey gives a critical reading of Jackson's video in his article. Reading the video under the proviso of psychoanalysis, he insists that it visually does what feminist film theorists have been wanting. Yet the video advances a pleasure element that feminism rejects.

67. I thank my students in UCLA's 98T "Representations of Women of Color in Visual Culture" class (spring 1997) for forcing me to rethink this area.

68. Marla L. Shelton, "Is Whitney Everywoman? Whitney Houston and the Icon of the Black Woman in Popular Culture," *Screening Noir* (spring 1995): 3.

69. The language and tone of her comment comes out of a Southern blues tradition. One example appeared in script/lyrics David Alan Grier parodied as an old blues singer on *In Living Color.*

70. John Leland, "Our Bodies, Our Sales," *Newsweek,* January 31, 1994, 56.

71. Franklin won a Grammy for Best R&B Female Vocal Performance. The other Grammy went to the writers (Narada Michael Walden and Jeffrey Cohen) for Best Song of the Year. See <http://music.com/showcase/urban/arethafranklin.html> (accessed October 17, 2000).

72. Mellencamp, *High Anxiety,* 286.

73. Ross returned to public consciousness in an expansive way with both her honoring in VH-1's "Divas Live" and the announcement of her 2000 Diana Ross and the Supremes concert tour. While the VH-1 special was a success, Ross found the nation not particularly receptive to her concert tour. Despite its publicity sweep, the tour folded midway.

74. Rubey, "Voguing," 884.

75. Tricia Rose, *Black Noise: Rap Music and Black Culture in Contemporary America* (Hanover, N.H.: Wesleyan University Press, 1994), 56. Since 1998, however, this has changed. Napster provided a means for consumers to access new music directly. Supplying music over the Internet, coupled with consumers' new ability to burn CDs, made music freely accessible. In 2000 the Supreme Court ruled that Napster infringed on copyright laws. Despite appeal, the verdict held. Yet the technology marched on, with corporations and legislators scrambling to catch up.

76. Fredric Jameson, "Postmodernism and Consumer Society," in *Postmodernism and Its Discontents,* ed. E. Ann Kaplan (London: Verso, 1988), 16.

77. Rose, *Black Noise,* 21.

78. Quoted in Brian Robbins, dir., *The Show,* Savoy Pictures (USA), 1995, 92 min., documentary film.

79. I am grateful to Katurah Cecilia Babb, Deputy Coordinator, Caribbean Policy Development Centre, for making the impact of structural adjustment very plain and pressing to me in her talk at the Barbados Summer Institute on Curriculum Transformation, June 20, 2000.

80. Quoted in Robbins, *The Show.*

81. Danyel Smith, "Ain't a Damn Thing Changed: Why Women Rappers Don't Sell," in *Rap on Rap: Straight-Up Talk on Hip-Hop Culture,* ed. Adam Sexton (New York: Dell, 1995), 125–126.

82. Patricia Hill Collins, "Learning from the Outsider Within: The Sociological Significance of Black Feminist Thought," *Social Problems* 33, no. 6 (December 1986): 42.

83. Valerie Smith, U.C.L.A.'s Feminist Theory series, Los Angeles, California, April 12, 1994.

84. Robin Roberts, "Music Videos, Performance, and Resistance," *Journal of Popular Culture* 25 (fall 1991): 150.

85. In addition, Queen Latifah stands as probably the most widely recognizable female rapper because of her longevity in the industry, her numerous film appearances, and her role as Khadijah James on *Living Single.* Plus that same rumor of lesbianism affected her rap, as well as her screen career. Interestingly, though, in 1996 she played a lesbian gangsta-wannabe in F. Gary Gray's *Set It Off.*

86. Deborah Gregory, "The Queen Rules," *Essence,* October 1993, 114.

87. Patricia Hill Collins, *Black Feminist Thought* (New York: Routledge, 1991), 94.

88. Ed Guerrero, *Framing Blackness: The African American in Film* (Philadelphia: Temple University Press, 1993), 98.

89. See my article "I Got Your B!" <http://www.volume.com> (accessed November 2000). In 1991 Bytches with Problems surfaced with a new meaning and empowerment of *bitch.* Like Boss they used *bitch* as a site of contest. Within the realms of sex, money, and female interaction, these Bytches insisted on *bitch* as a form of reaction and fighting power. In their opening track they reconstructed a scenario in which one member has a verbal altercation with a male, resulting in his physically attacking her. She leaves, returns with her

posse and her guns, and shoots up the place. The chorus follows: "All you motherfuckers better watch your back, cuz we comin' back strapped." By the mid 1990s these Bytches had dropped from the musical landscape.

90. Quoted in Michael Small, "Salt-N-Pepa Shake It Up, Laying a Cold Rap on Men," *People's Weekly,* April 18, 1988, 113.

91. Nataki H. Goodall, "Depend on Myself: T.L.C. and the Evolution of Black Female Rap," *Journal of Negro History* 79, no. 1 (winter 1994): 89.

92. Arceneaux, "Remix as Cultural Critique," 120.

93. bell hooks, *Yearning,* 92.

94. Danyel Smith, "MC Lyte," *Rolling Stone,* September 16, 1993, 17.

95. MC Lyte, *"Ruffneck,"* Atlantic Records, 1993, video.

96. Smith, "MC Lyte," 17.

97. Brett Pulley, "How a 'Nice Girl' Evolved into Boss, the Gangster Rapper," *Wall Street Journal,* February 3, 1994, 1A.

98. Ibid., 10A.

99. Boss (Lichelle Laws), *"Run, Catch, and Kill,"* Mercury Records, 1994, video. This video was part of a sound track for the film *Mi Vida Loca,* directed by Allison Anders. It is not a part of her initially released recording *Born Gangstaz.*

100. See Rose's *Black Noise;* see also her "Never Trust a Big Butt and a Smile," *Camera Obscura* 23 (1990): 117, 126–127.

101. Carol J. Clover, *Men, Women, and Chainsaws: Gender in the Modern Horror Film* (Princeton: Princeton University Press, 1992), 17.

102. Audre Lorde, *Sister Outsider* (Trumansburg, N.Y.: Crossing Press, 1984), 133.

103. Da Brat, *Sony Official Da Brat* <http://www.dabrat.com> (accessed October 5, 2000).

104. *Ally McBeal,* writ. Shelly Landau and David E. Kelley, Fox, November 16, 1998.

105. Akissi Britton, "Deconstructing *Lil' Kim:* The Whole World Is Watching Kimberly Jones. So Why Isn't Anyone Telling Her What She Needs to Know?" *Essence,* October 2000, 112.

106. Smooth sabotages her lyrics with her visual illustration. In her video *"Female Mac"* Smooth describes herself as a female mac (opposite of mac daddy), "walking like a gangster but more like a pimpstress." Camera angles massage, stroke, and virtually have intercourse with the women backup dancers while Smooth maintains her own self-styled, crotch-grabbing gyration on the ground. This video would seem a male fantasy run amok. Despite this she insists on an equality with male pimps. Smooth asserts that full control of the situation is within her power. Goodall parallels sexual-consequence lyrics with sex as weapon/revenge. She maintains that "these weapon/revenge songs do little to allay those fears, explicitly stating that women engage in sexual activity not for personal desire but out of the desire to control. They implicitly suggest that women are unable to gain this control in any other way" ("Depend on Myself," 89). In the video Smooth wears a baggy-jean outfit, alternating it with daisy-duke jean shorts unbuttoned in a tough, sexy way. In one scene she tosses her shoulder-length hair while walking a pit bull. With her legs and arms spread against a wall, she is sexed by the camera (with an in-and-out zoom). Simultaneously, Smooth assumes her parity when she says, "I'll roll a Lex while you roll your Mercedes."

107. Audre Lorde, "The Master's Tools Will Never Dismantle the Master's House," in *Sister Outsider* (Trumansburg, N.Y.: Crossing Press, 1984).

108. "Interview with Lil' Kim," *Atlantic Confidential with Dyana Williams* <http://media.atlantic-records.com/media/lil_kim> (accessed December 2000).

109. "Tracy Chapman: Matters of the Heart," video press kit, On the Scene Productions/Elektra, 1992.

110. Nelson George, "Tracy Chapman: Today's Black Woman," in *Buppies, B-Boys, Baps and Bohos: Notes of Post-Soul Black Culture* (New York: HarperPerennial, 1992), 113.

111. "Tracy Chapman: Matters of the Heart," video press kit, On the Scene Productions/Elektra, 1992, promotional videocassette.

112. Richard Harrington, "Wake-Up Call," *Washington Post,* February 13, 1994, G6.

113. Me'Shell NdegéOcello, "If That's Your Boyfriend," *Plantation Lullabies,* dir. Jean Baptiste Mondino, 1993.

114. Aufderheide, "Music Videos," 70.

115. Caldwell, *Televisuality,* 20.

116. Ibid., 362 n. 35.

117. Aufderheide, "Music Videos," 68.

118. Goodwin, *Distraction Factory,* 12.

119. Gan Su-lin, Dolf Zillman, and Michael Miltrook, "Stereotyping Effect of Black Women's Sexual Rap on White Audiences," *Basic and Applied Social Psychology* 19, no. 3 (September 1997): 381–399.

120. Rose, *Black Noise,* 146.

121. Quote by seventeen-year-old Jennifer Brannum in Donna Britt, "The Homegirls We Don't See," *Washington Post,* July 30, 1993, B1.

CHAPTER 4 ■ PUBIC HAIR ON MY COKE AND OTHER FREAKY TALES

1. *Webster's New International Dictionary,* 2d ed., s.v. "post-."

2. Teshome H. Gabriel, "Ruin and the Other: Toward a Language of Memory," in *Otherness and the Media: The Ethnography of the Imagined and the Imaged,* ed. Hamid Naficy and Teshome H. Gabriel (Langhorne, Pa.: Harwood Educational Publisher, 1993), 214.

3. Ibid., 218.

4. See Dates and Barlow, *Split Image,* esp. chap. 8.

5. Stuart Hall, "The Determinations of Newsphotographs," *Working Papers #3* (1972): 53–85; Stuart Hall, "The Whites of Their Eyes," in *The Media Reader,* ed. Manuel Alvarado and John O. Thompson (London: British Film Institute, 1990), 7–23.

6. Hall, "Whites of Their Eyes," 13.

7. Elayne Rapping, *The Looking Glass World of Nonfiction TV* (Boston: South End Press, 1987), 40–41.

8. Michele Wallace, "The Politics of Location: Cinema/Theory/Literature/Ethnicity/Sexuality/Me," *Framework* 36 (1989): 42–55.

9. To get a sense of the wide-ranging impact of the hearings see, e.g., Anita Hill, *Speaking Truth to Power* (New York: Doubleday, 1997); Anita Faye Hill and Emma Coleman Jordan, eds., *Race, Gender, and Power in America: The Legacy of the Hill-Thomas Hearings* (New York: Oxford University Press, 1995); Jane Mayer and Jill Abramson, *Strange Justice: The Selling of Clarence Thomas* (Boston: Houghton Mifflin, 1994); Toni Morrison, ed., *Race-ing Justice, Engendering Power: Essays on Anita Hill, Clarence Thomas, and the Construction of Reality* (New York: Pantheon, 1992); Sandra L. Ragan, ed., *The Lynching of Language: Gender, Politics, and Power in the Hill-Thomas Hearings* (Urbana: University of Illinois Press, 1996); Geneva Smitherman, ed., *African-American Women Speak Out on Anita Hill–Clarence Thomas* (Detroit: Wayne State University Press, 1995); Eloise Washington, *Uncivil War: The Struggle between Black Men and Women* (Chicago: Noble Press, 1996). Many other anthologies and texts dedicate themselves to this national news event.

10. Ernest Spaights and Ann Whitaker, "Black Women in the Workforce: A New Look at an Old Problem," *Journal of Black Studies* 25, no. 3 (January 1995): 283.

11. Recognizing that the lower and middle economic scales of Black women coalesce in

this statistical analysis, it still remains important to view both the disparities in income and net worth that exist across gender and race. If the analysis was extended, the findings would show that younger, less-educated women (largely Black and Latina) also sustain higher numbers of less income. The elevated figures come from Gracian Mack's article "More of Us Making Less," in *Black Enterprise,* October 1994, 48.

12. Naomi Wolf, *The Beauty Myth* (New York: William Morrow, 1991), 50.

13. Median income figures for 1998 were as follows: White men $31,980, White women and Black men $24,336, and Black women $20,800. See "Household Data Annual Averages," *Joint Center for Political and Economic Studies* <http://www.jointcenter.org/databank/databank/employ/earnings/full-T97-98.txt> (accessed January 8, 2001).

14. Karen W. Payne and Carlos A. Ugarte, "The Office of Minority Health Resource Center: Impacting on Health Related Disparities among Minority Populations," *Health Education,* December 1989, 6.

15. Ibid., 52.

16. U.S. Department of Health and Human Services, *Report of the Secretary's Task Force on Black and Minority Health* (Washington, D.C.: GPO, August 1985), 92.

17. See Table 11 of the Centers for Disease Control statistics <http://www.cdc.gov/hiv/stats/hasr/20l/table/htm> (accessed February 7, 2001). As of June 2000 there were 27,215 Whites, 71,741 Blacks, 24,710 Hispanics, 670 Asian/Pacific Islanders, and 399 American Indians/Alaskan Natives infected with HIV.

18. Anne McClintock, "The Angel of Progress," in *Colonial Discourse and Post-Colonial Theory,* ed. Patrick Williams and Laura Chrisman (New York: Columbia University Press, 1994), 295.

19. Caryl Rivers, *Slick Spins and Fractured Facts: How Cultural Myths Distort the News* (New York: Columbia University Press, 1996), 133.

20. On the economic disenfranchisement of Black women see K. Sue Jewell's chapter on affirmative action in *Mammy to Miss America.* Jewell describes African-American women's progress and the U.S. reaction to it.

21. Noble, *Beautiful, Also,* 314.

22. Caldwell, *Televisuality,* 13.

23. Kimberlé Crenshaw and Gary Peller, "Reel Time/Real Justice," *Denver University Law Review* 70, no. 2 (1993): 285–286, italics in original. Disaggregation is the breaking up of evidence (in this case the television narrative) piece by piece and assessing whether the evidence standing alone suffices to prove guilt.

24. Fiske, *Media Matters,* 33.

25. Ernie Sotomayor, "What Is News?" *Social Education,* March 1989, 161. By citing this reference I do not intend to foster a reception theory or to launch a communication study without a complete fleshing out of the implications. Sotomayor's observation serves simply to illuminate my understanding of television and uses of the medium by virtue of my being a television watcher myself.

26. Robert M. Entman, "African Americans according to TV News," *Media Studies Journal* 8, no. 3 (summer 1994): 32.

27. This is not to suggest that this was the first segment on race. Stories began airing with the civil unrest of the mid-1960s. Further, in 1986 Bill Moyers hosted a special PBS report called *The Vanishing Black Family,* which maintained that Black communities were crumbling largely because of Black women. The statement implies then that by 1992 news personnel believed that they firmly grasped the "pathology" of America's "problem people."

28. "LA Aftermath," narr. Jeff Greenfield, *Nightline,* ABC, May 8, 1992.

29. Fiske, *Media Matters,* 2.

30. *Chicago Defender,* September 19, 1983, 6.

31. See the *Los Angeles Sentinel,* September 22, 1983, A10.

32. See Russell, Wilson, and Hall, *Color Complex,* 152–153.

33. See bell hooks's chapter on Black beauty in her *Sisters of the Yam: Black Women and Self-Discovery* (Boston: South End Press, 1993).

34. Wolf, *Beauty Myth,* 14.

35. Sam Donaldson, *World News Tonight,* ABC, September 18, 1983.

36. Natasha B. Barnes, "Face of the Nation: Race, Nationalisms, and Identities in Jamaican Beauty Pageants," *Massachusetts Review* 35, nos. 3–4 (autumn–winter 1994): 477.

37. "Vanessa Williams," narr. Bob Berkowitz, *World News Tonight,* ABC, September 18, 1983, my italics.

38. Gray, *Watching Race,* 12.

39. Ibid.

40. Stuart Hall, "What Is This 'Black' in Black Popular Culture?" in *Black Popular Culture,* ed. Gina Dent (Seattle: Bay Press, 1992), 28.

41. Davies, *Black Women,* 7.

42. Miss America Organization <http://www.missamerica.com> (accessed February 9, 2001).

43. Colleen Ballerino Cohen, Richard Wilk, and Beverly Stoeltje, eds., *Beauty Queen on the Global Stage: Gender, Contests, and Power* (New York: Routledge, 1996), 2.

44. Ibid., 249.

45. Quoted in Frank Deford, *There She Is: The Life and Times of Miss America* (New York: Viking, 1971), 255.

46. Ibid., 250.

47. In 1970 Miss Iowa, Cheryl Brown, became the first Black Miss America contestant. *Chicago Defender,* September 19, 1983, 6.

48. Davies, *Black Women,* 12.

49. Nira Yuval-Davis, "Gender and Nation," *Ethnic and Racial Studies* 16, no. 4 (October 1993): 627.

50. NBC televised the 1996 Summer Olympic games held in Atlanta, as well as the 2000 Sydney, 1992 Seoul, and 1988 Los Angeles games.

51. The NBC news organization defended its decision to cover gymnastics extensively based on its surveys from previous Olympics. Yet I maintain that the network's privileging of particular events was predicated not only on assessed viewer taste but also on the racialized tastes of the broadcasters themselves.

52. bell hooks, *Yearning,* 62.

53. Barnes, "Face of the Nation," 473–474.

54. See David Theo Goldberg, *Racist Culture: Philosophy and the Politics of Meaning* (Oxford: Blackwell, 1993), 79.

55. "Vanessa Williams," narr. Bob Berkowitz, *World News Tonight,* ABC, September 18, 1983.

56. "Vanessa Williams," narr. John Palmer, *Nightly News,* NBC, July 23, 1984.

57. Williams appeared on national news outlets eight times as Miss America before 1984: Once on ABC's *World News Tonight,* thrice on NBC, twice on *The Nightly News,* and twice on the morning news show *Sunrise with Jane Pauley.* She also appeared on CNN.

58. ABC's *World News Tonight* aired from San Francisco because the program was covering the 1984 Democratic National Convention. The news of Williams's pictures usurped the election in importance over the following weekend. Interesting, too, was the reporting of the exact number of hours she had left to resign as opposed to saying three days. This phenomenon lent a modicum of seriousness and aggressiveness to the announcement.

59. "Vanessa Williams," narr. Steve Taylor, *World News Tonight,* ABC, July 20, 1984.

60. Ibid.

61. "Vanessa Williams," narr. Frank Casey, INN, July 20, 1984.

62. "Vanessa Williams," narr. Dan Rather, *Evening News*, CBS, July 20, 1984.

63. Ibid.

64. "Vanessa Williams," narr. Morton Dean, *Evening News*, CBS, July 22, 1984.

65. *Evening News* ran the story second, choosing to lead with an economics piece.

66. "Vanessa Williams," narr. John Palmer, *Nightly News*, NBC, July 23, 1984.

67. Ibid.

68. "Vanessa Williams," narr. Jeannie Most, CNN, July 23, 1984.

69. "Penthouse Sales Soar for Miss America Issue," *New York Times*, August 1, 1984, D17.

70. Bebe Moore Campbell, "A New Black Freedom: To Fail," *Washington Post*, July 29, 1984, C5.

71. "Miss America," narr. Dan Rather, *Evening News*, CBS, September 14, 1984.

72. "Miss America Pageant," *World News Tonight*, ABC, September 12, 1984.

73. "Vanessa Williams," narr. Stephen Geer, *World News Tonight*, September 12, 1984.

74. "Miss America," narr. Bob Simon, *Evening News*, CBS, September 14, 1984.

75. Ibid.

76. "Miss America," narr. Stephen Geer, *World News Tonight*, ABC, September 16, 1984.

77. In 1988 Vanessa Williams's first album, *The Right Stuff*, launched her onto the pop and r&b charts. Her follow-up effort, *The Comfort Zone* (1991), was a multimillion-dollar seller. *The Sweetest Days* (1994), *Star Bright* (1996), *Next* (1997), and *Greatest Hits—The First 10 Years* (1998) all followed. Williams appeared for nine months in the Broadway musical "Kiss of the Spider Woman" in 1994–1995 and won rave reviews. Her first film credit came as a patriotic, intelligent, and sexy computer informant in Chuck Russell's *Eraser* (1996), in which she starred opposite Arnold Schwarzenegger. She followed this debut with leading roles in *Hoodlum* (1997), *Soul Food* (1997), *Dance with Me* (1998), *Elmo in Grouchland* (1999), *Light It Up* (1999), and *Shaft* (2000). She has received two NAACP Image Awards, seven Grammy Award nominations and numerous New York Music Awards.

78. bell hooks, *Black Looks: Race and Representation* (Boston: South End Press, 1992), 75.

79. In a CNN report Black modeling agency owner Pat Evans revealed that the co-owners of Creative Artists Management proposed a merger with her agency pending the signing of Suzette Charles to Evans's agency. According to Evans the two knew about the Williams pictures because Tom Chiappel, the photographer, worked for them. Subsequent to Williams's dethroning, according to their vision, Charles would become Miss America and also a "hot commodity." The reporter indicated that they partially denied this accusation but subsequently sued Chiappel and *Penthouse* for excluding them from publishing profits. This scenario proves interesting here because it points again toward the idea that Williams's win had expressly larger implications for a supposedly postracist country.

80. "Controversy Not New to Pageant," *Washington Post*, July 24, 1984, A8.

81. See Paul Laurence Dunbar's poem "We Wear the Masks" in *The Complete Poems of Paul Laurence Dunbar* (New York: Dodd Mead, 1967), 112–113. As I indicated in chapter 1, although Black women may have occupied greater access to white-collar positions, Black men retained most positions of power, prestige, and compensation for their work.

82. Noble, *Beautiful, Also*, 115.

83. Stephen J. Wermiel, "Confirming the Constitution: The Role of the Senate Judiciary Committee," *Law and Contemporary Problems* 56, no. 4 (1993): 122.

84. Frantz Fanon, *Wretched of the Earth* (New York: Grove Weinfeld, 1963), 77.

85. "Questions and Answers," *Law Library Journal* 82, no. 193 (1990): 199.

86. Ibid., 198, my italics.

87. Sara Suleri, "Woman Skin Deep: Feminism and the Postcolonial Condition," in *Colonial Discourse and Post-Colonial Theory: A Reader*, ed. Patrick Williams and Laura Chrisman

(New York: Columbia University Press, 1994), 253. This law resembles America's Missouri Compromise (1820), which designated Black slaves as three-fifths of a person.

88. Anita Miller, ed., *The Complete Transcripts of the Clarence Thomas–Anita Hill Hearings: October 11, 12, 13, 1991* (Chicago: Academy Chicago, 1994), 6.

89. "Thomas," narr. Jim Wooten, *World News Tonight,* ABC, October 8, 1991. Quote from Thomas as read by John Danforth.

90. Mikhail Bakhtin, *Rabelais and His World,* trans. Helene Iswolsky (Cambridge, Mass.: MIT Press, 1968), 10.

91. Ibid., 34.

92. John Fiske, *Television Culture* (London: Methuen, 1987), 241.

93. Miller, *Complete Transcripts,* 118. Further testimony of Clarence Thomas took place at the Senate Confirmation Hearings, October 12, 1991.

94. Cripps, *Making Movies Black,* 253–254. Cripps discusses African-American positioning in McCarthy's HUAC hearings.

95. Quoted in ibid., 41.

96. Frantz Fanon, *Black Skin, White Masks* (New York: Grove Press, 1961), 63.

97. Crenshaw and Peller, "Reel Time," 293.

98. Noble, *Beautiful, Also,* 334.

99. Ibid.

100. Wermiel, "Confirming the Constitution," 137.

101. Sally Steenland, "On Trial: Courtroom Television," *Television Quarterly* 25, no. 4 (1992): 43.

102. Gray, *Watching Race,* 171–172.

103. Mona Fayad, "Reinscribing Identity: Nation and Community in Arab Women's Writing," *College Literature* 22, no. 1 (February 1995): 151.

104. "Anita Hill vs. Clarence Thomas: The Untold Story," narr. Michel McQueen, *Turning Point,* ABC, November 2, 1994.

105. Dan Quayle, "Restoring Basic Values: Strengthening the Family" (speech delivered at the Commonwealth Club of California in San Francisco, May 19, 1992).

106. Fayad, "Reinscribing Identity," 148.

107. Hall, "Whites of Their Eyes," 13.

108. Ibid.

109. United States Commission on Civil Rights, *Window Dressing,* 24.

110. Hayden White, *Tropics of Discourse: Essays in Cultural Criticism* (Baltimore: Johns Hopkins University Press, 1978), 107.

111. Richard Cloward and Frances Fox Piven, *Regulating the Poor: The Functions of Public Welfare* (New York: Vintage, 1993).

112. Jill Duerr Berrick, *Faces of Poverty: Portraits of Women and Children on Welfare* (New York: Oxford University Press, 1995), 5, my italics.

113. "American Agenda—Economy Welfare," narr. Rebecca Chase, *World News Tonight,* ABC, December 1, 1993.

114. Berrick, *Faces of Poverty,* 9.

115. Janet Staiger, *Bad Women: Regulating Sexuality in Early American Cinema* (Minneapolis: University of Minnesota Press, 1995), 21–22. Staiger traces early American notions of women's sexuality by highlighting the lengthy discourses on sexuality in the United States and the discourses circulating prior to the great social program's inception. Even Franklin Roosevelt, the initiator of these programs, spouted views on race suicide.

116. One example can be found in the news story "Unemployment/Wildcat Program." Reporter Marlene Sanders looked at a seven-month, New York City program designed to

help drug addicts, delinquent youth, former criminals, and welfare recipients. It featured a Black woman, who had begun procreating at age 15, and her four children. *Evening News*, CBS, August 7, 1982.

117. Nira Yuval-Davis, "Women and the Biological Reproduction of 'The Nation,'" *Women's Studies International* 19, nos. 1–2 (January–April 1996): 19.

118. Kathleen E. Powderly, "Contraceptive Policy and Ethics: Illustrations from American History," *Hastings Center Report* 25, no. 1 (January–February 1995), 39.

119. Ibid., 40.

120. "Massachusetts Welfare," narr. Lisa Myers, *Nightly News*, NBC, February 23, 1985. Connie Chung anchored.

121. "Wisconsin Workfare," *Evening News*, CBS, April 4, 1998.

122. Senate Committee on Labor: Human Resources Hearing on Title X, March 31, 1981.

123. Excerpt from Faye Wattleton's book, *Life on the Line*, quoted in *Ms.*, September–October 1996, 49.

124. Teshome Gabriel's "Third Cinema as a Guardian of Popular Memory: Towards a Third Aesthetics," in *Questions of Third Cinema*, ed. Jim Pines and Paul Willeman (London: British Film Institute, 1989), was useful in my thinking about popular memory vs. official, sanctioned historical accounts. Further, fictional narratives such as James Ivory's film *Jefferson in Paris* (1995) rewrite master-slave domination into consensual romance.

125. Rivers, *Slick Spins*, 208.

126. Ibid., 210.

127. "New Jersey Welfare Reform," narr. Stan Bernard, *Nightly News*, NBC, January 14, 1992.

128. See Julia R. Henly, "The Significance of Social Context: The Case of Adolescent Childbearing in the African-American Community," *Journal of Black Psychology* 19, no. 4 (November 1993); and Karin L. Brewster, "Neighborhood Context and the Transition to Sexual Activity among Young Black Women," *Demography* 31, no. 4 (November 1994).

129. Berrick, *Faces of Poverty*, 10.

130. Ibid., 15.

131. Entman, "African Americans," 34–35.

132. bell hooks, *Outlaw Culture* (New York: Routledge, 1994), 166–167.

133. "Campaign '84/Reaganomics," narr. Bill Plante, *Evening News*, CBS, August 20, 1984.

134. "Reagan News Conference/Homeless," narr. Richard Villariani, *Nightly News*, NBC, November 20, 1986.

135. Fiske, *Media Matters*, 107.

136. See Berrick, *Faces of Poverty*, 20.

137. Andrea Mitchell, narr., *Nightly News*, NBC, September 27, 1988.

138. Rivers, *Slick Spins*, 202.

139. "Assignment America: A Mother's Wish," narr. Bob Dotson, *Nightly News*, NBC, March 17, 1989.

140. Fiske, *Media Matters*, 42.

141. Ibid., 46.

142. However, none of the Miss Americas since Williams have achieved the material or cultural success that she has.

CHAPTER 5 ▪ YOU'D BETTER RECOGNIZE

1. Sojourner Truth, *Narrative of Sojourner Truth* (Boston: printed for the author, 1850).

2. The ideas of Jean-François Lyotard's postmodernism are well described in Steven Best

and Douglas Kellner, *Postmodern Theory: Critical Interrogations* (New York: Guilford, 1991), 165.

3. See Du Bois, *Souls of Black Folk*, 215.

4. Evelyn J. Hinz, "What Is Multiculturalism? A 'Cognitive' Introduction," *Mosaic* 29, no. 3 (September 1996): xiii.

5. Nicholas C. Cooper-Lewter and Henry H. Mitchell, *Soul Theology: The Heart of American Black Culture* (San Francisco: Harper and Row, 1986), 5–6.

6. Unlike others of her stature, Winfrey achieved ideological proportions similar to the concepts of the American dream, nation, capitalism, and democracy.

7. I am not suggesting that the United States held a monopoly on television talk. However, the talk show's contemporary articulation made it a uniquely American genre.

8. See Wayne Munson, *All Talk: The Talkshow in Media Culture* (Philadelphia: Temple University Press, 1993), 61.

9. Sara Welles, "Taming the TV Talk Show," *Television Quarterly* 28, no. 3 (summer 1996): 41–48.

10. Winfrey was not the first African-American woman to have a television talk show. Della Reese had a combination talk-variety show called *Della* (1969–1970).

11. Gloria-Jean Masciarotte, "C'mon, Girl: Oprah Winfrey and the Discourse of Feminine Talk," *Genders* 11 (fall 1991): 82.

12. Ibid., 88.

13. Ibid., 103.

14. Munson, *All Talk*, 15.

15. Ibid., 10.

16. Ibid., 5.

17. Laurie L. Haag, "Oprah Winfrey: The Construction of Intimacy in the Talk Show Setting," *Journal of Popular Culture* 26, no. 4 (spring 1993): 115.

18. Ibid., 120.

19. Munson, *All Talk*, 6–7.

20. Gray, *Watching Race*, 174.

21. Janice Peck, "Talk about Racism: Framing a Popular Discourse of Race on Oprah Winfrey," *Cultural Critique* 27 (spring 1994): 120.

22. Dana-L. Cloud, "Hegemony or Concordance? The Rhetoric of Tokenism in 'Oprah' Winfrey's Rags-to-Riches Biography," *Critical Studies in Mass Communication* 13, no. 2 (1996): 115–137.

23. Debbie Epstein and Deborah Lynn Steinberg, "All Het-Up! Rescuing Heterosexuality on the *Oprah Winfrey Show*," *Feminist Review* 54 (autumn 1996): 88–111.

24. Mimi White, *Tele-Advising: Therapeutic Discourse in American Television* (Chapel Hill: University of North Carolina Press, 1992), 186 n. 9.

25. Peck, "Talk about Racism," 104.

26. Ward Churchill, "White Studies: The Intellectual Imperialism of U.S. Higher Education," in *Beyond Comfort Zones in Multiculturalism: Confronting the Politics of Privilege*, ed. Sandra Jackson and José Solís (Westport, Conn.: Bergin and Garvey, 1995), 18.

27. Robert La Franco and Josh McHugh, "Piranha Is Good," *Forbes*, October 16, 1995, 66–67.

28. Ibid.

29. See <http://www.forbes.com/finance/lists> (accessed February 15, 2001).

30. Steve McClellan, "Look Who's Talking: Potential for High Ratings at Relatively Low Cost Attracts New Talk Shows," *Broadcasting*, December 14, 1992, 22–23.

31. "King World Agrees to Pay $150 Million in 'Oprah' Deal," *Wall Street Journal,* September 25, 1998, B7. Her contract was then renegotiated and extended to 2004.

32. Of the $200 million, King World banks roughly 35 percent for distribution fees. Cynthia Littleton, "Oprah to Talk through '02," *Variety,* September 28–October 4, 1998, 69.

33. Richard Katz and Cynthia Littleton, "Oxygen Moves Forward with Oprah," *Variety,* November 30–December 6, 1998, 25.

34. Littleton, "Oprah to Talk," 69.

35. Stephen Braun, "The Oprah Seal of Approval," *Los Angeles Times,* March 9, 1997, Calendar sec., 81.

36. Ibid.

37. Winfrey's Web presence is ubiquitous. A Google search for "Oprah Winfrey" brings up more than 105,000 pages. See, among others, a tribute to her by a fan <http://www.geocities.com/Hollywood/Lot/2891/oprah.html> (accessed November 19, 2001); and Mr. Showbiz's biographies on entertainers et al. like Oprah <http://www.mrshowbiz.go.com/celebrities/people/oprahwinfrey/index.html> (accessed October 2000); to find The Oprah Winfrey Show on international television schedules see <http://www.eurotv.com/rtv5.htm> (accessed November 19, 2001).

38. See John Fiske, "The Cultural Economy of Fandom," in *The Adoring Audience: Fan Culture and Popular Media,* ed. Lisa A. Lewis (London: Routledge, 1992), 30.

39. James R. Walker, "More Than Meets the Ear: A Factor Analysis of Student Impressions of Television Talk Show Hosts," paper presented at the 74th Annual Meeting of the Speech Communication Association, New Orleans, November 3–6, 1988, *ERIC,* ED 299630.

40. Richard Dyer, *Stars* (London: British Film Institute, 1979), 183.

41. Cloud, "Hegemony or Concordance?" 119.

42. An alternative version of King World and Winfrey's meeting suggests that her agent approached King World about distributing the program.

43. Du Bois, *Souls of Black Folk,* 14.

44. "Gun Control," *The Oprah Winfrey Show,* syndicated program, June 27, 1989.

45. Quoted in Thomas Morgan, "Oprah Winfrey: Troubled Youth to TV Host and Nominee," *New York Times,* March 4, 1986, 26.

46. As late as 1997, even in her slimmed-down, healthy version, Winfrey returned to her outreach mainstay, weight. In the March 5, 1997, *Oprah Winfrey Show* she retraced the moment she decided to change her lifestyle. She aired a portion of the skit done by the *In Living Color* cast satirizing her persona and the discussion of her weight around the dinner table in *The Nutty Professor* as different lows and highs of her weight roller coaster.

47. Butler, "Redesigning Discourse," 15.

48. This phrase comes from George Lipsitz, *The Possessive Investment in Whiteness: How White People Benefit from Identity Politics* (Philadelphia: Temple University Press, 1998).

49. Terry Eagleton, *Literary Theory: An Introduction* (Minneapolis: University of Minnesota Press, 1983), 101.

50. Peter Wollen, *Signs and Meaning in the Cinema* (Bloomington: Indiana University Press, 1972), 122.

51. Cloud, "Hegemony or Concordance?" 119.

52. "MTV Dance Party," *The Oprah Winfrey Show,* syndicated, August 7, 1991.

53. Rubey, "Voguing," 901–902.

54. Madonna's pussy is apparently so powerful that full texts are dedicated to its examination. See, e.g., Lisa Frank and Paul Smith, eds., *Madonnarama: Essays on Sex and Popular Culture* (Pittsburgh: Cleis, 1993); and Matthew Rettenmund, *Encyclopedia Madonnica* (New York: St. Martin's, 1995).

55. Andrew Ferguson, "Bad Girls Don't Cry," *National Review,* May 30, 1994, 72.

56. Albert J. Raboteau, "Fire in the Bones: African-American Christianity and Autobiographical Reflection," *America,* May 21, 1994, 4.

57. "The Sacrament of Penance," *New Advent* <http://www.newadvent.org/cathen/11618c.htm> (accessed July 22, 2001).

58. Morgan, "Oprah Winfrey," 26.

59. In 1995 Jonathan Schmitz murdered his best friend, Scott Amedure, three days after the two appeared on the *Jenny Jones* show. On the episode Amedure confessed that he had romantic feelings for Schmitz. Schmitz was convicted twice (the first time it was overturned) in 1999. Subsequently, the Amedure family won a $25 million lawsuit against *Jenny Jones* and its parent Warner Bros. in a Missouri court.

60. Quoted in Bob Longino, "Channel Surfer Oprah Exhorting Fans to 'Change Your Life,'" *Atlanta Journal and Constitution,* September 10, 1998, D6.

61. For proof of Winfrey's spiritual determination see her official Web site at <http://www.oprah.com>.

62. See "Christian Leaders Consult with Clinton," *Christian Century,* December 6, 1995, 1169.

63. "Oprah Winfrey," *Current Biography Yearbook* (New York: H. H. Wilson, 1987), 611. The writer compiled the biography from several sources, including the *Chicago Tribune, Ebony, New York Daily News, Miami Herald, Newsweek, Washington Post,* and Robert Waldon's book *Oprah!*

64. I thank Michelle Fang from my U.C.L.A. course, "Representations of Women of Color in Contemporary Visual Culture," spring 1997, for alerting me to this discrepancy.

65. One key issue Black women noticed about Winfrey's Sophia was the color of her skin. As extensively discussed in two previous chapters, the melanin quotient always plays a role in the way Colored people perceive themselves and certainly in the way that they are visualized.

66. Bobo, *Black Women,* 110.

67. Cooper-Lewter, *Soul Theology,* 1.

68. James Ayer, "Mark 3:20–35: Between Text and Sermon," *Interpretation: A Journal of Bible and Theology* 51, no. 2 (April 1997).

69. "Coming Out Day for Abusive Parents," *The Oprah Winfrey Show,* syndicated program, January 13, 1992.

70. Louise Kiernan, "Oprah's Poverty Program Stalls: Despite High Hopes, Only 5 Families Graduate in 2 Years," *Chicago Tribune,* August 27, 1996, N1.

71. In the opening Winfrey portrays a girl in her late teens or early twenties. The spectator may mark some incongruity as a result of the disparity between Winfrey's actual thirty-five-year-old body and the age of the character. Also, by the time the program ends, she appears to be seventy-five instead of the fifty that she should have been.

72. The film was the subject of twenty-four television news magazine pieces and eleven magazine covers. Frank Rich, "The Oprah Gap," *New York Times,* December 12, 1998, A21.

73. The first week *Beloved* garnered $8 million and placed number five in terms of box office receipts. By the end of the second week ticket sales had dropped 50 percent. Because films exploring African-American themes are marketed almost exclusively domestically, the film was a financial failure. "*Beloved* It's Not," *Economist,* November 21, 1998, 3–4.

74. Raphael Shargel, "Epic Mice," review of *Beloved, New Leader,* November 30, 1998, 18–19.

75. Rich, "Oprah Gap," A21.

76. For this academic view see Epstein and Steinberg, "All Het Up!"

77. Tom Shales, "Oprah's Preachiness Becoming a Turn-Off," *Atlanta Journal and Constitution,* November 5, 1998, D6.

78. *Ricki Lake* began in 1993. The show targets a young audience but concentrates on the eighteen-to-thirty-four-year-old demographic.

79. Jill Nelson, "Talk Is Cheap," *Nation,* June 5, 1995, 800.

EPILOGUE

1. Unfortunately, Miss Cleo didn't "keep it real" enough for Missouri attorney general Jay Nixon. Nixon said that "Miss Cleo should have seen this coming," as his office filed two suits against the company that promotes her, Access Resources Services, for fraud. For the less clairvoyant see the details in "Missouri Files Fraud Lawsuit against TV Psychics" at <http://www.cnn.com/2001/law/07/25/psychic.lawsuit/index.html> (accessed July 25, 2001).

2. Maurice Merleau-Ponty, *The Primacy of Perception,* ed. James M. Edie (Evanston, Ill.: Northwestern University Press, 1964), 5.

3. "Daydream," *Newsradio,* NBC, November 13, 1996.

4. "Last Rites," *ER,* NBC, October 1999.

5. "Humpty Dumpty," *ER,* NBC, November 18, 1999.

6. Interestingly, *Strong Medicine* is executive produced by Whoopi Goldberg, who makes guest appearances on the program.

7. Nielsen Media Research, *Report,* 42. "All others" were Caucasians and Hispanics.

8. For example, in 1996 Janet Jackson signed an $80 million recording contract with Virgin Records, the largest in the history of the music industry.

9. Meredith Brooks, "Bitch," on *Blurring the Edges,* Capitol Records, 1997.

10. Noella Cain is a Black music connoisseur and the aunt who schooled me on 1950s and 1960s Texas blues.

11. Newt Gingrich, *World News Tonight,* ABC, January 12, 1995.

12. "The Talk of TV—A Chat with Oprah Winfrey," *Day One,* January 5, 1995, Transcript #172-3, 8:00 P.M.

13. John McWhorter, "Gimme a Break!" review of *Primetime Blues: African-Americans on Network Television,* by Donald Bogle, *New Republic,* February 27, 2001 <http://www.tnr.com> (accessed April 2, 2001).

14. Ibid.

15. John Fiske believes that not in this lifetime are we likely to see considerable change. John Fiske, conversation with author, University of Queensland, Brisbane, Australia, December 2000.

16. Brent Owens, dir., *Pimps Up, Hoes Down,* HBO, 1998, documentary.

17. Quote of Julie Scelfo, in "The Contender," *Newsweek,* January 8, 2001, 48.

18. Reggie Rock Bythewood, dir., *Dancing in September,* HBO, 2001, cable motion picture.

19. Quote of Judy Goodwin, "Disney Angers Rights Group," *Arizona Republic,* August 24, 1999, B6.

20. Shannon Mcrac, "Flesh Made World: Sex, Text, and the Virtual Body," in *Internet Culture,* ed. David Porter (New York: Routledge, 1997): 73–86.

21. Barry Garron, "Novel Ideas," *Billboard,* April 22, 2000, 5–11.

REFERENCES

Abt, Vicki, and Leonard Mustazza. *Coming after Oprah: Cultural Fallout in the Age of the TV Talk Show.* Bowling Green, Ohio: Bowling Green State University Press, 1997.

Allen, Robert C., ed. *Channels of Discourse, Reassembled: Television and Contemporary Criticism.* Chapel Hill: University of North Carolina Press, 1992.

Amdur, Meredith. "Action-Hour Appeal Is Worldwide." *Broadcasting and Cable,* August 29, 1994, 39.

Ansa, Tina McElroy. *Ugly Ways.* New York: Harcourt Brace, 1993.

Arceneaux, K. C. "The Remix as Cultural Critique: The Urban Contemporary Music Video." *Popular Music and Society* 16, no. 3 (fall 1992): 109–124.

Arnheim, Rudolf. *Film as Art.* Berkeley: University of California Press, 1957.

Atkin, David. "The Evolution of Television Series Addressing Single Women, 1966–1990." *Journal of Broadcasting and Electronic Media* 35, no. 4 (fall 1991): 517–523.

———. "An Analysis of Television Series with Minority-Lead Characters." *Critical Studies in Mass Communication* 9, no. 4 (1992): 337–349.

Aufderheide, Pat. "Music Videos: The Look of the Sound." *Journal of Communication* 36, no. 1 (winter 1986): 57–78.

Ayers, James. "Mark 3:20–35: Between Text and Sermon." *Interpretation: A Journal of Bible and Theology* 51, no. 2 (April 1997): 178–182.

Bakhtin, Mikhail. *Rabelais and His World.* Trans. Helene Iswolsky. Cambridge, Mass.: MIT Press, 1968.

Banks, Ingrid. *Hair Matters: Beauty, Power, and Black Women's Consciousness.* New York: New York University Press, 2000.

Barnes, Natasha B. "Face of the Nation: Race, Nationalisms, and Identities in Jamaican Beauty Pageants." *Massachusetts Review* 35, nos. 3–4 (autumn/winter 1994): 471–492.

Bernardi, Daniel, ed. *The Birth of Whiteness: Race and the Emergence of U.S. Cinema.* New Brunswick, N.J.: Rutgers University Press, 1996.

Berrick, Jill Duerr. *Faces of Poverty: Portraits of Women and Children on Welfare.* New York: Oxford University Press, 1995.

Best, Steven, and Douglas Kellner. *Postmodern Theory: Critical Interrogations.* New York: Guilford, 1991.

Bobo, Jacqueline. *Black Women as Cultural Readers.* New York: Columbia University Press, 1995.

Bobo, Jacqueline, and Ellen Seiter. "Black Feminism and Media Criticism: 'The Women of Brewster Place.'" *Screen* 32, no. 3 (autumn 1991): 286–302.

Boddy, William. *Fifties Television: The Industry and Its Critics.* Chicago: University of Illinois Press, 1993.

Bogle, Donald. *Blacks in American Films and Television: An Illustrated Encyclopedia.* New York: Simon and Schuster, 1988.

———. *Toms, Coons, Mulattoes, Mammies, and Bucks: An Interpretive History of Blacks in American Films.* New York: Continuum, 1991.

Boskin, Joseph, and Joseph Dorinson. "Ethnic Humor: Subversion and Survival." *American Quarterly* 37 (spring 1985): 81–97.

Brewster, Karin L. "Neighborhood Context and the Transition to Sexual Activity among Young Black Women." *Demography* 31, no. 4 (November 1994): 603–614.

Britton, Akissi. "Deconstructing *Lil' Kim:* The Whole World Is Watching Kimberly Jones. So Why Isn't Anyone Telling Her What She Needs to Know?" *Essence,* October 2000, 112–115, 186.

Brooks, Tim, and Earle Marsh. *The Complete Directory to Prime Time Network and Cable TV Shows: 1946–Present.* New York: Ballantine, 1995.

Brown, Malaika. "Sisterhood Televised: Yvette Lee Bowser and the Voice She Listens To." *American Visions* (April–May 1995): 42–43.

Browne, Nick. "The Political Economy of the Television (Super) Text." In *American Television: New Directions in History and Theory,* ed. Nick Browne. Langhorne, Pa.: Harwood Academic, 1994.

———, ed. *American Television: New Directions in History and Theory.* New York: Harwood Academic, 1994.

Bullough, Vern L., and Bonnie Bullough, *Cross Dressing, Sex, and Gender.* Philadelphia: University of Pennsylvania Press, 1993.

Butler, Jeremy G. "Redesigning Discourse: Feminism, the Sitcom, and *Designing Women.*" *Journal of Film and Video* 45, no. 1 (spring 1993): 13–26.

Butsch, Richard. "Class and Gender in Four Decades of Television Situation Comedy: Plus ça Change . . ." *Critical Studies in Mass Communication* 9, no. 4 (1992): 387–399.

Caldwell, John Thornton. *Televisuality: Style, Crisis, and Authority in American Television.* New Brunswick, N.J.: Rutgers University Press, 1995.

Campbell, Bebe Moore. "A New Black Freedom: To Fail." *Washington Post* (July 29, 1984): C5.

Cepeda, Raquel. "Money, Power, Elect: Where's the Hip-Hop Agenda?" *Essence,* August 2000, 117–118, 163–164, 166–168.

Chernoff, John Miller. *African Rhythm and African Sensibility: Aesthetics and Social Action in African Musical Idioms.* Chicago: University of Chicago Press, 1979.

Christian, Barbara. *Black Feminist Criticism: Perspectives on Black Women Writers.* New York: Pergamon Press, 1985.

Churchill, Ward. "White Studies: The Intellectual Imperialism of U.S. Higher Education." In *Beyond Comfort Zones in Multiculturalism: Confronting the Politics of Privilege,* ed. Sandra Jackson and José Solís. Westport, Conn.: Bergin and Garvey, 1995.

Cloud, Dana L. "Hegemony or Concordance? The Rhetoric of Tokenism in 'Oprah' Winfrey's Rags-to-Riches Biography." *Critical Studies in Mass Communication* 13, no. 2 (1996): 115–137.

Clover, Carol J. *Men, Women, and Chainsaws: Gender in the Modern Horror Film.* Princeton: Princeton University Press, 1992.

Cloward, Richard, and Frances Fox Piven. *Regulating the Poor: The Functions of Public Welfare.* New York: Vintage, 1993.

Cohen, Colleen Ballerino, Richard Wilk, and Beverly Stoeltje, eds. *Beauty Queen on the Global Stage: Gender, Contests, and Power.* New York: Routledge, 1996.

Collins, Patricia Hill. *Black Feminist Thought.* New York: Routledge, 1991.

———. "Learning from the Outsider Within: The Sociological Significance of Black Feminist Thought," *Social Problems* 33, no. 6 (December 1986): S14–S32.

Cooper-Lewter, Nicholas C., and Henry H. Mitchell. *Soul Theology: The Heart of American Black Culture.* San Francisco: Harper and Row, 1986.

Crenshaw, Kimberlé, and Gary Peller. "Reel Time/Real Justice." *Denver University Law Review* 70, no. 2 (1993): 283–296.

Cripps, Thomas. *Making Movies Black: The Hollywood Message Movie from World War II to the Civil Rights Era.* New York: Oxford University Press, 1993.

———. *Slow Fade to Black: The Negro in American Film, 1900–1942.* New York: Oxford University Press, 1993.

Cross, Brian. *It's Not about a Salary . . . Rap, Race and Resistance in Los Angeles.* London: Verso, 1993.

Dates, Jannette L., and William Barlow. *Split Image: African Americans in the Mass Media.* Washington, D.C.: Howard University Press, 1990.

Davies, Carole Boyce. *Black Women, Writing, and Identity: Migrations of the Subject.* New York: Routledge, 1994.

Deford, Frank. *There She Is: The Life and Times of Miss America.* New York: Viking, 1971.

Denisoff, R. Serge. *Inside MTV.* New Brunswick, N.J.: Transaction, 1988.

Department of Labor. *The Negro Family: The Case for National Action.* Washington, D.C.: GPO, 1965.

Dickerson, Sandra A. "Is Sapphire Still Alive? The Image of Black Women in Television Situation Comedies in the 1990s." Ph.D. diss., Boston University School of Education, 1991.

Douglas, Susan. "Sitcom Women: We've Come a Long Way. Maybe." *Ms.,* November 1995, 76–80.

Du Bois, William Edward Burghardt (W.E.B.). *The Souls of Black Folk.* 1903. Reprint, New York: Norton, 1999.

Dunbar, Paul Laurence. "We Wear the Masks." In *The Complete Poems of Paul Laurence Dunbar.* New York: Dodd Mead, 1967.

Dyer, Richard. *Stars.* London: British Film Institute, 1979.

Eagleton, Terry. *Literary Theory: An Introduction.* Minneapolis: University of Minnesota Press, 1983.

Edwards, Audrey. "From Aunt Jemima to Anita Hill: Media's Split Image of Black Women." *Media Studies Journal* (winter–spring 1993): 214–222.

Ellison, Ralph. *Invisible Man.* New York: Quality Paperback Book Club, 1947.

Ely, Melvin Patrick. *The Adventures of "Amos 'n' Andy": A Social History of an American Phenomenon.* New York: Free Press, 1991.

Entman, Robert M. "African Americans according to TV News." *Media Studies Journal* 8, no. 3 (summer 1994): 29–38.

Epstein, Debbie, and Deborah Lynn Steinberg. "All Het-Up! Rescuing Heterosexuality on the *Oprah Winfrey Show.*" *Feminist Review* 54 (autumn 1996): 88–111.

Fanon, Frantz. *Black Skin, White Masks.* New York: Grove Press, 1961.

———. *Wretched of the Earth.* New York: Grove Weinfeld, 1963.

Farley, Christopher John. "Black and Blue." *Time,* November 22, 1993, 80–81.

Fayad, Mona. "Reinscribing Identity: Nation and Community in Arab Women's Writing." *College Literature* 22, no. 1 (February 1995): 147–160.

Ferguson, Andrew. "Bad Girls Don't Cry." *National Review,* May 30, 1994, 72.

Feuer, Jane. "Genre Study and Television." In *Channels of Discourse, Reassembled: Television and Contemporary Criticism,* ed. Robert C. Allen. 2d ed. Chapel Hill: University of North Carolina Press, 1992.

Fine, Marlene G., Carolyn Anderson, and Gary Eckles. "Black English on Black Situation Comedies." *Journal of Communication* 29, no. 3 (summer 1979): 21–29.

Fiske, John. "The Cultural Economy of Fandom." In *The Adoring Audience: Fan Culture and Popular Media,* ed. Lisa A. Lewis. London: Routledge, 1992.

———. *Media Matters: Everyday Culture and Political Change.* Minneapolis: University of Minnesota Press, 1994.

———. *Reading Television.* New York: Methuen, 1978.

———. *Television Culture.* New York: Routledge, 1987.

Forman, Ruth. *We Are the Young Magicians.* Boston: Beacon Press, 1993.

Frankenberg, Ruth. *White Women, Race Matters.* Minneapolis: University of Minnesota Press, 1993.

Frazier, E. Franklin. *Black Bourgeoisie.* London: Collier, 1969.

Frazier, June M., and Timothy C. Frazier. "*Father Knows Best* and *The Cosby Show:* Nostalgia and Tradition in the Sitcom Tradition." *Journal of Popular Culture* 27, no. 3 (winter 1993): 163–172.

Freeman, Michael. "It's the Hour of the Hour." *Mediaweek,* June 6, 1994, 18–20.

Freeman, Mike. "Ratings Block Minority Syndicators." *Broadcasting and Cable,* September 27, 1993, 30–31.

Fuller, Linda K. *"The Cosby Show": Audiences, Impact, and Implications.* New York: Greenwood Press, 1992.

Fusco, Coco. "About Locating Ourselves and Our Representations." *Framework* 36 (January 1989): 7–14.

Fusfeld, Daniel R., and Timothy Bates. "Black Economic Well-Being since the 1950s." In *A Turbulent Voyage: Readings in African American Studies,* ed. Floyd W. Hayes III (San Diego, Calif.: Collegiate Press, 1997).

Gabriel, Teshome H. "Ruin and the Other: Toward a Language of Memory." In *Otherness and the Media: The Ethnography of the Imagined and the Imaged,* ed. Hamid Naficy and Teshome H. Gabriel. Langhorne, Pa.: Harwood Academic Publisher, 1993.

———. "Third Cinema as a Guardian of Popular Memory: Towards a Third Aesthetics." In *Questions of Third Cinema,* ed. Jim Pines and Paul Willeman. London: British Film Institute, 1989.

Gaines, Jane. "White Privilege and Looking Relations: Race and Gender in Feminist Film Theory." *Cultural Critique* 4 (fall 1986): 59–79.

Galster, George C. "White Flight from Racially Integrated Neighborhoods in the 1970s: The Cleveland Experience." *Urban Studies* 27, no. 3 (June 1990): 385–399.

Gan Su-lin, Dolf Zillman, and Michael Miltrook. "Stereotyping Effect of Black Women's Sexual Rap on White Audiences." *Basic and Applied Social Psychology* 19, no. 3 (September 1997): 381–399.

Gates, Henry Louis, Jr., and Nellie Y. MacKay, eds. *The Norton Anthology of African American Literature.* New York: Norton, 1997.

George, Nelson. *Blackface: Reflections on African-Americans and the Movies.* New York: HarperPerennial, 1992.

———. *Buppies, B-boys, Baps, and Bohos: Notes of Post-Soul Black Culture.* New York: HarperCollins, 1992.

Giddings, Paula. *When and Where I Enter: The Impact of Black Women on Race and Sex in America.* New York: Bantam Books, 1984.

Gladney, Marvin J. "The Black Arts Movement and Hip-Hop." *African American Review* 29, no. 2 (summer 1995): 291–301.

Glazer, Nathan. "The Hard Questions: Life in the City." *New Republic,* August 19, 1996, 37.

Glennon, Ivy. Review of *Women Watching TV: Gender, Class and Generation in the American TV Experience,* by Andrea Press. *Journal of Communication* 44, no. 1 (1994): 180–183.

Goldberg, David Theo. *Racist Culture: Philosophy and the Politics of Meaning.* Oxford: Blackwell, 1993.

Goodall, Nataki H. "Depend on Myself: T.L.C. and the Evolution of Black Female Rap." *Journal of Negro History* 79, no. 1 (winter 1994): 85–93.

Goodwin, Andrew. *Dancing in the Distraction Factory: Music Television and Popular Culture.* Minneapolis: University of Minnesota Press, 1992.

Gow, "Making Sense of Music Video-Research during the Inaugural Decade." *Journal of American Culture* 15, no. 3 (fall 1992): 35–43.

———. "Music Video as Communication: Popular Formulas, Energy, Genre." *Journal of Popular Culture* 26 (fall 1992): 41–70.

Gray, Herman. "African-American Political Desire and the Seductions of Contemporary Cultural Politics." *Cultural Studies* 7, no. 3 (October 1993): 364–373.

———. "The Endless Slide of Difference: Critical Television Studies, Television, and the Question of Race." *Critical Studies in Mass Communication* 10, no. 2 (June 1993): 190–197.

———. *Watching Race: Television and the Struggle for "Blackness."* Minneapolis: University of Minnesota Press, 1995.

Gregory, Deborah. "The Queen Rules." *Essence,* October 1993, 56–58, 114–115, 118.

Guerrero, Ed. *Framing Blackness: The African-American Image in Film.* Philadelphia: Temple University Press, 1993.

Haag, Laurie L. "Oprah Winfrey: The Construction of Intimacy in the Talk Show Setting." *Journal of Popular Culture* 26, no. 4 (spring 1993): 115–121.

Haggins, Bambi L. "Banter, Banter, Banter, Kiss: Evolution and Intransigence in Romantic Comedy." Paper presented at the Society for Cinema Studies Conference, Dallas, Tex., March 1, 1996.

———. "There's No Place Like Home: The American Dream, African-American Identity, and the Situation Comedy." *Velvet Light Trap* 43 (spring 1999): 23–36.

Hall, Ronald. "The Bleaching Syndrome: African Americans' Response to Cultural Domination vis-à-vis Skin Color." *Journal of Black Studies* 26, no. 2 (November 1995): 172–184.

Hall, Stuart. "Cultural Identity and Cinematic Representation." *Framework* 36 (1989): 68–81.

———. "The Determinations of Newsphotographs." *Working Papers in Cultural Studies #3* (1972): 53–85.

———. "What Is This 'Black' in Black Popular Culture?" In *Black Popular Culture,* ed. Gina Dent. Seattle: Bay Press, 1992.

———. "Whites of Their Eyes." In *The Media Reader,* ed. Manuel Alvarado and John O. Thompson. London: British Film Institute, 1990.

Hamamoto, Darrell Y. *Nervous Laughter: Television Situation Comedy and Liberal Democratic Ideology.* New York: Praeger, 1989.

Hansen, Miriam. *Babel and Babylon: Spectatorship in American Silent Film.* Cambridge: Harvard University Press, 1991.

Harris, Joanne. "Why Not Just Laugh? Making Fun of Ourselves on Television." *American Visions,* April–May 1993, 38–41.

Haynes, Karima A. "Miss America: From Vanessa Williams to Kimberly Aiken." *Ebony,* January 1994, 42.

Heath, Rebecca Piirto. "What Tickles Our Funny Bones." *American Demographics* (November 1996): 48.

Heaton, Jeanne Albronda. *Tuning in Trouble: Talk TV's Destructive Impact on Mental Health.* San Francisco: Jossey-Bass Press, 1995.

Heintz-Knowles, Katherine E., McCrae A. Parker, Patti Miller, Christy Glaubke, Sierra Thai-Binh, and Tristan Sorah-Reyes. *Fall Colors: 2000–01 Prime Time Diversity Report.* Oakland, Calif.: Children Now, 2001.

Henly, Julia R. "The Significance of Social Context: The Case of Adolescent Childbearing in the African-American Community." *Journal of Black Psychology* 19, no. 4 (November 1993): 461–477.

Herbert, Solomon. "The Women of Brewster Place." *Essence,* November 1988, 39.

Higgins, John M. "Johnson Taking BET Private." *Broadcasting and Cable,* March 23, 1998.

Hill, Anita. *Speaking Truth to Power.* New York: Doubleday, 1997.

Hill, Anita Faye, and Emma Coleman Jordan, eds. *Race, Gender, and Power in America: The Legacy of the Hill-Thomas Hearings.* New York: Oxford University Press, 1995.

Hill, George H. *Ebony Images: Black Americans and Television.* Carson, Calif.: Daystar, 1986.

Hill, George H., Lorraine Raglin, and Chas Floyd Johnson. *Black Women in Television: An Illustrated History and Bibliography.* New York: Garland, 1990.

Hinz, Evelyn J. "What Is Multiculturalism? A 'Cognitive' Introduction." *Mosaic* 29, no. 3 (September 1996): vii–xiii.

hooks, bell. *Ain't I a Woman: Black Women and Feminism.* Boston: South End Press, 1981.

———. *Art on My Mind: Visual Politics.* New York: New Press, 1995.

———. *Black Looks: Race and Representation.* Boston: South End Press, 1992.

———. "Making Movie Magic." Introduction to *Reel to Real: Race, Sex, and Class at the Movies,* by bell hooks. New York: Routledge, 1996.

———. *Outlaw Culture: Resisting Representations.* New York: Routledge, 1994.

———. *Sisters of the Yam: Black Women and Self-Discovery.* Boston: South End Press, 1993.

———. *Talking Back: Thinking Feminist, Thinking Black.* Boston: South End Press, 1982.

———. *Yearning: Race, Gender, and Cultural Politics.* Boston: South End Press, 1990.

Hunter-Gault, Charlayne. *In My Place.* New York: Farrar, Straus, Giroux, 1992.

Hurston, Zora Neale. "The Pet Negro System." In *I Love Myself,* ed. Alice Walker. Old Westbury, N.Y.: Feminist Press, 1979.

Hutchinson, Janice Faye. "The Hip Hop Generation: African American Male-Female Relationships in a Night Club Setting." *Journal of Black Studies* 30, no. 1 (September 1999): 62–84.

Jameson, Fredric. "Postmodernism and Consumer Society." In *Postmodernism and Its Discontents,* ed. E. Ann Kaplan. London: Verso, 1988.

———. *Postmodernism, or, The Cultural Logic of Late Capitalism.* Durham, N.C.: Duke University Press, 1991.

Jaynes, Gerald David, and Robin M. Williams Jr., eds. *A Common Destiny: Blacks and American Society.* Washington, D.C.: National Academy, 1989.

Jeffries, John M. "Discussion." In *Slipping through the Cracks: The Status of Black Women,* ed. Margaret C. Simms and Julianne M. Malveaux. New Brunswick, N.J.: Transaction, 1987.

Jewell, K. Sue. *From Mammy to Miss America and Beyond.* New York: Routledge, 1993.

Jhally, Sut. *DreamWorlds II: Desire/Sex/Power in Music Video.* Media Education Project. 1995.

Jhally, Sut, and Justin Lewis. *Enlightened Racism: "The Cosby Show," Audiences, and The Myth of the American Dream.* Boulder, Colo.: Westview, 1992.

Johansson, T. "Music Video, Youth Culture and Post Modernism." *Popular Music and Society* 16, no. 3 (fall 1992): 9–22.

Jones, Felicia G. "The Black Audience and the BET Channel." *Journal of Broadcasting and Electronic Media* 34, no. 4 (fall 1990): 477–486.

Joyrich, Lynne. "Critical and Textual Hypermasculinity." In *Logics of Television,* ed. Patricia Mellencamp. Bloomington: Indiana University Press, 1990.

Kaplan, E. Ann. "Is the Gaze Male?" *Powers of Desire: The Politics of Sexuality,* ed. Ann Snitow, Christine Stansell, and Sharon Thompson. New York: New York University Press, 1983.

———. *Rocking around the Clock: Music Television, Postmodernism, and Consumer Culture.* New York: Methuen, 1987.

Kaye, Jeffrey. "Color Bars." *MacNeil/Lehrer NewsHour,* KCET, January 28, 1993.

Kinder, Marsha. "Music Video and the Spectator: Television, Ideology and Dream." *Film Quarterly* 38 (fall 1984): 2–15.

King, Norman. *Everybody Loves OPRAH! Her Remarkable Life Story.* New York: William Morrow, 1987.

Kolawole, Helen. "Booting Booti Off the Box: What's behind the Female Flesh Cavorting around Swimming Pools in the Endless Stream of Rap and R&B Videos?" *Voice*, June 18, 1996.

Kubey, Robert, Mark Shifflet, Niranjala Weerakkody, and Stephen Ukeiley. "Demographic Diversity on Cable: Have the New Cable Channels Made a Difference in the Representation of Gender, Race, and Age? *Journal of Broadcasting and Electronic Media* 39, no. 4 (fall 1995): 459–471.

La Franco, Robert, and Josh McHugh. "Piranha Is Good." *Forbes*, October 16, 1995, 66–67.

Laing, Dave. "Music Video: Industrial Product, Cultural Form." *Screen* 26, no. 2 (March–April 1985): 78–83.

Larson, Stephanie Greco. "Black Women on *All My Children*." *Journal of Popular Film and Television* 22, no. 1 (spring 1994): 44–48.

Leibman, Nina C. *Living Room Lectures: The Fifties Family in Film and Television.* Austin: University of Texas Press, 1995.

Leland, John. "Girl Groups: Our Bodies, Our Sales." *Newsweek*, January 31, 1994, 56.

Levy, Steven. "Ad Nauseam: How MTV Sells Out Rock and Roll." *Rolling Stone*, December 8, 1983: 33–34.

Lewis, Lisa A. "Consumer Girl Culture: How Music Video Appeals to Girls." In *Television and Women's Culture: The Politics of the Popular,* ed. Mary Ellen Brown. London: Sage, 1990.

———. "Form and Female Authorship in Music Video." In *Television: The Critical View,* ed. Horace Newcomb, 5th ed. New York: Oxford University Press, 1994.

———. *Gender Politics and MTV.* Philadelphia: Temple University Press, 1990.

Lipsitz, George. *The Possessive Investment in Whiteness: How White People Benefit from Identity Politics.* Philadelphia: Temple University Press, 1998.

Livingstone, Sonia, and Peter Lunt. *Talk on Television: Audience Participation and Public Debate.* New York: Routledge, 1994.

Lorde, Audre. *Chosen Poems Old and New.* New York: Norton, 1982.

———. *Sister Outsider: Essays and Speeches.* Trumansburg, N.Y.: Crossing Press, 1984.

Lubiano, Wahneema. "Black Ladies, Welfare Queens, and State Minstrels: Ideological War by Narrative Means." In *Race-ing Justice, En-gendering Power: Essays on Anita Hill, Clarence Thomas, and the Construction of Social Reality,* ed. Toni Morrison. New York: Pantheon, 1992.

———. "But Compared to What? Reading Realism, Representation, and Essentialism in *School Daze, Do the Right Thing,* and the Spike Lee Discourse." *Black American Literature Forum* 25, no. 2 (summer 1991): 253–282.

MacDonald, J. Fred. *Blacks and White TV: African Americans in Television since 1948.* Chicago: Nelson-Hall, 1992.

Malveaux, Julianne. "Section Introduction." In *Slipping through the Cracks: The Status of Black Women,* ed. Margaret C. Simms and Julianne M. Malveaux. New Brunswick, N.J.: Transaction, 1987.

Mapp, Edward. "Black Women in Films." *Black Scholar* 4, nos. 6–7 (March–April 1973): 42–46.

Marc, David. *Comic Visions: Television Comedy and American Culture.* Boston: Unwin Hyman, 1989.

Masciarotte, Gloria-Jean. "C'mon, Girl: Oprah Winfrey and the Discourse of Feminine Talk." *Genders* 11 (fall 1991): 81–110.

Mattick, Paul, Jr. "A Spurned Woman." *Arts Magazine,* January 1992, 17–18.

Mayer, Jane, and Jill Abramson. *Strange Justice: The Selling of Clarence Thomas.* Boston: Houghton Mifflin, 1994.

McClellan, Steve. "Look Who's Talking: Potential for High Ratings at Relatively Low Cost Attracts New Talk Shows." *Broadcasting,* December 14, 1992, 22–23.

McClintock, Anne. "The Angel of Progress." In *Colonial Discourse and Post-Colonial Theory,* ed. Patrick Williams and Laura Chrisman. New York: Columbia University Press, 1994.

Mcrac, Shannon. "Flesh Made World: Sex, Text, and the Virtual Body." In *Internet Culture,* ed. David Porter. New York: Routledge, 1997.

McWhirter, Darien A. *The End of Affirmative Action: Where Do We Go from Here?* New York: Birch Lane Press, 1996.

Means Coleman, Robin R. *African American Viewers and the Black Situation Comedy: Situating Racial History.* New York: Garland, 1998.

Medhurst, Andy. Introduction to *The Colour Black: Black Images in British Television,* ed. Therese Daniels and Jane Gerson, 15–21. London: British Film Institute, 1990.

Meehan, Eileen. "Conceptualizing Culture as Commodity: The Problem of Television." In *Television: The Critical View,* ed. Horace Newcomb. New York: Oxford University Press, 1994.

Mellencamp, Patricia. *High Anxiety: Catastrophe, Scandal, Age, and Comedy.* Bloomington: Indiana University Press, 1992.

———, ed. *Logics of Television: Essays in Cultural Criticism.* Bloomington: Indiana University Press, 1990.

Mercer, Kobena. *Welcome to the Jungle: New Positions in Black Cultural Studies.* New York: Routledge, 1994.

Merleau-Ponty, Maurice. *The Primacy of Perception.* Ed. James M. Edie. Evanston, Ill.: Northwestern University Press, 1964.

Miller, Anita, ed. *The Complete Transcripts of the Clarence Thomas–Anita Hill Hearings: October 11, 12, 13, 1991.* Chicago: Academy Chicago, 1994.

Moore, F. Michael. *Drag! Male and Female Impersonators on Stage, Screen, and Television: An Illustrated World History.* Jefferson, N.C.: McFarland, 1994.

Moore, Melvin M. "Blackface in Prime Time." *Small Voices and Great Trumpets: Minorities and the Media,* ed. Bernard Rubin. New York: Praeger, 1980.

Moraga, Cherríe, and Gloria Anzaldúa, eds. *This Bridge Called My Back: Writings by Radical Women of Color.* New York: Kitchen Table/Women of Color Press, 1983.

Morgan, Joan. "The Bad Girls of Hip-Hop," *Essence,* March 1997, 76–77, 132, 134.

———. *When Chicken Heads Come Home to Roost: A Hip-Hop Feminist Breaks It Down.* New York: Simon and Schuster, 1999.

Morley, David. *Television, Audiences, and Cultural Studies.* New York: Routledge, 1992.

Morrison, Toni. *Playing in the Dark: Whiteness and the Literary Imagination.* Cambridge: Harvard University Press, 1992.

———, ed. *Race-ing Justice, En-gendering Power: Essays on Anita Hill, Clarence Thomas, and the Construction of Reality.* New York: Pantheon, 1992.

Morse, Margaret. "Talk, Talk, Talk." *Screen* 26, no. 2 (March–April 1985): 2–15.

Morton, Patricia. *Disfigured Images: The Historical Assault on Afro-American Women.* New York: Greenwood, 1991.

Munson, Wayne. *All Talk: The Talkshow in Media Culture.* Philadelphia: Temple University Press, 1993.

Naficy, Hamid. *The Making of Exile Cultures: Iranian Television in Los Angeles.* Minneapolis: University of Minnesota Press, 1993.

Naylor, Gloria. *The Women of Brewster Place.* New York: Viking, 1980.

Nelson, E. D. (Adie), and B. W. Robinson. "Reality Talk or Telling Tales? The Social Construction of Sexual and Gender Deviance on a Television Talk Show." *Journal of Contemporary Ethnography* 23, no. 1 (April 1994): 51–78.

Nelson, Janie. "Attitude-Behavior Consistency among Black Feminist and Traditional Black Women." Ph.D. diss., Kent State University, 1981.

Nelson, Jill. "Talk Is Cheap," *Nation,* June 5, 1995, 800–802.

Newcomb, Horace, ed. *Television: The Critical View.* 5th ed. New York: Oxford University Press, 1994.

Newcomb, Horace, and Robert S. Alley, eds. *The Producer's Medium: Conversations with Creators of American TV.* New York: Oxford University Press, 1983.

Noble, Jeanne. *Beautiful, Also, Are the Souls of My Black Sisters: A History of the Black Woman in America.* Englewood Cliffs, N.J.: Prentice-Hall, 1978.

Nobles, Wade W. "African Philosophy: Foundations for Black Psychology." In *A Turbulent Voyage: Readings in African American Studies,* ed. Floyd W. Hayes III. San Diego, Calif.: Collegiate Press, 1997.

Painter, Nell Irvin. "Hill, Thomas, and the Use of Racial Stereotype." In *Race-ing Justice, Engendering Power: Essays on Anita Hill, Clarence Thomas, and the Construction of Social Reality,* ed. Toni Morrison. New York: Pantheon, 1992.

Patterson, James T. *America in the Twentieth Century: A History.* New York: Harcourt Brace College, 1994.

Patterson, Lillie, and Cornelia H. Wright. *Oprah Winfrey: Talk Show Host and Actress.* Hillside, N.J.: Enslow, 1990.

Payne, Karen W., and Carlos A. Ugarte. "The Office of Minority Health Resource Center: Impacting on Health Related Disparities among Minority Populations." *Health Education,* December 1989, 6–8.

Peck, Janice. "Talk about Racism: Framing a Popular Discourse of Race on *Oprah Winfrey.*" *Cultural Critique* 27 (spring 1994): 89–125.

Person, James E., Jr., ed. *Statistical Forecasts of the United States.* Detroit: Gale Research, 1993.

Peterson-Lewis, Sonja, and Shirley A. Chennault. "Black Artists' Music Videos: Three Success Strategies." *Journal of Communication* 36, no. 1 (winter 1986): 107–114.

Pieterse, Jan Nederveen. *White on Black: Images of Africa and Blacks in Western Popular Culture.* New Haven, Conn.: Yale University Press, 1992.

Powderly, Kathleen E. "Contraceptive Policy and Ethics: Illustrations from American History." *Hastings Center Report* 25, no. 1 (January–February 1995): S9–S11.

Prakash, Snigdha. "Viacom-BET." *All Things Considered.* National Public Radio, November 3, 2000.

Press, Andrea. *Women Watching Television: Gender, Class, and Generation in the American Television Experience.* Philadelphia: University of Pennsylvania Press, 1991.

Priest, Patricia Joyner. *Public Intimacies: Talk Show Participants and Tell-All TV.* Cresskill, N.J.: Hampton Press, 1995.

Quayle, Dan. "Restoring Basic Values: Strengthening the Family." Speech delivered at the Commonwealth Club of California in San Francisco, May 19, 1992.

"Questions and Answers." *Law Library Journal* 82, no. 1 (winter 1990): 197–200.

Rabinovitz, Lauren. "Sitcoms and Single Moms—Representations of Feminism on American TV." *Cinema Journal* 29, no. 1 (1989): 3–19.

Raboteau, Albert J. "Fire in the Bones: African-American Christianity and Autobiographical Reflection." *America,* May 21, 1994.

Ragan, Sandra L., ed., *The Lynching of Language: Gender, Politics, and Power in the Hill-Thomas Hearings.* Urbana: University of Illinois Press, 1996.

Randolph, Laura B. "The Real-Life Fresh Prince of Bel Air: Television and Recording Tycoon Benny Medina Proves That Hollywood Life Can Be Stranger Than Hollywood Fiction." *Ebony,* April 1991, 30–38.

Rapping, Elayne. *The Looking Glass World of Nonfiction TV.* Boston: South End Press, 1987.

Regester, Charlene. "Lynched, Assaulted, and Intimidated: Oscar Micheaux's Most Controversial Films." *Popular Culture Review* 5, no. 2 (February 1994): 47–55.

Reid, P. M. "Racial Stereotyping on TV: A Comparison of the Behavior of Black and White Television Characters." *Journal of Applied Psychology* 64 (October 1979): 465–471.

Richards, Larry. *African American Films through 1959: A Comprehensive, Illustrated Filmography.* Jefferson, N.C.: McFarland, 1998.

Richardson, Bill. *Guy to Goddess: An Intimate Look at Drag Queens.* Berkeley: Ten Speed Press, 1994.

Rivers, Caryl. *Slick Spins and Fractured Facts: How Cultural Myths Distort the News.* New York: Columbia University Press, 1996.

Roberts, Robin. "Ladies First: Queen Latifah's Afrocentric Feminist Music Video." *African American Review* 28, no. 2 (summer 1994): 245–257.

———. *Ladies First: Women in Music Videos.* Jackson: University Press of Mississippi, 1996.

———. "Music Videos, Performance, and Resistance: Feminist Rappers." *Journal of Popular Culture* 25 (fall 1991): 141–152.

Robbins, Brian, dir. *The Show.* Savoy Pictures, 1995.

Rose, Tricia. *Black Noise: Rap Music and Black Culture in Contemporary America.* Hanover, N.H.: Wesleyan University Press, 1994.

———. "Never Trust a Big Butt and a Smile." *Camera Obscura* 23 (1990): 109–131.

Ross, Andrew. "Back on the Box." *Artforum,* May 1995, 17.

Rowe, Kathleen. "Roseanne: Unruly Woman as Domestic Goddess." In *Television: The Critical View,* ed. Horace Newcomb. Oxford: Oxford University Press, 1994.

———. *The Unruly Woman: Gender and the Genres of Laughter.* Austin: University of Texas Press, 1995.

Rubey, Dan. "Voguing at the Carnival: Desire and Pleasure on MTV." *South Atlantic Quarterly* 90, no. 4 (fall 1991): 871–906.

Russell, Kathy, Midge Wilson, and Ronald Hall. *The Color Complex: The Politics of Skin Color among African Americans.* New York: Anchor Books, 1993.

Schulman, Norma. "The House that Black Built." *Journal of Popular Film and Television* 22, no. 3 (fall 1994): 108–115.

Scott, Gini Graham. *Can We Talk? The Power and Influence of Talk Shows.* New York: Insight Books, 1996.

Scott-Heron, Gil. "The Revolution Will Not Be Televised." In *The Norton Anthology of African American Literature,* ed. Henry Louis Gates Jr. and Nellie Y. McKay. New York: Norton, 1997.

Shargel, Raphael. "Epic Mice." Review of *Beloved,* by Toni Morrison. *New Leader,* November 30, 1998, 18–19.

Sharkey, Betsy. "Give Them What They Want." *Mediaweek,* May 27, 1996, 26–30.

———. "Teen Angel: Singing Sensation Brandy Is Lifting." *Mediaweek,* February 19, 1996, 20–23.

Shelton, Marla L. "Is Whitney Everywoman? Whitney Houston and the Icon of the Black Woman in Popular Culture." *Screening Noir* 1, no. 1 (spring 1995): 3–5.

Shohat, Ella, and Robert Stam. *Unthinking Eurocentrism: Multiculturalism and the Media.* London: Routledge, 1994.

Simms, Margaret C., and Julianne M. Malveaux. *Slipping through the Cracks: The Status of Black Women.* New Brunswick, N.J.: Transaction, 1987.

Small, Michael. "Salt-N-Pepa Shake It Up, Laying a Cold Rap on Men." *People,* April 18, 1988, 113–114.

Smith, Barbara, ed. *Home Girls: A Black Feminist Anthology.* New York: Kitchen Table/Women of Color Press, 1983.

Smith, Clay J. "Open Letter to the President on Race and Affirmative Action." *Howard Law Journal* 42, no. 1 (fall 1998): 27–58.

Smith, Danyel. "Ain't a Damn Thing Changed: Why Women Rappers Don't Sell." In *Rap on Rap: Straight-Up Talk on Hip-Hop Culture,* ed. Adam Sexton. New York: Dell, 1995.

———. "MC Lyte." *Rolling Stone,* September 16, 1993, 17.

Smith-Shomade, Beretta E. "Rock-a-Block, Baby! Black Women Disrupting Gangs and Constructing Hip-Hop Gangsta Film." *Cinema Journal* (Forthcoming, 2002).

Smitherman, Geneva. *Talkin and Testifyin: The Language of Black America.* Detroit: Wayne State University Press, 1986.

———, ed. *African-American Women Speak Out on Anita Hill–Clarence Thomas.* Detroit: Wayne State University Press, 1995.

Sotomayor, Ernie. "What Is News?" *Social Education,* March 1989, 161–163.

Spaights, Ernest, and Ann Whitaker. "Black Women in the Workforce: A New Look at an Old Problem." *Journal of Black Studies* 25, no. 3 (January 1995): 283–296.

Spigel, Lynn. "Television in the Family Circle: The Popular Reception of a New Medium." In *Logics of Television,* ed. Patricia Mellencamp. Bloomington: Indiana University Press, 1990.

Stanal, Jerry. "Beautiful: A Desperate Man's Search for Meaning at the Miss America Pageant." *LA Weekly,* October 11–17, 1996, 26–33.

Staiger, Janet. *Bad Women: Regulating Sexuality in Early American Cinema.* Minneapolis: University of Minnesota Press, 1995.

Stalter, Katharine. "Striving for Balance in the '90s." *Film and Video,* February 1993, 50–57.

Steenland, Sally. "On Trial: Courtroom Television." *Television Quarterly* 25, no. 4 (1992): 39–43.

Suleri, Sara. "Woman Skin Deep: Feminism and the Postcolonial Condition." In *Colonial Discourse and Post-Colonial Theory: A Reader,* ed. Patrick Williams and Laura Chrisman. New York: Columbia University Press, 1994.

Taylor, Ella. *Prime-Time Families: Television Culture in Postwar America.* Berkeley: University of California Press, 1989.

Teinowitz, Ira, and Michael Wilke. "Cable Net to Accept Spirits Ads: Move by Black Entertainment TV Follows DISCUS Ending Its Ban." *Advertising Age,* November 11, 1996, 1.

Thompson, Heather Ann. "Rethinking the Politics of White Flight in the Postwar City." *Journal of Urban History* 25, no. 2 (January 1999): 163–198.

Trinh, T. Minh-ha. "Not You/Like You: Post-Colonial Women and the Interlocking Questions of Identity and Difference." In *Making Face, Making Soul—Hacienda Cara: Creative and Critical Perspectives by Feminists of Color,* ed. Gloria Anzaldúa. San Francisco: Aunt Lute, 1990.

———. *When the Moon Waxes Red: Representation, Gender, and Cultural Politics.* New York: Routledge, 1991.

Truth, Sojourner. *Narrative of Sojourner Truth.* Boston: Printed for the author, 1850.

Turner, Patricia A. *I Heard It through the Grapevine: Rumor in African-American Culture.* Berkeley: University of California Press, 1993.

Udovitch, Mim. "The Girlie Show." *Rolling Stone,* October 14, 1993, 67, 69–70.

United States Commission on Civil Rights. *Window Dressing on the Set: An Update.* Washington: GPO, 1979.

U.S. Department of Commerce. *Statistical Abstract of the United States, 1994.* Washington, D.C.: GPO, 1994.

U.S. Department of Health and Human Services. *Report of the Secretary's Task Force on Black and Minority Health.* Washington, D.C.: GPO, August 1985.

Waldron, Robert. *Oprah!* New York: St. Martin's Press, 1987.

Walker, James R. "More Than Meets the Ear: A Factor Analysis of Student Impressions of

Television Talk Show Hosts." Paper Presented at the 74th Annual Meeting of the Speech Communication Association, New Orleans, November 3–6, 1988. *ERIC,* ED 299630.

Wallace, Michele. *Black Macho and the Myth of the Superwoman.* New York: Dial, 1978.

———. "The Politics of Location: Cinema/Theory/Literature/Ethnicity/Sexuality/Me." *Framework* 36 (1989): 42–55.

Washington, Eloise. *Uncivil War: The Struggle between Black Men and Women.* Chicago: Noble Press, 1996.

Waters, Harry F., and Janet Huck. "Networking Women." *Newsweek,* March 13, 1989, 48.

Waxler, Caroline. "Bob Johnson's Brainchild." *Forbes,* April 22, 1996, 98–100.

Welles, Sara. "Taming the TV Talk Show." *Television Quarterly* 28, no. 3 (summer 1996): 41–48.

Wermiel, Stephen J. "Confirming the Constitution: The Role of the Senate Judiciary Committee." *Law and Contemporary Problems* 56, no. 4 (1993): 121–145.

West, Cornel. *Race Matters.* Boston: Beacon Press, 1993.

White, Armond. "In Living Color." *Rolling Stone,* October 14, 1993, 73, 76–77.

White, Hayden. *Tropics of Discourse: Essays in Cultural Criticism.* Baltimore: Johns Hopkins University Press, 1978.

White, Mimi. *Tele-Advising: Therapeutic Discourse in American Television.* Chapel Hill: University of North Carolina Press, 1992.

Wilson, Hugh A. "Does Affirmative Action for Blacks Harm Whites? *Western Journal of Black Studies* 22, no. 4 (winter 1998): 218–225.

Wolf, Naomi. *The Beauty Myth.* New York: William Morrow, 1991.

Wollen, Peter. *Signs and Meaning in the Cinema.* Bloomington: Indiana University Press, 1972.

"*The Women of Brewster Place.*" *Ebony,* March 1989, 122–126.

Wong, William. "Covering the Invisible 'Model Minority.'" *Media Studies Journal* 8, no. 3 (summer 1994): 49–59.

Young, Lola. "Review." *Screen* 37, no. 4 (winter 1996): 400–408.

Yuval-Davis, Nira. "Gender and Nation." *Ethnic and Racial Studies* 16, no. 4 (October 1993): 621–633.

———. "Women and the Biological Reproduction of 'The Nation.'" *Women's Studies International* 19, nos. 1–2 (January–April 1996): 17–24.

Zook, Kristal Brent. *Color by Fox: The Fox Network and the Revolution in Black Television.* New York: Oxford University Press, 1999.

———. "Straight Expectations: Black Women and the Hair Product That Seduced and Betrayed." *LA Weekly,* March 10–16, 1995: 16–20.

INDEX

affirmative action, 16, 18–19, 45, 113, 193n44
ageism, 90
agency, definition of, 23
Aid to Families with Dependent Children (AFDC), 138, 143
Aiken, Kimberly, 60
Ajaye, Franklyn, 38
Alexander, Erika, *see Living Single*
Alexander, Khandi, 179
Ali, Tatyana M., *see Fresh Prince of Bel-Air*
Allan, Blaine, 74
Allen, Jonelle, 33
Allen, Woody, 32
All in the Family (TV series), 28, 30, 68
Ally McBeal (TV series), 49, 102
Amen (TV series), 54, 57
American Bandstand (TV music show), 77
Amos, John, 30, 30*fig.*, 193n31, 196n25
Amos 'n' Andy (radio series), 11, 29
Amos 'n' Andy (TV series), 5, 11, 33, 34
Angelou, Maya, 19, 31
Any Day Now (TV series), 180, 194n58
Arceneaux, K. C., 82, 97
Arie, Indie, 104–105
Arnheim, Rudolf, 46, 83
Arnold, Tichina, *see Martin*
Arsenio Hall Show, The (TV variety series), 19
Arthur, Bea, 30, 30*fig.*
Atkin, David, 31
Atlantic Starr, 71
audience: Black, and response to Blacks on TV, 27, 195n5, 196n23; for Fox Broadcasting, 35–36; for *Ricki Lake*, 216n78; for situation comedy, 28
Aufderheide, Pat, 69, 74, 107
Avery, James, *see Fresh Prince of Bel-Air*

Badu, Erykah, 104–105
Bagley, Ross, *see Fresh Prince of Bel-Air*
Baker, Houston, 19
Baker, Josephine, 10, 191n8
Bakhtin, Mikhail, 131
Baldwin, James, 105
Banks, Ingrid, 64
Banks, Tyra, 60, 67
Barnes, Natasha, 117–118
Barr, Roseanne, 161
Baudrillard, Jean, 114

beauty pageants, 118–119. *See also* Miss America Pageant; Miss America Pageant, 1983
Beavers, Louise, 10, 11
Beloved (film), 156, 171–172, 175, 215nn71–73
Benson, George, 79
Benson (TV series), 199n72
Bentley, Lamont, 45, 46*fig.*
Berrick, Jill Duerr, 138, 139
Berry, Halle, 60, 159
BET, *see* Black Entertainment Television
Beulah Show, The (TV series), 5, 8, 11, 33, 199n72
Beyer, Troy, 194n58
Birth of a Nation, The (film), 9
bitch, as term, 94–96
Black English, 58
Black Entertainment Television (BET), 1, 19, 24; founding of, 71–72; and music video, 85; purchase of holdings of, 72–73; *Rap City* program on, 78; role in Black music video dissemination, 72, 73
Black family, 16, 22, 192n23, 208n27
Black female: agency of, in television news, 146; contemporary role of, in film, 21; contemporary role of, on TV, 21; disparity with Black male, 21–22, 23; in dramatic series, 194n58; invisibility of, in early film, 10–11; invisibility of, in early radio, 11; and myth of ascension to power at Black male's expense, 21, 22; nonpresence of, in film, 32; nonpresence of, on TV, 33; objectification of, 22–23, 67–68; powerlessness of, in early film, 9–10, 11; professional, 129 (*see also* Hill, Anita); role of, in early film, 9–10. *See also* Black family; Black female, representation in situation comedy; stereotype, of Black female
Black female, representation in situation comedy: body size, 60–61; characterization, 50–56, 97, 199n82; class, 56–58; cultural logic of objectification of, 67–68; hair issues, 61–64, 199n87; language issues, 58–59; as prophetess, 197n37; skin tone issues, 59–61; work role, 49–50. *See also* Black female; stereotype, of Black female

ABOUT THE AUTHOR

Beretta Eileen Smith-Shomade is an assistant professor of media arts at the University of Arizona. Her research and teaching focus on the intersections of representation, identity, and audience in popular culture. She is also a video documentarian.